# Raising Children
# with Character

## About the Author

Elizabeth Berger, M.D., is a board-certified child and adolescent psychiatrist with more than twenty years' experience treating children and families in community settings, hospitals, and private practice. She has been a member of the faculty of the Columbia University College of Physicians and Surgeons, Northwestern University Medical School, University of Cincinnati College of Medicine, and MCP-Hahnemann School of Medicine. Dr. Berger has appeared in numerous panels and public forums, as well as on radio and television, addressing parents' concerns about their children. She lives in Elkins Park, Pennsylvania, with her husband and two teenage children.

# Raising Children with Character

## Parents, Trust, and the Development of Personal Integrity

Elizabeth Berger, M.D.

JASON ARONSON INC.
Northvale, New Jersey
London

Cover art entitled "Golden Rule" printed by permission of the Norman Rockwell Family Trust. Copyright © 1961 the Norman Rockwell Family Trust.

Production Editor: Judith D. Cohen

This book was set in 11 pt. Fairfield Light by Alpha Graphics of Pittsfield, NH and printed and bound by Book-mart Press, Inc. of North Bergen, NJ.

**Library of Congress Cataloging-in-Publication Data**

Berger, Elizabeth.
   Raising children with character : parents, trust, and the
development of personal integrity / Elizabeth Berger.
      p.  cm.
   Includes bibliographical references and index.
   ISBN 0-7657-0214-2 (alk. paper)
   1. Personality development.  2. Child rearing.  3. Parent and
child.  I. Title.
BF723.P4B47   1999
649'.7—dc21                                                    98-53684

Printed in the United States of America on acid–free paper. For information and catalog write to Jason Aronson Inc., 230 Livingston Street, Northvale, NJ 07647-1726, or visit our website: www.aronson.com

To M. L. B., who has faith

# Contents

My son, keep your father's commandments;
Do not forsake your mother's teaching.
Tie them over your heart always.

—Proverbs 6:20

# Preface

This is the book I was always looking for and could never find—one that spoke directly to ordinary parents about their long-term hopes for their children's spirits as full human beings, and to clinicians who counsel parents and children encountering difficulty along that path.

This book grows out of my life-experience as a mother, child psychiatrist, and educator. It is intended for both therapists and parents—indeed for anyone concerned with the well-being of young people—to address these questions:

- How do children grow in their minds and hearts to be rich inside?
- What is the parents' role in this process?
- What are the common stumbling blocks to a parent's good intentions?

To answer these questions, I have sought to combine the best of many schools of thought in a way that focuses on the child's eventual personal maturity—his character—and the role of the parent's intimate involvement in evoking, supporting, and enhancing it. This is of course a very different approach from eliminating "negative behaviors" through management techniques. But an emphasis on one or the other perspective really depends on what one is after. I have found ordinary parents, as well as parents seeking treatment, to be deeply interested in understanding their children's emerging character, once they come to identify its development as one of their goals. The therapist who assists distressed families is, in a certain way, doing the same thing—recruiting the wise and mature aspects of the child's and the parent's personalities as allies in an effort to understand and surmount their difficulties.

The parent seeking advice is reassured to hear, "Oh, he'll grow out of it!"—that a troublesome aspect of the child's behavior is normal. But it goes so much further for the parent to understand *why* it is normal, to see the behavior as an example of a broader element of childhood, to grasp the underlying principles. This helps the parent anticipate and support the child's development in other areas. It builds up the parent's faith in himself, in the child, and in their relationship.

Likewise, the therapist may advise the parent to perform or refrain from performing some particular act. The parent may take the advice at face value, on the expert's authority. But the parent's own authority is enhanced when his parenting is put in a larger context, *when he understands why* it is often helpful to pursue certain approaches to children and why it is often unconstructive to pursue others.

My goal is thus to identify general themes in the emotional dialogue between parent and child—the music behind the specific words—that contribute to the forward direction of the child's character growth. For this reason I have painted with a rather broad brush, describing "the wise parent" in abstract and idealized terms. This is not to imply that flesh-and-blood parents must measure up to a superhuman ideal, but to suggest that it can be greatly helpful for parents *to have some sort of ideal in mind*. Indeed, what seems to produce today so much insecurity in many good parents, such a fear of "making mistakes," is often the lack of an overarching mission—a clear vision of what, after all, the parent is aiming for. My intent in this book has been to articulate such a vision, a philosophy of childrearing that is both technically and spiritually sound and that speaks to our craving not only for facts, but for meaning.

I refer often to both "the parent" and "the child" as "he," to spare endless repetition of awkward phrases such as "himself or herself." The English language allows for no entirely satisfactory solution to this problem. Naturally, real children are as often female as male. The real-life caretaking parent today, however, is still far more often female. By using "he" to represent "any parent," I hope to convey my conviction that the intimate care of children is as much the father's concern as the mother's.

The book's organization follows the unfolding of personality development in non-technical terms: early childhood, school-age, and adolescence. There are in addition subjects that recur throughout development, and discussion of these concepts is interposed within the chronology.

I have attempted to translate psychological ideas back into plain English, in a way close to the actual experience of ordinary parents, to aid clinicians who would like to help parents understand psychic entities such as "ambivalence," "regression," or "projection" without getting overly caught up in the technical vocabulary. Within the text, I make reference to a core list of pioneering authors who—though perhaps imperfectly—first gave us these ideas and revolutionized our understanding of childhood. As examples, *vignettes* of ordinary day-to-day situations highlight some of the typical issues that perplex parents, and *clinical cases* illustrate the treatment of troubled youngsters and their families. Details from actual cases have been combined and disguised; names have been changed to protect the privacy of real individuals.

It goes without saying that many disturbed children suffer from disorders that are largely the consequence of abnormal neuroanatomy or biochemistry—deficits that all the parent's wisdom and self-sacrifice in the world cannot completely repair. The parent's understanding can, however, go a long distance to improve the child's chances for personal fulfillment in life, despite the child's "diagnosis."

Indeed, my focus on those *factors the parent can do something about* inherently downplays all of the factors that the parent can't at the moment do much to change. Parents are not magicians, despite the fact that some experts, the general public, and parents themselves seem quick to find fault with the parent whose child presents problems. No parent can be responsible for all of the external factors that will have great impact on his children's lives and their characters. It is for this reason that while any parent can take personal pride in the child who fulfills his potential, no well-meaning parent should feel personally to blame for a child's disturbance. The well-meaning parent's deepest wish is *to make everything all right for his child*—but it must be recognized that doing so may sometimes be beyond everyone's powers.

Finally, I wish to acknowledge my great debt to the many teachers, colleagues, and patients whose ideas I have inherited, borrowed, and made my own. I thank my editors, Judith Cohen and Cindy Hyden, for their spirited and perceptive advice, and my dear friends Gunnbjorg Lavoll, M.D. and Jeffrey Mitchell, Ph.D., for their careful critique of the manuscript. Above all I thank my husband Marc for his endless encouragement, enthusiasm, and practical support.

# 1

⁓

# Why Character Counts

## A PARENT'S DEEPEST CONCERN

Only one thing concerns parents more than their children's present behavior, and that is their child's future qualities as a human being. Every parent is eager to see his child grow up to be brave, responsible, trustworthy, and kind. The fact that parents want so passionately to see their children become really fine people is itself a wonderful thing, a sign of their hopefulness and inherent commitment to morality.

Parents seem to know in their hearts that what really counts is not so much the child's surface troubles of the moment, but what these troubles mean for the person the child will become. The worried parent says "My child hits!" but what lurks in the back of the parent's mind is the more profound anxiety, "and what kind of person will he turn out to be if this keeps up?"

The parent's goal is not only to control a child's immediate behavior but to respond to it so as to bring out the best in the child's personality over the long run. It is in fact because of their devotion to this long-term agenda that most parents are able to call upon great fortitude in facing all of the difficulties, frustrations, and backsliding that typify childhood. With confidence in the child's emerging character, parents discover within themselves a tolerance and understanding for all of the childish behaviors that so try anyone's patience.

## DEFINING CHARACTER

Character is not an esoteric notion. Its meaning is perhaps clearest in the down-to-earth qualities of personal goodness and strength so close to all of our hearts as a nation. An upright character is our fundamental American value, and strikes an easily recognized note for most parents. In fact, *character* is everywhere—men and women most admired in our country's history are the very embodiment of strong character qualities: courage, ingenuity, loyalty, responsibility, and altruism. These values emerge in our greatest documents—the speeches of Abraham Lincoln and Dr. Martin Luther King, Jr. Popular books, movies, and TV shows are unified by these themes: the good guy displays these virtues and battles the bad guy. The underdog defeats the larger villain through his pluck, common sense, and determination. On a more sophisticated level, the good guy battles within himself and becomes a better guy. The Hollywood movies and human interest stories in the newspaper that illustrate these dramas may not be great works of art, but they are great works of cultural self-definition. The American consensus around *who we want to be* is beyond controversy—it can be exploited, stereotyped, and satirized, but it continues to unite and inspire us. We are one people because we value this—the steadfast heart of the noble everyman.

Can we be more specific about the nature of the character that we hold so dear? What we mean by character, perhaps foremost, is the capacity to know right from wrong and to act from a position of moral conscience. Beyond that, we mean courage, realism, and the ability to accept loss squarely. We also mean creativity, empathy, and the capacity to love. We mean a respect for the human condition, a commitment to other human beings and to our ideals. These qualities are what prepare a young person for the eventual demands of adulthood, for being a good parent and a fine citizen.

Further, although people of character share qualities in common, part of the meaning of character lies in its *individuality*. This acknowledges that each person is irreplaceable and precious in his or her own singular way, and unlike every other person. A person's character is in this sense related to his soul or spirit, intangible and absolute.

Character involves *the fundamentals of living*. It is the sum of a person's responses to the profound polarities of human existence: love and hate, man and woman, life and death. And finally, character involves an *inner struggle*—between work and play, self and others, a future goal and an impulse of the moment.

We can translate these qualities into more psychological language by suggesting that strength of character involves achieving a fair balance between protecting one's self-interest and a concern for others, taking into account a sensible appraisal of reality as well as an awareness of ethical principles.

## CAN CHARACTER BE TAUGHT?

It is not uncommon for a parent to feel overwhelmed with the responsibility of "teaching" everything to his child. Such a parent is a bit like one sensitive girl of 10 who worried that her children might never learn to talk. After all, she had never taught anyone to talk before. What if she couldn't do it? How would the children ever learn? So many words! So much grammar! Where would she begin?

It was a relief to this future mother to be told that babies begin to talk not because they are taught, but because they are loved. She was comforted to hear that infants already have inside just what they will need in order to talk and walk, to master the world around them, and in time to master themselves, so long as they are cherished and protected from harm in all the ordinary ways.

Indeed, most childish errors need no particular correction. At a certain age every small child is likely to say, "I runned all the way." The parent is not required to point out to the child that "ran" is the proper word. Simply by interacting with the child, and especially by responding to what the child is eager to say with genuine enthusiasm, the parent encourages the child to master language, including irregular verbs. This learning process has a life of its own.

Thus it is with parents' concern to "teach" character values. There is nothing wrong with teaching children—on the contrary, parenthood involves a great deal of teaching—pots are hot, the street is dangerous, and hitting isn't allowed—conveying all of these useful specifics demands a large part of the parent's energy. And of course, the parent may hold valuable discussions with his child on the abstract subjects of truth, commitment, and ideals. But the child's inner capacity for these things has taken shape long before his ability to discuss them. *Parents can be reassured that it is through the intimacy of the ordinary day that the child's potential for morality, devotion, and idealism is stimulated and enhanced.*

Character development is not by and large the result of special lessons. It is *embedded in and the product of the child's growth.* The totality of the process of child development—especially in the preschool years—gives structure and depth to a child's character. What parents do—and, particularly, the spirit in which they do it—makes up the raw material from which the child's values develop.

# 2

## Intimacy from Birth through Preschool

### THE LOVE RELATIONSHIP IS
### THE CHILD'S PRIMARY VALUE

The value the parents place on the child is his first "value," and helps define the child's image of himself from the very beginning. We notice that the process of loving the child gets started before the inception of his separate existence, with the twinkle in the eye of the man and woman who wish for a child. The prospective parents prepare themselves with all the many notions involved in having a baby. For both men and women, this is weighted with considerable meaning from their own childhoods, distilled from their fundamental love relationships with their parents, siblings, and others. All of this becomes part of the value their new baby has for them, and the value they discover in their baby. For many people, raising children is the central fulfillment of life itself. It is observed—because the baby itself inherits long-standing and, as it were, archaic parts of the personality—that parents normally seem to overvalue their own baby. It is easy for outsiders to feel that they've even gone a little overboard. This special value is conveyed to the baby in a thousand ways, in the music of one's voice, in touch, in the process of taking care of the baby's physical needs. This is more an art than a science, more a celebration than a lesson: "I feed you because I love you!" sings the mother's heart, as it did when she cradled her doll years ago.

The baby, meanwhile, is forming attachments and ideas in response, with language only catching up with these developments much later. We can say that early on in life there is a beginning idea or sense of "myself," an idea of the loved "someone else," and a feeling that links these two images. Scientists who study infants are beginning to ac-knowledge what parents have known all along: that the baby on his side of the equation, even in the very first days and weeks of life, is quite complicated in his capacity to love and be loved, to respond to the environment, and to interact on a unique, intimate level. The newborn is already a psychological person. The brilliant smile that infants de-velop at 2 or 3 months heralds an even richer and more conversational love relationship.

Very early—around 8 months of age—babies begin to comprehend that other people understand their ideas and emotions. At this time babies begin to show powerful loyalty for certain loved persons and may display worry or outrage at the close approach of strangers.

From the age of a year and a half, the child begins to use symbols for ideas in his own mind, and speaks in two- and three-word phrases. Complex social emotions can be expressed nonverbally, such as em-barrassment, envy, and empathy. The age of 2 heralds the emergence of pride, shame, and guilt. The child has entered the social environ-ment as a separate entity, aware that the meeting ground between the wishes of others and his own needs must be negotiated. He already has a considerable repertoire of intimate interpersonal skills.

Although on one hand grounded in the baby's neurological connec-tions that are present and continue developing from birth, this remark-able personal growth is dependent on the participation of loving adults who respond to the child and care for its body and spirit. Parents do not interact with their infant because they understand the sequence of development intellectually. They do it because they love their infant, and because of the intense pleasure that getting to know, feeding, car-ing for, and playing with their infant gives them. The experience is personal, emotional, and intimate for both parent and child. For the parents of a new baby, it is as if the entire world has been emptied of its importance, all of which has been poured into the existence of their little pride and joy.

There is no question that *the parents' love for a child is the most powerful element in the formation of his character*. The extraordinary quality and force of ordinary parents' love for their children is, however, rather underplayed in our conscious awareness. We take it for granted. It is obvious most prominently in its frustration: the heartbreak of couples who cannot conceive, or the unspeakable anguish of those who have lost a child through death. It is a curious thing that poets of all ages find endless opportunity to celebrate romantic love between men and women, but few poets celebrate the devotion of parents to their children.

The love of a baby involves not just the love of the idea of the baby, but the love of its body. Those tiny fingers and toes! The luscious smell of its little soft neck. The absurd superiority of one's own delicious baby over everyone else's baby. Puritanical ideas make some people blush to recognize it, but the personal and physical fulfillment for parents in feeding, loving, and caring for their babies shares some of the qualities of longing and excitement of adult romantic love.

The irreplaceable uniqueness and profundity of feeling in the bond between infants and their parents is worth stressing because it is the overall atmosphere in which specific development (language, motor skills, intellect, and emotion) unfolds, giving a personal coloration and tone to the entire process. One also notes that the parents' joy acts as a counterweight to the considerable frustration, tedium, lost sleep, and anxiety involved in being responsible for their baby. Their love prepares them for the emotional endurance and self-discipline that they will be called upon to demonstrate.

To express the scope of parents' dedication, in a rather simplistic way, one might observe that it is parents who would choose to give their child the single remaining seat in the lifeboat of a sinking ship, rather than take it for themselves. Any ordinary parent would give his life for his child. This emotional reality, although not often explicit, is the very core of a child's psychological life. It is out of this fundamental experience of having *received devotion* that the child begins to achieve the capacity to be devoted. It is the beginning of character.

## THE PROBLEM OF LOVE AND HATE

This experience is not all roses, since in any ordinary day stormy situations disrupt the scenes of bliss. We see this when the infant is shrieking with hunger. The baby experiences only the need for a meal, and ideas of love or contentment are for the moment lost. In the regularity of the satisfaction of need, and the human magic that goes with it, however, the baby begins to form more consolidated, complex, and durable concepts of *satisfactions that are anticipated* and the people who bring these satisfactions. It goes without saying, of course, that real life regularly offers inevitable frustrations as well as satisfactions; this is why everyone accepts a crying infant in the movie theater as a natural thing. It often makes people smile. It's all right as long as Mommy or Daddy is near. *The parent's goal is not that the infant never experiences unsatisfied need, but that the satisfaction comes reliably and promptly enough so that the baby does not despair.* We find here the origins of joy, of optimism, of faith, and of friendliness. They grow in the baby as a consequence of his being alive and loved, and because need was relieved.

In the natural course of things there is more love than rage and hate, but that does not make the rage and hate disappear. All infants experience despair and outrage and a sensation of helplessness in response to ordinary frustrations. There is plenty of frustration built into reality under the best of circumstances. The infant also has a tendency to see all good things, as well as all bad, as coming from the powerful parents.

Before the child is 2, he faces an additional vexing and peculiar problem: the growing awareness that the loved person who relieves desire and the hated person who frustrates desire are indeed the very same person. Wrestling with the emotional attachment to someone who is alternatively loved and hated, and transforming it into an image of someone who contains both good and bad qualities simultaneously, is part of the work of early childhood—a task that often persists incomplete throughout life. From this complicated inner realization comes *the capacity for forgiveness and toleration.*

Likewise, well before 3, the child begins to understand that he himself can be alternately good and bad—that the same little self who so brilliantly mastered the use of a fork in the morning, to everyone's admiration, went on at lunch to pull the cat's tail, strictly for spite. At some point, probably before 2 and certainly before the child's language can express the sentiment, the child begins to *be sorry,* to regret his own destructiveness. He shows the awareness that he has a real impact on the feelings of others. He sees that he can make other people feel angry or sad or hurt, and feels bad about it.

## DEPENDENCE AND INDEPENDENCE

All of this happens at the same time that the child is attaining the capacities—walking, talking, feeding himself—that allow for increased physical independence. In that independence, however, the child is thrown back upon his inner resources to draw upon the self-esteem, the courage, and the friendliness that have grown there, laid down in memories of being cared for lovingly. Yet, the ability of the toddler to draw upon these good things inside is quite limited. It is as if the inner image of the parents' enthusiasm fades, and the child loses heart. His face crumples. All of a sudden he needs to find the real parent and bury his face in his mother's lap. It is this alternating push towards autonomy and pull towards dependency that gives the 2- and 3-year-old a contradictory, back-and-forth quality.

*The memory of parental warmth and imagination animates the child's inner life as the child begins to experience himself as a separate being.* This is the process involved in to-and-fro activities in which loss and recovery are enacted repetitively. The peek-a-boo game is a straightforward example of this kind of play, where the loved parent comes and goes. There are versions of this game where the child is relatively passive, bubbling over with joy when the adult "reappears." In other variants, the youngster takes charge of events, and orchestrates the disappearance of the adult or inanimate object that represents the parent. We see this behind the toddler's joy in tossing stuffed animals out of his crib, or cups and spoons off his high-chair tray. This is more than a game; it is the child's way of taking charge of intimacy.

Biological maturation of the brain has allowed the infant to register with increasing sophistication the idea that objects continue to exist, though temporarily out of sight. The child knows that a ball that has rolled under the couch is still there, although unseen. The growing implications of this development has great impact on the infant's capacities for human relationships. Locating where parents are and, in particular, exerting control over their comings and goings begin to take on enormous importance.

*As the toddler's recognition of his separateness, dependency, and relative helplessness sinks in, his natural reaction is to lay hold of and dominate the parent.* This gives the love relationship of the toddler its characteristically bullying flavor—his wish to be close to the parent is often flooded with the sadistic urge to control and punish the wayward adult. To force the adult to submit serves to deny the painful truth that human beings are truly separate from one another. The child can be quite the tyrant, surprised and outraged at the inevitable disloyalty of his subject that confronts him at every turn. The toddler becomes aware of the impulse to hurt. The child's natural impulse to hurt is not the result, as people sometimes think, of his being neglected and abused. It is the result of his having been loved, and loving back. All this gives the child quite a bit to mull over.

Indeed, the urge to dominate, punish, and control other people—particularly loved ones—is a profound one in human nature; it has its origin in a phase of childhood before the personality has made its peace with separateness, and before it has learned to achieve its goals through the use of language and compromise.

The parent's availability is necessary as a psychological safety net for the toddler because he can't realistically sustain his independence for very long. He is still little and not very competent. The toddler is a person of ups and downs, sometimes angry at the parent—as if it were the parents' fault that he needed them! The "terrible two's" (which can be reexperienced at any age) refers to this eternal psychological dilemma: the urge to be mighty and brave "all by myself," and the craving to be small and protected and have one's needs met by others.

The stormy emotions of this age range reflect the great pushing and pulling within the child to be masterful one moment, helpless and dependent the next. The strain of this is felt by the parent, too—this is why a youngster in the midst of this struggle is so exhausting. The sensitive parent has an intuitive understanding of when to step in and when to butt out; in this way, the child can take pride in the success as his own, despite the parent's participation.

### *Vignette*

*Watch James (age 2) buttoning his shirt. He is joyous when he masters the first button, but there's trouble ahead: button two won't easily go through the hole. After pushing unsuccessfully for a while, he glares at mother, as if to say "make it work." Mother reaches to help but James pulls away angrily. Now mother is to blame. He turns his back to her and struggles some more, then he breaks down in frustration: "You do it!" Mother fixes it. A tear falls. James has retouched the bedrock of babyhood, like the bottom of a swimming pool. Sighing, with new dignity, he takes in hand the third button.*

These intense and ordinary moments are repeated countless times in the course of a day. It is indeed especially through the routine of daily life, rather than special experiences, that the child grows emotionally. The child gains confidence by leaning against the parent's greater capacities and expertise, but also by pushing the parent away, as if to say, "Get lost! I'm in charge here!" We notice there is a certain paradox involved: the parent who is pushed away already has been taken in. The fact that the parent and child already have been securely attached to each other is what allows the child to safely push the parent away. This tends to happen especially once the child has absorbed the parent's guidance—the child becomes a little expert himself. The achievement at the end of the day is not just about buttons, it's about the child's sense of independence and responsibility; it's about recognizing one's need for others and taking ownership of one's accomplishments. It's about pride and patience and ambition and love.

Mother knows that James needs two contradictory things at once: for her to endorse his independence and for her to button the button. It would be an unusual thing for a mother to experience this contradiction intellectually; mothers usually don't think through this kind of challenge on a conscious level. Mothers know this emotionally and intuitively, which is where it counts. *Responding to the child's conflicting needs takes an enormous amount of emotional work.* That is why being with a child who is in the throes of this problem is so draining and requires so much patience.

We should note, too, that this is an active kind of patience, not just like waiting patiently for a bus: the needed qualities have more to do with the parent's courage, endurance, and loyalty. It requires, perhaps above all, mother's faith in human nature, her faith in her child's spirit and its potential for growth. From a physical standpoint, it is easy to put a shirt on a child. Doing it right psychologically takes both deep motivation and the strength of character to do it in such a way that the child is enriched by the experience as well as actually dressed. In this way, we might say there is a transmission of character from one generation to another.

Many of these issues are played out in an especially visible way in the course of toilet training. Originally the child enjoys the process of eliminating his urine and bowel movement at the best possible time (for him). The substance produced is good; it is warm; it is mine. It has interesting properties when you spread it around.

A thunderous shock is in store for the baby whose mother indicates that these products are not valuable to her at all. She may turn up her nose at them, and suggest in various ways that the dirty diaper, the waste product, or even his delight in it is "bad." The child's dilemma is to choose between two incompatible aims: preserving the pleasure of eliminating when it pleases him most, or winning the parent's admiration. Of course, *the wise parent understands that this is an evolving conflict within the child, not a power struggle between the parent and child.*

As in every imitation of adult behavior, something of the unsocialized pattern of the infant is relinquished here in favor of the pleasure in mastery of the act itself and the doors it may open in the real world, the inner pleasure and pride in being "just like" the parent, and the pleasure in pleasing an appreciative audience. The selfish, personal pleasure of making a mess at will is forgone, forgotten, or disguised in other forms. The toilet-trained child becomes eligible for all kinds of new adventures, as well as reaping general admiration for being a fine fellow.

## THE PARENT INSIDE

For our purposes, it is the child's inner world that is illuminating, as he proceeds along the way to attaining greater mastery, because this is the domain of values. We can overhear the drama, very often, as the small child addresses his stuffed animal or doll, reassuring, scolding, cajoling, or teasing, "Do this, don't do that." The parent, with his agenda and habits of mind, has inhabited the child's emotional being and become part of it, speeches and all. The youngster struggling with learning to tie his shoelaces will perhaps mouth under his breath, "bunny ears, bunny ears," preserving the encouraging parent within. The child whispers, "now look both ways," incorporating the protecting parent's guidance even as he continues to hold the parent's hand at the curb.

The child tells himself, "Mommy is right here." He begins to take over the functions of soothing himself, providing for himself the relief of anxiety or hurt that used to be mother's role. Thus the paradox: the more richly and securely the child is loved while dependent, the more his independence of spirit can blossom at a later time.

*Establishment of the inner presence of the guiding and comforting parent is one of the most significant emotional achievements of early childhood.* This presence becomes the anchor of the child's ability to soothe and manage himself, and to tolerate anxiety, sadness, and anger. All day long the parent provides a view of the world and the child within it that reinforces the child's ability to wait, to tolerate frustration, and to foresee solutions down the path. The ordinary empathy of parents leads them to do this naturally, without any specific awareness of this in mind. Mother says to the impatient child, "Oh, dinner will be ready soon" or "Daddy can fix it" or "Don't worry—we'll find it later." These constantly murmured words explain the universe—the loud noise isn't dangerous, it's only the garbage truck—but they also encourage the child's growing capacity to endure the stresses and dilemmas of daily life, because they mean these problems can be understood, grappled with, and mastered.

The child is equipped with powerful impulses to imitate and absorb the attitudes, ideas, and actions of loved persons. In this way, the parent's ordinary commentary is a vehicle not only for information, but for attitude and growth of feeling as well. The parent says, "See the leaves fall? It's autumn!" The parent conveys not only the fact that the seasons change, but also whatever *emotion* is present in the parent—delight, excitement, love of nature. This feeling is mingled with closeness involved in shared experiences—the bond of cherished intimacy and tenderness between the parent and the child.

This is a great wellspring of personal strength for the child, who may then carry with him throughout life traces of interwoven memory—of the passage of seasons, of leaves, and of being loved. The fact that most adults specifically remember very little of their early childhood does not mean that these experiences are lost on the child. They continue to exert force on the child's character as *the stuff of an inner life*—the ability to be alone, to make one's experience meaningful to oneself, and to feel truly alive. The capacity for solitude is based on the sense of deep meaningfulness of the life process, an outgrowth of this dialogue.

## ROMANCE IN THE NURSERY

The most fascinating subjects for the preschool child are those things most near at hand—the human body and its various potentials, and the human psyche and its relationships. The child's imagination struggles all day long to piece these mysteries together as he lives among others. This great drama includes what adults classify as the facts of sexual reproduction, but it is much broader, and encompasses where people come from, where they go when they die, how they come together, what makes them stick together, and how loving and hating fit in with coming and going.

These are, of course, primarily the issues that continue to concern all of us as human beings throughout the life cycle, because they are the very stuff and substance of our existence. *It is in early childhood that people form their first notions about these great fundamentals; it is in our earliest family experiences that we lay down the framework for our later potential as physical and psychological creatures.*

The idea of having a baby does not start in adulthood; in fact, the wish for a baby is one of the earliest ideas a person may have. Even babies are quite interested in having babies, as is revealed in their play.

Eric at 16 months reacted to the arrival of his newborn sister that morning from the hospital by putting a doll in his shirt, proudly strutting around pregnant, and giving birth on the floor. He then marched his "baby" and a carton of the sister's diapers to the front door, where he deposited them—indicating that he had had enough of the new baby. It was time for her to leave now. This toddler's behavior displays the way in which a child's psychological understanding and capacity to communicate symbolically outstrip his ability to use words. Naturally, any child's sexual ideas are typically rather garbled from the perspective of scientific fact—as can be seen in the common childhood belief that the mother becomes pregnant by eating something, or that birth takes place through the belly button.

The point is not that young children have a great store of accurate wisdom about reproduction, but that they have a great sensitivity to and awareness of human emotion, especially concerning the eternal situations of love and hate, birth and death. We can see evidence that Eric had two intentions in mind: he wanted to do what his mother had done in producing the baby, and he wanted to get rid of the rival. These wishes, though bound to be frustrated in the here-and-now situation, live on in the personality; they are transformed in indirect ways into the stuff of living—to other forms of creativity and competition, and, eventually, into fatherhood itself.

*It is not principally how parents explain the facts of life but how they live the facts of life that shapes and colors the small child's view of the life cycle and his role in it.* From earliest childhood, the parents' identities, goals, and values are absorbed by the young individual. Part of this may be intentional teaching, but the essence of it is imitative. The core of imitation is the child's *wanting to be*—to be like, to have within himself the voice and presence of the loved parent.

The child's great desire is to be *just like* the parents. His desires are still close to magical wishes—he is a firm believer that hoping something should be so or playing that something should be so makes it so in reality. This belief comes face to face with new complexities, with the child's evolving recognition of the distinctions of girl, boy, man, and woman. We know that babies too young to talk are aware of themselves as either girls or boys, but the implications of this do not start to sink in until they begin to practice their romantic arts on their parents. While children of both sexes crave physical closeness from both mother and father, for the 3- and 4- year old there is a new additional quality of seduction that enters the child's emotions towards both parents, particularly the parent of the opposite sex. Coyness, charm, and the wish to captivate an audience are stimulated.

Like the shrieking baby in the movie theater, the 3-year-old boy who announces his plans to marry his mother makes us grin. We are happy to see such juicy evidence of life; at the same time we hope that he will not be too unmercifully crushed by the realization that, alas, this cannot be. First, there is the obstruction that Mom is already married to Dad, whom one can not conveniently do away with, both because he is powerful and because he is also good to have around, even loved. The possibility of rivalry—even in the very back of the little boy's mind—opens the door for much reflection on his torn loyalties, his sense of his own villainy, and his fears of retaliation. The boy has new opportunities to feel lonely and defiant, to recall other anxieties experienced in earlier contexts, and to rework them on the stage of this troubling new soap opera.

The 3-year-old girl similarly loves her mother and has the ambition of possessing her. Without losing this loyalty (indeed because of it), the little girl aims to do and be what Mommy is—and to show that she can do a better job at it. She will marry Daddy and be the perfect wife. But the mother is also loved, and mother's disapproval, for any reason, is upsetting. The idea of having Daddy all to herself brings on the possibility of losing the loved mother and of facing the angry mother. For the little girl the notion of having a baby of her own begins to take on more pressing importance. Commonly this is mixed up with the fantasy of stealing it from mother, or fearing mother would steal it from her child, or sharing it with mother peaceably. Marrying, owning, and making babies become the absorbing interest of small children of both genders.

It should be noted that the sense of sexual identity, of role, and of romantic yearning is fixed and absolute only in theory. The little boy and girl both remain loyal, in part, to the parent of the same sex. They aim at times to exclude the parent of the opposite sex, although generally in a less noticeable form. These contradictions live within the child harmoniously side by side, and enrich the personality.

The ambition to fill the shoes of the loved parent (doing what the parent does) cannot entirely escape encountering the staggering idea of getting rid of the rival. Because children think magically, their notions of death are fluid and flexible—slaying the rival is quite compatible with needing him the next moment. Of course, the idea of doing away with the parent is not fully embraced by the child's personality as a whole. It may make its clear appearance only at moments when the child is bitterly angry at that parent. The ordinary ups and downs of a toddler's day may provide numerous opportunities for such moments, however. The small boy is disappointed in Daddy, who has been busy on the telephone, and who then gives the boy a sharp rebuke at the third interruption. "I hate you," his little son yells, looking daggers.

The toddler's normal exploration of his own body and the activities of elimination, bathing, and changing lead to the discovery of the child's version of sexual pleasure that results from handling his genitals. Unlike the excitement of physically mature persons that leads to orgasm, a child's sexual desire has nowhere to go. It is bound to be frustrated. The physical yearning and excitement of a toddler's genital explorations is tied up in his mind in a vague way with the people the toddler loves, and adds a new depth of romantic passion to this love.

Parents generally convey to small children the message that masturbation is not to be done publicly—it pertains to one's "private parts." Straightlaced parents may communicate this without themselves being fully aware that the issue has surfaced. During this period, children gain increased pleasure and applause in exhibiting publicly the attractiveness of their bodies, and their growing abilities in general. "Showing off" makes its appearance.

The child of this age is alert enough to observe that little girls and little boys are built differently. At a certain phase, the appearance of the little girl's genitals is regularly misinterpreted by small children of both sexes to lack something. The observed differences are easily woven into the child's understanding of sex in an anxiety almost universal in the nursery-age range, that the female genital has been injured or mutilated. Many children assume the girl had a penis at one time, but lost it—perhaps as a punishment. The child's preoccupations during this period of development, the physical potential for sexual excitement, and the emotional ambition to possess the parents romantically come

together in a new anxiety: the possibility of loss of the genital as a punishment for sexual rivalry or masturbation. A little boy may fear the loss
of his penis, and a little girl may worry about where hers went. Each
child needs reassurance that the child is perfect and intact and will
stay that way, just as he or she is.

Ordinarily, these developments pass under the noses of parents
without coming into clear focus, and often strike people as quite pre-
posterous when they are discussed explicitly. There are several reasons
for this. First, it is the nature of memory to lose a firm grasp of events
in our preschool years, so that as adults we cannot readily identify our
own recollections of this age. In addition, old-fashioned ideas of "sin"
make us most uncomfortable with the idea that children have sexual
sensations in their bodies or sexual wishes in their minds. Moreover, a
child's sexual excitement is not focused, as is an adult's: it tends to
include many things, such as eating, dancing, jumping around, and
sometimes spanking. (We notice that adults tend to preserve echoes
of these elements in activities that are precursors to romance.)

The child's use of language, in addition, is not sophisticated enough
to convey these themes directly. Lacking a grown-up vocabulary, children use the language of symbols. Thus we may see bits and pieces of
the story rather than the logical whole. Children may not comment on
the puzzling differences between the appearance of boys' and girls'
bodies, yet they may go through a period of worry about other things
that seem broken or defective. Kathleen, age 3, was endlessly preoccupied with a decorative fountain in the park—sometimes the water
was spouting out, sometimes not. She asked over and over with evident fright what had happened to the fountain. Her parents, who an-
swered her questions repeatedly, were perplexed at the intensity of her
concern and their inability to reassure her. Other children will object
strenuously to being offered a cookie that is broken, or focus nervously
on a remote possibility of injury to their bodies. Sometimes they tempt
fate with repeated acts of risk-taking, as if to flout injury and prove that
their bodies are intact no matter what.

*What is called for, of course, is not that parents understand child psy-
chology on a technical level, but that they respond to their child moment
to moment with ordinary support and empathy.* Their boy may not announce boldly, "Mommy is all mine!" but his behavior may convey this.

Such a child may be quite irritating, expertly commanding Mommy's indulgent attention just when Dad would like it for himself. It is entirely normal that the father feels put out by the little charmer, but it is important that he tolerate this with a certain humor rather than a bitterness that suggests that the little boy is a real rival. The child's aggression and magical assertion of power of course needs to be realistically contained so that safety and sanity prevail. This can happen without puncturing the child's balloon, so to speak.

Likewise, the mother of a 3- or 4-year-old girl may need to call upon inner forbearance. There are times when the little girl reproaches her mother severely, when only Daddy can provide comfort. These moments may be especially puzzling to the mother if she has been the major caregiver.

## CHARACTER AT THE CLOSE OF
## THE PRESCHOOL PERIOD

Although as adults most people remember only sketchy events from the period before the age of 5, this is not because nothing has happened. On the contrary, what has taken place is a process of emotional growth that will have immense consequences for what kind of person the child becomes. One can see that the development of *the capacity to feel for others* is a product of the young child's ordinary experience of being cared for lovingly. The wish to give, to share, to "make up," and to nurture have their roots in receiving regular care performed out of love. Impulses of genuine generosity, being sorry, and forgiving come from inside and are obvious in the behavior of small children without their having been taught. Routinely meeting the child's hunger, thirst, fatigue, or being too hot or too cold *at the time that it is felt*, so that relief of the need is related both to the person and to an appreciation of the person's intent—this is the beginning of hope, good fellowship, and trust.

In addition to this, the preschool youngster has had to make peace with the frustration of fundamental wishes, at least in terms of the magical possession of either parent. The child has slowly and painfully come to see that things are not *so* simply because he announces that they are so. Mommy and Daddy remain, indeed, married to one another. They seem to like it that way. The child has been "put in his place." Every effort is made so that this is not a humiliating defeat, but the child remains, in fact, a small child in a big world where adults are in charge. The youngster thus becomes something of a realist; one must accept facts for what they are.

The child has had to grapple with his own destructive feelings and to see that they do not, in themselves, do catastrophic harm. His intermittent hostility to each parent has been endured, and everyone has survived. His anger at his parents and his love for them have come together as a bittersweet lesson. The child recognizes that other people are not extensions of his wants, but want things for themselves that may even exclude him for a time. The loved person is separate from the child and has a life of his or her own. With this realization comes the increasing capacity to tolerate frustration in human relationships and to accept partial and postponed fulfillment of satisfactions. The child learns to wait. He learns to be "nice." From this too comes the experience of remorse for harboring destructive feelings towards loved persons, and a sense of concern and responsibility.

The child's direct romantic aspirations have been put on hold. In the process, the child's love for the parent, his discovery of gender differences, and his personal experience of erotic feeling have been brought together. The result is that the child's sexual identity, his need for love, and his capacity for biological excitement are now linked. This lays the groundwork for the future experience of mature intimacy, where sexual sensations (which come and go) and spiritual commitment (which is enduring) can be joined in one lifetime relationship.

Of course, the child continues to be more or less joyously in love with both parents—a feeling accompanied by the tenderness and pride so typical of the state of love. The little girl thinks her mother is the prettiest lady in the world, the very best mother; she plays the piano more beautifully than anyone else possibly could. Likewise her father is the most courageous and important man on earth. Out of this come a thousand childhood offerings of love: a flower, a kiss, a cherished secret. In this we see a reciprocal effect of the parents' overvaluation of the baby; the child overvalues his particular parents as unique, special, and ideal.

The child's capacity to idealize the parents in spite of the inevitable everyday disappointments and the parents' actual ordinariness is of crucial importance to his character because it establishes the future capacity for idealization and idealism. This is necessary for all mature forms of emotional commitment. Later experiences of falling in love will inherit the same coloration of uniqueness and joy: only the beloved could possibly be so enchanting and endearing! This is the miracle of romantic love, in which average men and women find in one another absolutely unique, precious, and irreplaceable charms. The capacity for idealization that has its roots in childhood ardor is what sustains adult love over a lifetime; the stability of the parents' love for each other and for the child is experienced by the youngster as eternal. The legacy of this childhood experience is the ongoingness of the child's mature choices, his conviction that a devotion once fixed is everlasting.

The idealization of the parents will also be transferred in various partial ways to teachers, friends, and other new faces. Because the parents loved and were loved by the child, the outside world opens up with possibilities. The child can invest himself in relationships through thick and thin, and tolerate some measure of disappointment within the context of a broader loyalty. His character is thus prepared for a fidelity in human relationships that does not shatter with every minor tribulation; he is willing to connect with strangers, and optimistic about finding something valuable in the connection.

Importantly too, the child's devotion to his parents is eventually re-experienced in relation to abstractions, to ideas and ideals. Often the parents' traditions are loved in a direct fashion; specific memories of the parents' activities and beliefs are embraced. Thus we find individuals loving their religion, their country, or their system of ethics because this is what their parents valued; they feel closer to the parents (perhaps even despite the physical absence of the parents) through devotion to these beliefs. The parents' love for the child is kept externally alive through shared investment in emotionally meaningful ideals. Here we see the transmission of values imbued with the power of the parents' love.

Indeed, the capacity for all idealism is rooted in the child's idealization of his parents, even when the idealism produces conflict with the actual parents. The youngster's enthusiasm to "save the world," so typical of adolescents, grows out of the character traits of compassion, devotion, and idealism that are rooted in the love relationship with the parent (as well as the competitiveness that is part of that love relationship); this often leads to ironies, as when the adolescent's specific beliefs clash with parental ideas.

The child's idealization of the parents is matched by a corresponding sensation of great self-importance. As one little boy of 2 expressed vigorously, "I'm going to put my pee-pee and potty all over the whole world!" The parents' attentiveness and tenderness towards the child allows the gradual transformation of his sense of all-powerful grandeur to a more realistic view, although the universal language of love always endorses his claim to be "the best little boy in the whole world." The gradual deflation of the child's impossibly grand view of either his parents or himself is not, however, the parents' responsibility, insofar as the inevitable frustrations and failures of realistic circumstances make the youngster's actual limitations all too plain to him.

*The parents' job is to smooth over the discontinuity between the child's perception of his magical powers and his perception of his actual childish ineptitude.* This is easily done by the parent who steps in to assist the child in moments of his helplessness, yet maintains the emotional position of the child's supreme importance, because that too is what the parent feels. This process is most overt in the nursery period but is actually carried forward throughout the child's development into adolescence and even beyond.

The parents' role is to knit together into one whole the two polar experiences the child encounters, often many times in the course of a day: all-powerful joy and love, and all-powerful grief and hate. Parents do this naturally, because they find *the whole child* endearing and worth it. This role is, however, enormously taxing and emotionally depleting; if there is more than one child, the caregiving adults will have an even greater personal need of support and replenishment.

It is here that the child begins to achieve a view of himself that is sustained and does not crumble with every loss and frustration. This forms a core of self-esteem that is visible later in diverse qualities: levelheadness under fire, optimism in the face of loss, and equanimity amid stress. The youngster becomes prepared for the preservation of his own emotional stability in the ups and downs of living. This has great implications in terms of the youngster's ability to regulate his own mood.

The parents' joy in the child provides the nourishment that permits him to tolerate the growing recognition that he is not, indeed, the literal center of the universe—only the center of his parents' universe, perhaps, and that only in a fundamental way, not in a way that gives him magical control over their every move. All of these experiences contribute to the character of the child as the preschool period draws to a close.

## READINESS FOR SCHOOL

The child setting out for kindergarten is at a crossroads; he is pretty well glued to his parents, but he is also on the threshold of a larger world. He is ready for it. All along, *the intense emotional relationships the child has formed with his family during the preschool years, and the child's efforts to understand the ins and outs of these relationships, have been the workshop of his growing character.* As the youngster comes of school age, he is already equipped in fundamental form with the qualities of warmth, imagination, responsibility, and a sense of a personal future.

We recognize that his personality is still rudimentary and that in functioning it easily backslides and breaks down. We readily observe that every kindergarten child retreats into babyish reactions to various stresses, probably many times each day. He goes to pieces and falls apart. However, the continued presence of the kernels of maturity keep him moving forward. After the retreat into babyishness, there is a forward advance along the growing edge of the youngster's personality, reinforced by the continuing availability of parents.

The character qualities emerging in the child entering school have been transmitted through the deeply personal intimacy of daily life with parents who provide physical care, love, and stability in the nursery years. While meeting the physical needs of the child's growing body, they have also provided for the needs of his growing heart and spirit, although perhaps not noticing that they have done so.

We also observe that this system is of necessity quite robust—perfection is neither attainable nor required. The ordinary accidents and irregularities of life naturally interfere with the absolute availability of any pair of parents. On average, children manifest a great resilience to imperfection and delay, so long as the basics are reliable. And it should go without saying that to fill the role of parent it is not necessary to be the actual biological parent, but the psychological parent. There is a certain poignancy when the parent sees his very own DNA, and that of his spouse and forebears, express itself in the shape of a child's hands and nose—and very often in the shape of his personality. In ordinary circumstances, this adds a depth to the child's attachment in both directions, just as the experiences of pregnancy, labor, birth, and breast-feeding add a dimension of depth to a mother's love. But anyone can fill the bill beautifully if the human commitment, devotion, and availability are there. All that is needed is that the adults respond to the child as any ordinary parents would do, because loving that child is the most important thing in their lives. Fortunately, many persons have this to give to a child who is not biologically their own, just as, sadly, there are some biological parents who do not have this to give to their own children.

The child is prepared to go to school at the closure of nursery age because his character has grown to encompass the rudimentary functions of managing himself for several hours at a time. This has been a passionate process, based on deep attachments that now continue to influence him from inside when the actual parents are absent. What follows, from kindergarten to the beginning of the teenage years, is a long period of consolidation of these developments. When the child first begins school, his toleration for handling excitement, frustration, and uncertainty is rather limited. The day needs to be fairly short and the teacher needs to step in, from time to time, as a substitute parent for the child who is "falling apart." The function of elementary school is to give children an opportunity to exercise limited, step-by-step independence from their parents, through extending and deepening their capacity for constructive human relationships and the process of education.

Of course, children have been learning all along. The kind of learning that takes place before elementary school is immense, but it is not education in the narrow sense. What a baby, a toddler, or a 4-year-old learns is personal and universal, and cannot be separated from the concept of play. A small child's struggle to draw a human form so that it expresses the action or emotion that he holds in his mind's eye demonstrates this kind of activity; muscle, vision, and the child's creative spirit come together on the plane of discovery that is both generic to all human beings since the beginning of time and idiosyncratic to the particular child. The child is magical; he is open to everything.

Neurological developments allow for a different kind of learning to begin at the age of 6 or 7. The child's thinking has become more realistic. He can think ahead; he can study; he understands that the world is made up of interlocking systems and he locates his place within the scheme of things. He acknowledges the claims of an outer impersonal reality that obeys its own laws. He is ready to submit to the outer world, to authorities, to the sphere of laws that apply equally to everyone. At this age one can make headway teaching a child a specific discipline: a craft, a religion, an academic subject like history or mathematics. The child becomes proud of his industriousness. The idea of work becomes relevant—whether it is actual adult work (harvesting a crop), or working on or toward something (learning to read). The magical thinking that surrounded the nursery child like a kind of radiant cloud—"I am King Kong!" or "I am going to marry Daddy!"—is gradually transformed into increasingly realistic planning. Many wishes are pushed out of the present and into the future. Unrealistic goals are assessed as such and laid aside.

At the close of the preschool period, the child still maintains curiosity about babies and producing them, but the goals of adult roles—marriage and children—are postponed. They are shifted into the future. It is in this context that a child begins to possess a uniquely personal future, to construct his future, and to construct himself in such a way as to inhabit the future of his own hopes. He begins to plan. It is as if the child has negotiated a trade-off between immediate wishes and far-off ones that promise deeper and more grown-up satisfactions. This is the beginning of planning for a future, of the child's engaging in tasks that do not have direct gratification. He begins to apply himself. These crucial steps are reflected in the child's statement that begins, "When I grow up . . ."

The self-regard of the school-aged child is thus somewhat measured, and ebbs and flows in accordance with the self's perceived success in relation to an idealized self, and to various goals and standards. It is here that the child's character begins to resemble that of an adult, at least in form, as he acquires a conscience-like concern inside that observes him at all times, like the parent used to do, and deals out a sense of pride or dismay as befits the occasion.

A person whose behavior is led by his larger personal goals has a kind of constancy and integrity—we are likely to say he is true to himself.

## Clinical Considerations

On the path from birth to kindergarten, the child undergoes an extraordinary development, a flowering of biological and psychological growth. The preceding chapter described this process, focusing on the growth of the child's inner resources—his character—his ability to be generally loving, responsible, and optimistic. The professional clinician will recognize the debt here to the structural concepts of the id, the ego, and the superego, as well as the framework of unfolding psychosexual development, as these entities take shape through the child's interactions with the environment (S. Freud 1917). This environment includes the parents' conscious and unconscious attitudes as they libidinalize his body and spirit through caring for him.

The infant grows cognitively but also emotionally, through stages of bonding, to the achievement of psychological separateness (Mahler et al. 1975). Defensive operations of the ego progress from primitive projection, introjection, and splitting to the acquisition of defenses that involve acknowledgment and mastery of reality (A. Freud 1936). Thought evolves from the primary process of magical wishes and dreams to include also the secondary process, in which the laws of reality are given their due. The child's inner world becomes peopled with increasingly stable images (symbolic representations) of himself and others, linked by both positive and negative affects (Jacobson 1964).

The normal child's internalized objects, the parental "goodness" inside, provides solace to him when the real parent is experienced as temporarily "bad," frustrating, or absent (Klein 1932). These images of self and other—the residue of memory and fantasy formed in the early relationships—take shape as the child's *character*, a personal and relatively enduring way of experiencing the world and responding to it

(Fenichel 1945). The introjected objects become firmer and more realistic over time, providing the child an increasing capacity to tolerate solitude, delay, and disappointment in actual persons. Thus the child gradually comes to terms with his own greed, envy, and aggression, as well as with the limitations inherent in all of reality. All of this is presumed when we say that a particular child is ready for school.

## Case

*Mrs. Gilbert brought her 5-year-old son Ted to therapy because, as she explained with an embarrassed smile, "I just can't control him." Ted was a strapping boy with a loud, bragging manner and a high IQ; he had been enrolled in a nursery school program for gifted children, where he was increasingly aggressive and defiant of direction. His development had been unremarkable, although he had a bold boisterous temperament and a tendency to hit and shove both other children and his parents. But Ted had another, anxious side; this Ted bit his nails, suffered from frequent nightmares, and had various long-standing fears (of security guards at shopping malls, of noisy lawn mowers, of lightning).*

*Mrs. Gilbert was now visibly pregnant with her second child, and Ted was almost abusive to her—playfully ramming into her stomach full force, and calling her a "fat cow" (she had a chronic problem of controlling her weight). Mrs. Gilbert was a homemaker with a college degree. Her husband was a university professor and a "nervous" individual. Mrs. Gilbert doubted he had the time to participate in the treatment. Her older brother had been an outstanding student, but had committed suicide by jumping from a dormitory window at the age of 19 after suffering several years of mental illness and many psychiatric hospitalizations.*

*The therapist observed Mrs. Gilbert and Ted together in the office. It was striking that Ted's frequent attempts to violate both his mother's feelings and her body were met with an anxious smile and a measure of ineffective, limp pleading. When Ted pushed and insulted her, she would throw a childlike glance at the therapist, as if hoping he would do something to rescue her. The therapist made a mental note of his own emotional reactions: at first he had been* enraged and appalled at Ted's "conscienceless" attacks—he had felt an impulse to physically overpower this sassy, boastful youngster. Yet when he watched mother and son together, he suddenly felt a surge of sympathy for Ted and anger at his mother for putting up no resistance to his assaults. He felt a little like smacking her himself.

Mother—by no means a stupid woman—was a classic enabler, just as Ted was classically spoiled. She offered Ted no help in curbing, redirecting, or experiencing remorse for his aggression. When the therapist succeeded in luring the elusive father into the office, he was surprised to see that the father also had a clear, if somewhat intellectualized, understanding of this interaction: "He hits her because she lets him." All the same, father saw his own role as a reporter or observer, rather than a participant.

The therapist attempted to teach Mrs. Gilbert new ways to set limits on Ted's hostile behavior. Although over a period of some weeks she made a mighty effort to duplicate the therapist's techniques, somehow she always managed to undercut herself. It was as if she herself were of two minds about it. There was no change in Ted's symptoms.

Recognizing that Mrs. Gilbert was unable to make use of practical advice, the therapist met with her individually and explained kindly that he had come to wonder whether certain personal troubles interfered with her ability to follow through on her conscious intention to respond more appropriately to Ted's aggression. Her eyes filled with tears and she said softly, "I knew it was that." The therapist then expressed hope that Mrs. Gilbert could surmount these problems through understanding herself better. Even before he could finish, however, Mrs. Gilbert began to pour out her fears that Ted would eventually be like her brother, brilliant but destructive to himself and everyone around him.

She proceeded to describe, over the next several sessions, how her own girlhood had been dominated by her brother's illness. He would storm and shout, at times striking her to the ground with his fists. Her parents had been utterly helpless whenever this happened.

Deep down she nursed the painful idea that they excused the brother's behavior because they valued him ("the genius") more than her, and that they were willing to stand by and allow him to hurt her. She felt she had sacrificed her youth to her brother's illness and

*that his suicide had enshrined him permanently as a tragic martyr.
She had never admitted to herself how abandoned and angry she had
felt during these hard years.*

*Similarly, Mrs. Gilbert had never recognized how her current
family reproduced these traumatic features—amidst males of great
intellect and little empathy, she passively absorbed the blows, hoping to be rescued. Like her parents, her husband stood by without
stepping in. She realized, saying this, that nevertheless she had been
accustomed to leaning on her husband in many ways, as if he were
a parent and she were a child.*

*At the same time, she began to view Ted in a new light: not as a
powerful, intimidating, masterful force, but as a little boy overwhelmed and distressed by his own anger, jealousy, and anxiety. As
her recognition of the legitimacy of her own aggressive feelings grew,
her appraisal of her son's aggression became more realistic. Gradually, her very voice and body posture took on a firmer quality with
him and in general.*

*She now communicated to Ted in a thousand small ways that
he could, should, and would refrain from hurting people. At the
same time, her warmth and empathy for him also became more
vigorous. Meanwhile, the therapist met with both Ted and mother
together to facilitate Ted's expression of emotion in more adaptive
ways. In this therapy threesome, Ted drew pictures of bombs, of
fighting animals—and then an elaborate drawing of a special flower
that felt unloved by the rain "because there were other flowers pop-
ping up all over the place."*

Ted's problems illustrate the importance of the child's resolution
of the oedipal struggle to the development of a workable conscience
and ego ideal. At the beginning of treatment, Ted was not a very nice
boy. He was not interested in being nice; he did not struggle very effectively within himself to be a good person, but projected this struggle
onto security guards as harsh authorities who might attack him from
outside.

The therapist had an inkling from many of her remarks that Mrs.
Gilbert had been more than a little enthralled with her ill brother, whom
she also pitied and feared. Her view of herself as female was colored

by an unconscious fantasy of masochistic surrender to a violent male; yet in this passivity there was a certain grandiosity too—only she, secretly the strong one, could tolerate the brother's abuse, which in a sense she deserved. Because of her sense of guilt, Mrs. Gilbert was *too* nice— afraid of her own deeply repressed aggression and ashamed of her romantic feelings. She was afraid of wanting anything for herself.

Ted's developmental claims to own and dominate his mother then intensified these conflicts—she could not presume to contain his aggression, but she would passively submit to and absorb it. As a child, she had felt guilty over needs of her own that took away attention from her brother; she felt particularly guilty now that Ted had the evidence, so visible in her pregnancy, of her sexual activity with her husband and her disloyal wish to have a second child. It was indeed her primitive fear that Ted might kill her unborn child that made her seek treatment. Ted, in turn, was in the grips of his own phallic grandiosity; his mother's doormat-like acquiescence to his omnipotence confused and overstimulated him.

The therapy did not need to bring all of these issues to consciousness and resolution; what was necessary was that Mrs. Gilbert express some of her long-stifled emotions in relation to her brother and her parents. This itself helped her to separate the past from the present, and to experience less inhibition of her own self-protective aggressive impulses. She was then better able to limit her son's grandiosity, rather than to be cowed by it. Her new way of responding to Ted encouraged him to internalize these limits, to master his own oedipal jealousy, and to articulate symbolically concerns about being lovable despite the threat posed by his mother's pregnancy. Of course, as a result he was in fact much easier to love, a much nicer boy.

This case illustrates how a parent's neurotic conflicts may interfere with establishment of appropriate parent–child boundaries, resulting in the youngster's excessive anxiety and behavioral acting out. Through treatment, the parent was able to contain (but also to enjoy) the child more energetically, which in turn permitted the child to grow to be more self-critical, self-contained, and emotionally expressive.

This case also demonstrates how successful child treatments often include the parents. *The well-intentioned parent is hungry for company in doing a better job with the child and eager to talk with the child's thera-*

*pist*. Often, as here, the parent carries within himself a considerable burden of psychic pain—a dominating personal problem that is indirectly very relevant to the child's dilemma. An imaginative and flexible therapist aims to illuminate for the parent how these two realms are interrelated: in this endeavor, the therapist is guided by the material presented, rather than by preconceived recipes for isolated treatment modalities. It is often possible for the parent, as a consequence, to experience great relief in other areas of living, although the treatment has been geared principally toward helping the parent respond more sensitively to the child's needs.

# 3

*ঙ*

# On the Parent's
# Good Authority

## AUTHORITY AS CHARACTER

Mom and Dad of the old American dream were strong, kind, and stead-fast. Their leadership in the drama of daily living was vivid, intimate, and inspiring. They loved life, each other, and their children. These simple devotions made them deeply respectful of all people, large and small. They took joy in responsibility and pride in the work that went with it. They bore their sorrows with dignity, without self-pity or envy. As a result, you wanted to be like them and to do what they did.

These idealized parent figures had the kind of natural authority that brings out the best in their children's character. They may not have had any unusual talents, training, or resources; they may never have given the issue of their own authority a moment's thought. Neverthe-less, their actions showed constancy of purpose because of their deep commitments and beliefs.

*The very essence of the parent who is a strong authority figure is faith: faith in the existence of human goodness, faith in the forces of growth and forward development within the child, and faith in himself as a resource-ful, self-reliant, and capable adult.* This is indeed just the kind of author-ity that many parents today would so dearly love to feel they have. If we wish to understand what enhances and what undermines parental authority, we need to focus not on particular techniques but on the parents' overall outlook and spirit. These are the aspects of the parents' character that give their authority its meaning.

What are the strong parent's goals when exercising authority? Of course, *the most fundamental goal of authority is to make sure that the child is safe*. We see this in action when a toddler is about to get himself into potential danger and the parent swoops him up off his feet out of harm's way. When children first become mobile but are too little to use their own judgment, the parent's day involves quite a bit of this kind of authority, which is physical as well as mental.

A parent who is determined not to let a toddler play in the street simply doesn't let it happen. He gives it no opportunity to happen. This goes for a whole world full of potentially unsafe situations. The wise parent is tactful at these times, because he instinctively understands that "making" a child do something always carries the disadvantage of getting a child's back up, of infuriating a little person who is eager to do things "all by myself." Thus he aims wherever possible to control the situation, rather than to control the child. Nonetheless he has no compunction against using force when necessary to lift the child out of a dangerous situation. Parents don't let their tots set the living room curtains on fire, or fling forks at their grandma at dinner. This may be more a question of the parent being quick and vigilant rather than physically stronger than the child, but when children are very little the physical strength of the parent is always there to back up the parent's ability to make the child safe. When all else fails, the adult extracts the child from the situation, containing him.

Long after the child has become large enough to give the parent quite a run for his money physically, the parent is still able to "make" the child do things in the child's best interest. A child may come home from school one day completely fed up with the second grade. All the same, he still needs to return to school the next day. A parent experiencing a moment of personal insecurity might be intimidated by the child and react as if the child were a grown-up. Long negotiations may follow on the value of education. Another parent who feels temporarily inadequate and pushed against the wall may overreact to his own helplessness with aggression and begin to shout. The wise parent sympathizes with the child's distress, and remarks mildly that tomorrow is a long way off.

The parent and child must both respect the laws of reality; the parent makes this happen in the name of safety. A child needs to be vaccinated, and to come into the house at dinner time, and to do a hundred things he'd be disinclined to do, if no one "made" him. Children like and need to be "made" to do things that establish a wholesome routine, and give them a sense of security and reliability. Thus the empathic parent maintains a reasonable level of order and organization within the home because the provision of predictability in the environment contributes to his child's sense of security. The child can see that the rules are there to help people, including himself.

*The rhythm of living and the music the parent brings to it are themselves aspects of the parent's soothing and caring.* For example, children need to go to bed at a certain time each night because otherwise they are tired the next day. They are too little to accomplish this on their own so that parents need to put them to bed. A child responds, above all, to the spirit in which this is done; children respond differently to a parent who grimly deprives them of staying up than to a parent who enjoys tucking them tenderly into their beds on time.

To the degree that children are little and dependent, they need to feel that parents are structuring and supervising daily life and making decisions for them, in their best interest, and that the parents have no lingering doubts about their right and ability to enforce these decisions. It's like the authority a policeman has to divert traffic on Main Street because of a downed power line—he doesn't have to discuss it or defend it; he just does it.

Sooner or later, of course, the parent needs to use his authority to help the child learn to manage himself, to help the child gradually take over the functions of the parent. This is a very different aspect of the parent's authority from making the child safe, because no force on earth can make a child manage himself. The child has to want to do it and he has to know how. The child needs both inspiration and information. This is the second element of a parent's authority.

*Helping a child learn to manage himself is perhaps the greatest challenge of parenthood, and takes forbearance, self-discipline, energy, and wisdom.* This is the sphere of the parent as expert, experienced in the laws of nature and of living. The parent teaches, inspires, models, and suggests. This is less like the authority of the policeman, and more like the authority of the wise elder. If you had a problem with butterflies, for example, you would consult an authority on butterflies. He can't "make" you solve your problem, but probably he can help you solve it yourself.

The kind of expertise offered by the parent is the expertise of a person who has seen not one or two examples of something, but hundreds of them. What the child needs is not some sort of scientific, professional, technical expertise, but expertise at general living. Why does the world act as it does? Why are people the way they are? What shall I make of this—a flat tire, a bloody nose, a dead bird? The endless "why" questions of the small child represent his insatiable craving for his parent's wisdom, his readiness to be apprenticed to the craft of mastering the ways of the external world and his own personal reactions to it.

A strong parent is comfortable using his authority to do what is necessary to make the child safe, since without safety there isn't anything of much value. He exercises his authority to create a special environment within which the child can explore the world in companionship with the parent. The wise parent works hard to minimize conflicts with and constraints applied directly to the child; he invests in this effort because he knows that it is his positive rapport with the child that sets the stage for a more profound and lasting kind of parental authority— offering leadership and guidance to his child's developing character. This interaction depends above all on a deeply intimate love relationship. Its success or failure rests to a great extent on the parent's faith in that love and its power to evoke in the child future capacities that are not immediately evident. Character, after all, is a long-term project.

### Vignette

*Emma in her high chair throws mashed bananas on the floor. Mommy suggests that Emma not do this (maybe she suggests this quite energetically). When Mommy says, "No, no. We don't throw food," it is above all a piece of wisdom, a gift, from an authority on table manners. The goal is not to "make" the child stop throwing food this very instant. The goal is to contribute to a general trend away from food throwing—if not today, perhaps tomorrow. We notice that the more pleasant the parent is while delivering this wisdom, the more likely it is to capture Emma's attention and stick in her mind as advice worthy of following. But right now Emma is too pleased with her newly discovered ability to pitch bananas on the floor to pay heed. How wonderful to control whether the bananas are up here or down there! It has the same satisfaction as the game of making parents disappear and reappear, and the same vague delicious undercurrent of bullying and dominating those one loves. Look! It makes Mommy go up and down too, right after those bananas. Up and down! There is also the fun of making a mess. Emma crows with delight.*

If Emma's mother is a woman of faith, she will trust that Emma will not throw bananas when she is ready for her high school commencement, or even next year. A good-natured and experienced parent tolerates (or at any rate survives) the child's use of food as a dramatic foil and as a plaything, despite its being a nuisance, knowing that this is the way it is with babies. The parent has empathy for the child, and laughs along with her, even as she tries to look sober and disapproving. Mother understands that this is a phase, and that once it arrives it cannot be made to go away by force, and that once it is gone nothing can bring it back. Mother knows that she is not responsible for making Emma stop throwing food this particular afternoon. Mother knows this because she is aware of the potential growth as it unfolds within the child and she has faith in that process.

Authority is above all a manifestation of the parent's own maturity of character. Maintaining appropriate authority over a child draws powerfully upon the parent's resources of patience, self-discipline, empathy, and optimism. We observe correspondingly a certain *loss of authority* whenever the parent runs out of patience or faith, or inner strength.

## THE PARENT'S TEMPER

The most universal factor that undermines parental authority is the momentary outburst of the parent's own temper and despair. The ideal parent is easy to recognize, but not so easy to be. Real human beings are not paragons, and all of us have many moments of anger, hopelessness, childishness, and foolishness. A wise parent is not especially free of these moments; all parents experience them on a daily basis. *What makes a parent wise is his ability to recover his equilibrium from these moments without getting too carried away with them, his capacity to get back in the driver's seat as the grown-up.*

If Emma's mother is a perfectly normal person having a hard day, it is possible she may run out of patience with the messy child and bananas all over the floor. Out slips a harsh word and a nasty look. The fun is over. Emma freezes, regarding her mother with a look of surprise and hurt. Perhaps her mother has just mopped the floor and sees all her work ruined. Perhaps she is embarrassed to have a kitchen that does not look tidy and clean and feels it reflects poorly on her. Perhaps Emma's triumphant pleasure in bullying her mother to and fro all afternoon has hit a nerve—Mother fumes, "Is this child making a mess on purpose?" Perhaps the child's obvious immaturity, the great distance ahead between her actual behavior and the aim of graceful table manners, suddenly overwhelms her mother with a sense of futility. These ordinary human reactions disrupt her authority and undermine her positive contribution, in the moment, to the long-term goal of Emma managing her own table manners.

With frustration and stress comes loss of perspective. This is inevitable. Every parent feels strong chaotic emotions of helplessness and resentment throughout the day as he is buffeted by the demands of family life.

It is helpful for the parent to understand that these feelings are natural, normal, and inevitable. At the same time, we must observe that the common denominator of these reactions is that *they temporarily bring the parent down to the child's level.* The parent, in these moments, has lost touch with his higher mission as a parent. He is busy feeling exasperated, overwhelmed, and abused. He is feeling sorry for himself. It is as if, for the moment, the tables were turned: the parent looks at the child in the high chair with anger and hurt and demands, "Why aren't you being nicer to me?"

It is in this frame of mind that the parent has momentarily relinquished his authority. He is down there head-to-head, nose-to-nose with the child, feeling not like the child's wise protector, but like the child's rival. He feels like a victim. This happens to us all. What parent has not been brought to his knees psychologically by a thirty-five-pound child?

A real flesh-and-blood parent is bound to feel this way towards his own children quite frequently because the deep intimacy of the parent's bond with his child reaches down into the parent's own personality, into layers where every parent is vulnerable to powerful, primitive, negative emotions of anger, envy, and helplessness, as well as powerful emotions of love. No one can get your goat like your own child! Sometimes parents feel foolish and guilty about this, because they observe that the baby-sitter and the child get along without these storms of feeling. But this only tells you that the baby-sitter and the child are connected to each other superficially, rather than profoundly—that their relationship, while pleasant, is not as deeply intimate as the parent's with his child.

A parent with a strong sense of self-reliance, of faith in human nature, and of trust in his child's ongoing development, will try to contain himself at these moments of resentment and despair, and will often succeed, because he knows they do not represent the mature side of his own personality. The parent needs to make an active effort to do so, and this self-discipline is taxing. Of course, no parent can control himself perfectly, so that there will be plenty of occasions when the parent acts on his feelings of anger and helplessness—when he loses his temper and says and does things motivated by his own childish impulses to "get back" at his vexing offspring. The mature parent regrets these angry words and deeds because he knows they are intended to hurt and because they lack real authority. He knows they do nothing to contribute to his child's self-control because they are evidence of his own imperfect self-control. All the same, he accepts the validity of his anger and wishes to retaliate as a part of being human. Temper got the better of him. He is sorry, and he communicates this to the child simply and directly. He apologizes.

*For the parent to acknowledge and accept responsibility for his temper, his own lack of perfection, is one of the most important things a parent can do for the child's growing character.* The parent's apology communicates to the child that we are all in the same boat with this difficult business of managing ourselves, and that perfection is not a realistic goal. When the parent is sorry, it reestablishes his authority as a person who is helpful and wise, not a person who feels wounded, spiteful, and sorry for himself. It reestablishes his integrity. The parent's show of temper, followed by a genuine apology, is a great consolation to the child. It is the model of how people reestablish closeness and trust, despite moments of conflict and anger.

## THE ROLE OF EXTERNAL PRESSURES

Many outside forces and pressures can work to undermine a parent's authority, directly or indirectly—by undermining his ability to provide safety and supervision, his faith in his own goodness and adequacy as a person, his faith in human nature, or his faith in his child. It is not unreasonable to say that all factors that pervasively erode a parent's optimism and peace of mind will tend to impair the strength of his authority because it is the overstressed and depleted personality that reacts by getting down on the child's level rather than acting with wisdom and forbearance. It is the depleted personality that tends to remain on that level. It is here that external hardships exert some of their cruelest influence on families by diminishing the inner resources that a parent brings to his relationship with his child.

All the various causes of human misery—social upheaval, war, extreme poverty, or life-threatening illness, among other accidents and disasters—may cause parents to feel like helpless victims because, in truth, they actually are victims. It is easy for a parent at the end of his rope to lose patience with a child's demands and have a hard time mustering the resources to recover equilibrium. It is hard to feel optimistic and hard to maintain a child's physical safety when there is chronic anxiety about food, shelter, and survival. An adult who cannot manage to meet his children's basic needs is often hard pressed to manage his own emotions and to help small children manage theirs. A child throwing food in these circumstances would not be greeted with humor.

The modern parent whose life is overburdened, overextended, and rushed in more everyday ways may also feel eaten alive by his child's needs. This is the busy parent who, without intending to do so, has become the prisoner of his own lifestyle. He is not, in any absolute sense, a victim, yet he is boxed in by the consequences of his own choices. His inner resources are depleted. Without recognizing it, this parent may react by exerting a disapproving moral pressure on the child to not need the parent. The parent can't afford for the child to backslide, to fall apart, to be babyish. The parent's reality is overly stressful to begin with, so that the child's "nonsense" is readily experienced as a personal insult, a self-indulgence, and an administrative disaster. This places a demand upon the child to act like a miniature adult. This is not realistic; the child is bound to fail.

The overstressed parent may not have what it takes to adequately supervise and guide the child—whether these resources lie in the arena of time, money, or patience and equanimity. The parent has too many other children, or too many other obligations. He's in a squeeze. He has not been able to budget for the actual size and timetable of the child's needs.

## FEELINGS OF VICTIMHOOD

The parent's authority comes out of the strong, resourceful, and empathic parts of his character. When his reactions are generated by less mature parts of his personality, there is a loss of real authority and sometimes a grim attempt on the parent's part to substitute something else in its place. This is clearest in the extreme case of the parent whose character is practically dominated by a sense of personal injury, inadequacy, and resentment—the parent who chronically feels like a victim.

The origin of these strong negative feelings is often the parent's childhood, when he suffered some significant trauma or loss that produced a great sense of helplessness or anger. These feelings then became the permanent framework of the parent's view of himself and the world. It is true that another child may have been the victim of similar forces and yet have emerged with a different outlook on life altogether. The point is that the adult's sense of suffering had its origin in a response to a reality, an actual deprivation.

At some point in time, that person's attitude of helplessness and resentment could have been expressed in words, creative play, or art, and he might have felt relief and moved on. Some additional factor prevented this from taking place, so that the person's personality became paralyzed around his anger and hurt, without full recognition and expression of what it meant. Perhaps the child concluded that speaking directly of his feelings—or even identifying them, which needs to happen first—was unacceptable.

The early absence of a deep, supportive love relationship in which the person could have communicated and worked through his distress seems to be another necessary feature of the trauma; one might also say that the absence of the intimate relationship itself was the heart of the real trauma, and the focus on the precipitating hardship only a way of making sense out of the feelings of hurt. The true deprivation was that the child had no one to share his pain and make its burden lighter.

Thus we see dramatic differences among individuals who have survived a particular hardship. Middle-aged people today can sometimes see this in the variety of their parents' responses to the Great Depression. Sometimes one comes upon individuals who can't get beyond the outrage of having had very little in 1933; they have to remind their children at every turn that they kept their own clothes in an apple-crate when they were little, and had to pee in an outhouse. Their offspring can't take ordinary pleasure in anything they possess because of the parent's envy; the child doesn't appreciate it enough that he has been provided with a real closet and a bathroom. The child is doomed to fail in this, no matter how appreciative he is, because he cannot fill the bottomless pit of the parent's sense of deprivation.

Most people, having suffered want during the Great Depression, don't need to relive it at every moment. Having survived hardship gives them a sense of pride, a compassion for the woes of the world, and a relish for ordinary joys. Curiously, they are often the very brothers and sisters of these unhappy individuals, sharing the same outhouse, though not perhaps the same human relationships with others at a crucial period. For them, that was then and this is now. For others, however, disappointments continue to be re-experienced, both in their deep lack of confidence in their own effectiveness and self-reliance and in their relationships with others. It is hard for such individuals to be truly intimate with anyone because they have trouble acknowledging and expressing their own emotions, and because they cannot trust anyone fully. This often leads to unsatisfactory marriages and a general confusion about what human beings need and can expect from one another.

To the degree that a parent's personality is dominated by feelings of victimhood, he is likely to experience an intense ongoing struggle with his child in all areas of authority. This parent experiences little faith in human nature, in himself, or in the child. He may not realize these things in so many words because these pessimistic attitudes seem to him only natural. He takes these assumptions for granted, and each reinforces the others. He has no great faith in the child's innate potential to develop and grow, or to profit from experience. As a result, he feels personally burdened with the overwhelming job of making all of these things happen himself by endless effortful pushing and pulling on the child. He envisions the child as a lump of clay to be pounded into shape rather than a living thing that spontaneously observes, learns, and responds. The very fact that the child has a mind of his its own is resented as the child's *resistance* to his parental authority, rather than welcomed as the source of the child's eventual self-mastery and genuine independence.

By the same token, the parent who feels like a chronic victim (while usually touchy about anything that seems like a criticism) has, at bottom, a low opinion of himself. He feels inadequate. He does not expect that his child would want to be like him; as a result, he cannot lead by example. It never occurs to him that the child could actively admire him so he has no confidence in this as a motivation for the child's behavior. He is left with no choice but to cause the child to experience something painful on purpose in hopes this will "teach him a lesson."

This parent lacks authority because he feels bitter, put-upon, and helpless, rather than active and effective. Whereas all of us descend to resentment and self-pity at moments of stress, the parent who feels like a perpetual victim dwells there permanently. He does not notice it, apologize for it, or seek to change it because he does not recognize it for what it is—his underlying attitude toward life. For him, it's just the way things are.

Because the parent who feels like a victim takes everything personally, the natural demands of parenthood feel to him like a special persecution. He resents that the child is allowed to be weak when he is expected to be strong. Because he is not stupid, he usually perceives that there is some sort of problem in the area of authority over his child. It becomes an "issue." *The difficulty is that the parent's resentments and passivity have interfered with his establishing genuine authority, which rests upon supervision and leadership.* He is left only with his anger and the domains that go with it—his wish to withhold, retaliate, control, punish, scold, or threaten the child. This is the idiom of the parent who aims to "show the child who's boss," who wants to "teach that child a lesson," and "give him what he deserves." Of course, every parent might say these words when he's mad, but the wise parent abandons them when he comes to his senses, because he knows they don't get anywhere. The parent who feels like a chronic victim sees these phrases as an ideology.

## *Clinical Considerations*

### Case

*Mr. Burke brought his twin boys, age 2½, to treatment, because they were "plain evil." He complained in bewilderment, "They just don't respect me." Mr. Burke was himself only 23, an unemployed roofer receiving disability payments for a back injury. He was thus in a position to be the at-home caretaker of his sons, motherless since the age of 5 months. Mrs. Burke had died at the wheel in an automobile accident. In saying this, Mr. Burke indicated with obvious discomfort that "alcohol had been involved." He had been with her in the car, and had also been drinking.*

*The tragedy had transformed him. He had vowed never to drink again and to devote himself to his infant boys. He dedicated himself to feedings, naps, and laundry; his sons' increasing independence, however, had led to difficulties that Mr. Burke had not anticipated. He described a perpetual struggle to teach his sons to listen and to mind. Because there were two of them—and because of his back problem—this was a challenge indeed. He spent much of his time barking "No!" and "Stop that!" to his frisky youngsters, and placing them angrily in their playpen, where they would weep and shriek interminably.*

*The therapist observed Mr. Burke with his sons. The moment the family entered the office, Mr. Burke said tensely, "Now sit down and don't start up with me." Very shortly, of course, the boys began to drift from their seats and explore the therapist's interesting office, but Mr. Burke jumped up and directed them to an empty spot on the carpet, reminding them with more anxiety than anger that they'd "better listen."*

*At last, Mr. Burke succeeded in placating the boys with crackers. One of the twins reached for another, making a demanding, grunting noise to signal his desire for it. With a look of grave disapproval, Mr. Burke declared sternly, "That's not how you ask for things!" holding the crackers aloft where the child could not reach them.*

*The therapist could see that this very young, socially isolated, and inexperienced father had very little idea of what normal children were like and very little understanding of how a parent's interactions with his children might encourage and support their development rather than perpetuate a wearying battle of wills. The therapist suggested a few hours of day care every day and parenting classes, to give Mr. Burke some time for himself and some exposure to basic information about children. She also continued to see Mr. Burke individually to assess the family's progress and to encourage him to empathize with the actual immaturity of his offspring.*

*These concrete measures went a good way toward reducing Mr. Burke's misery at home, but problems remained: his sons still gave him "a lot of mouth." He described, for example, how one of the sons had dropped a favorite stuffed bear down the cellar steps. The child could see it but not reach it. The boy had cried out excitedly to his father, "You better get that!" Mr. Burke was angry at the child's lack of "respect." He resolved to wait to get the bear until the child "decided to ask properly." When he explained this to the child, the little one had burst into tears.*

*The therapist again suggested, as she had before, that Mr. Burke's good intentions to raise well-mannered children had inspired him to set expectations that were completely over their heads. Why was he so focused on his children's "misbehavior"? To the therapist's surprise, Mr. Burke energetically responded that this was simply his "philosophy." Although he had come to treatment for advice, and ad-*

*mittedly knew next to nothing about child development, it was very clear that he nonetheless had extremely strong opinions about how children should be raised. These parenting classes were all very interesting, but in fact he didn't approve of their message at all—his kids were not going to be "babied!"*

The therapist recognized that something in Mr. Burke beyond a simple lack of information made him extremely anxious about his children's impulses, especially their aggression. She inquired with interest how it was that he had acquired his "philosophy."

Mr. Burke looked above all to his father as an example, and his relationship with him had been stormy. His father was a combat veteran of the Vietnam War and had returned from the service with many addictions, an irritable and suspicious man. Indeed, Mr. Burke had grown up in virtual terror of his father's wild rages. He described his mother as a weepy and ineffectual person who had divorced his father when Mr. Burke was 10 and had moved back to her own mother's home hundreds of miles away. Mr. Burke never could understand why she did not take him with her.

At around this time, however, Mr. Burke's father had begun to mellow; he ceased abusing drugs and eventually became a locally recognized union organizer. Today he was a colorful and charismatic man, and Mr. Burke felt he could never fill his shoes. He had regularly sent Mr. Burke money since his early widowhood. Mr. Burke was grateful and dependent upon him; in the end, he admired him as a good father.

The therapist surmised that while Mr. Burke loved this latter-day father, who was after all a decent man and legitimately helpful to him, he also harbored very different feelings beneath the surface. Inside, Mr. Burke felt chronically inadequate, anxious, and angry; he suffered from a foggy but powerful conviction that he could never be good enough to please the explosive tyrant that his father had seemed to be when he was small.

And yet, it was hard to be angry at this man who, now middle-aged, was savvy and shrewd, and kind to Mr. Burke. The terrible and dangerous father, hated and feared, was a vague and remote memory, the stuff of nightmares. This dreadful father lived on, principally, in Mr. Burke's conflicted relationship with his own sons.

*Again there was a father demanding the impossible, again a baffled child in tears.*

*This chaotic portrait of fatherhood explained many features of Mr. Burke's approach to his own sons, his frantic insistence on respect, good behavior, and control. At every moment, his sons were obligated to reassure him that he was good and in control as a father, just as they were good and in control as sons. These were exhausting, frustrating, and unachievable goals for all of them.*

*The resemblance to his father went further. As the therapist encouraged Mr. Burke to explain his past, he began to reveal how serious his own drinking problems had been. Before the fatal accident, he had received several DUIs. In fact, his driver's license had been revoked. Mr. Burke had never "noticed" how—just like his own father—he had been an addicted parent who then redeemed himself to become a better person, a good parent. The therapist pointed out this similarity. Mr. Burke fell silent.*

*After a long moment, he described in a shaking voice the night of the accident. The truth was, he said, that he himself had been the driver. He swerved to miss an oncoming car, then hit a tree, and the automobile overturned. He and his wife were thrown from the car. He was only superficially injured, but he could see that his wife had been killed.*

*Hours seemed to pass on the deserted roadway. He no longer felt drunk; he felt illuminated with a sudden clarity of purpose. He recognized that if he were found responsible for the accident, he would be jailed and his children would be left with no one. When the police arrived, he calmly explained that his wife had been the driver. The lie had never been questioned. In this evil act, good was born. He swore then that he would be a good father. He had kept his word.*

*Mr. Burke now began to speak about his late wife, about whom until now he had been curiously silent. He admitted an abiding sense of guilt and responsibility for her death. He confessed that he had been unhappy in his brief marriage; that he had in fact only married the woman because she was pregnant; and that, after her death, the sympathy of well-wishers had always caused him more pain than comfort. If they had only known how bad he really was!*

*With this unburdening, Mr. Burke was able to face more directly his grief and anger at his wife's death and resentment for the lonely responsibility he was left to carry. His wife had abandoned him, just as his own mother had long ago. He felt a sense of mourning for his own curtailed youth and a tender sadness for his sons. At the same time, he began to see their antics with more flexibility and humor, as the ordinary mischief of healthy individuals. Spontaneously, he began to speak of them by name as Sean and Keith, rather than simply as "the twins." They became increasingly actual persons, separate from him and from each other.*

This case illustrates the peculiar loyalty that parents may demonstrate to a "philosophy" of child-rearing, a philosophy that itself may be hidden and unquestioned, and may often prove to be ultimately derived from memories, wishes, and fears generated in their own childhoods. The philosophy often appears as a resistance to treatment—the patent's dogged unwillingness to benefit from the therapist's brilliant and enlightened advice. As such, it characteristically generates an annoyed impatience within the therapist: "Is this father an idiot? How can he think this way!"

The negative countertransference is often a useful clue to the nature of the patient's inner struggle. The therapist longs to push and berate the patient into a state of maturity that he is not yet able to achieve, just as the patient's parent (in the transference) pushed and berated the patient years ago. The patient unconsciously expects to re-experience the therapist as an uncanny repetition of his own parent, despite the fact that his conscious hope is to experience the therapist as something vastly different from his parent.

This readiness to experience the therapist as the unempathic parent acts as an inducement for the therapist to succumb to the temptation to scold, withhold, punish, or otherwise hurry the patient. Naturally, these approaches do not work in therapy, just as they do not work in child-rearing.

The patient's loyalty to a parenting philosophy is so often the loyalty of the patient to his own parents, or rather to a particular view of them and of himself, and to the degree that the philosophy is destructive, it suggests that the loyalty is a chaotic one and the inner relationship with the parent is conflictual and poorly integrated. In this case, Mr. Burke in effect had two fathers—the addicted one who inspired fear and hate and the sober one who inspired devotion. The unrealistic black-and-white quality of these images propelled Mr. Burke to see himself and his sons in terms that were similarly rigid and unrealistic. In particular, they left no room for *a growth process* involving imperfect and unsteady steps, sometimes forward, sometimes back, that nonetheless progresses overall in a positive direction.

# 4

## Building Self-Discipline

### CONTROL

The parent of strong authority keeps his small child from playing in the street. When he is older, the parent explains the potential dangers of cars; he does so lovingly, because the child is precious to him. As the child matures, staying out of the way of cars is a way of preserving forever within himself the love relationship with the parent; he manages himself in relation to dangers as the parent once did, with respect for his own body and respect for the reality of danger. Looking back, he respects his parent—not because the parent was intimidating, but because he was helpful and effective. The parent's legacy was to keep the child safe until he was mature enough to keep himself safe.

A parent with little faith in himself may not feel up to this challenge. He may feel overwhelmed by the need to keep the child safe; he may convince himself that this isn't really his responsibility—the child *ought* to "listen," even though the child clearly doesn't. The parent may resent the work of supervising the child, and such resentment makes it easy to lose his temper at the child who doesn't obey, who makes the job of supervision even harder. The parent may try to garner sympathy from those around him, as if to say, "Just look how hard I'm trying!" What is lost here is that the parent may not have truly dedicated himself to keeping the child safe. He may not consider this his goal. He may believe that making the child obey is his goal. This parent has the ambition to control the child's will, rather than control the situation. As a result, the child feels violated and provoked and even less inspired to comply.

A parent who feels depleted and victimized may have difficulty with any and all aspects of control. He may have trouble "making" his child do anything at all, although he always seems to be chasing around hollering after him. His small child frequently puts himself in danger, as if to say, "Aren't you going to do something about this?" The parent is full of threats, pleas, and arguments, but is somehow not taking direct action when action is called for. The parent takes the child's refusal to cooperate at face value, as if the child were an adult. When the child is injured, which often happens in this setting, the parent turns around and says, "See, I told you so." The child is not encouraged to respect this parent because the parent has not kept him safe.

Many good parents sincerely believe that their mission is somehow to get their children to "mind," to make them "obey," and to teach them to "listen." These attitudes, which run deep in our culture, are the remnants of a once dominant historical view of childhood: badness is simply born into children and has to be disciplined out of them; parenting is the story of how this is done.

It is an undisputed fact that real children—even the easiest of them—do not mind very reliably, or obey, or listen. Yet sometimes parents are frightened to abandon the goal of obedience because they see the only alternative as permissiveness—giving the small child permission to torture the cat or put finger paint on the walls. But permissiveness is an absence of real authority that deprives the child of clues as to what kind of behavior is bad for the cat or bad for the walls. The child needs the parent's leadership to master these important lessons, and achieving mastery takes time. Real authority requires a respect for this process and the reality of its time-frame.

The wise parent communicates these clues to the child, helping the child to understand what is bad for the cat, while seeing to it that in the meantime the cat is not hurt. The wise parent makes sure that the cat is not tortured, while recognizing that the child will not always obey. Indeed *the parent must fill the gap* between the obligations of reality (cats must not be tortured) and the child's capacity to deliver reliably on this obligation. Since the child is small, his compliance can only be partial. He may obey most of the time, if one is lucky, on a good day. This is all one can ask for.

The parent who aims to control his child and make him "mind" gets in the way of the child's finding out about reality and learning to deal with it effectively. The child is prevented from discovering reality because he is so busy fending off the parent. We see this when the parent of a toddler is insistent that he do things immediately the way the parent would, not the way the child would. The child approaches the food, the clothing, the bathroom, or whatever, trying to figure out how the stuff works; before he can get his hands into it, however, the parent interferes. This parent has no faith in the child's ability to confront reality and learn from it. To this parent, the process only makes a mess. The child's ineptitude makes the parent itch to get into the act. "Nothing doing," goes the tot, who wants to figure it out on his own. A parent whose feelings are hurt because his advice is not instantly taken retaliates by deserting the child. "Okay, big shot—solve this yourself."

This child is alternately smothered and left in the lurch. The abandonment brings the child running back to the parent, since after all he is little and dependent. But the parent tolerates the child only when the child is doing it "his way." This parent is both suffocating and indispensable.

One notices that these are the terms of relatedness that occur naturally in toddlerhood, when the child is bound to experience intimacy as a love–hate relationship. The parent who has his own problems with mature intimacy can't see this as the child's inner struggle. He readily takes it personally and responds on the child's level. A vigorous 2-year-old may rise to this challenge and become a wily and often triumphant enemy. A wide variety of family problems with toilet training, sleep, food, aggression, and later money and sexuality can been seen as variations on this underlying theme. *One can waste great quantities of energy talking about bowel movements or meals or money or sex when the parent's real difficulty is with his own authority.* The parent is having trouble responding to the child's need to be active and free while being contained, the child's need for autonomy in the midst of overall dependency. The parent who takes this personally needs to control the child completely or not at all.

## BEING RIGHT THERE

It is necessary, of course, that the situation be controlled by parents so that children are safely supervised and contained. If all else fails, this is accomplished by the parent being *right there*—a kind, strong, friendly presence that keeps the child's judgment firmly supported.

It is the parent who does not see his role as sticking by the child *right there* who sets the child up for failure. He tells the excited child to control himself; then the parent moves off, on to something else. The child falls apart and does not control himself. The parent is angry because the child has done what he was warned not to do, "behind the parent's back." It happened that way, however, only because the parent turned his back on the child at a time when the child needed the parent *right there*. The anger and the impulse to punish the child enter the picture when supervision at the outset would have done the job.

Much "misbehavior" results from the parent's neglecting to exercise authority in a way that the child can actually use in the first place. The parent's expertise has been offered, but not in a language the child understands. The child is "corrected" but not enlightened. The missing piece is the concrete guidance to the child: how the right thing is actually achieved. Doing this takes a great deal of time and energy, because the concept has to be presented in a way the child can profit from and make his own.

### *Vignette*

*Lydia (age 4) is at a crowded beach with her parents and other relatives, all adults. She plays alone nicely, making sand castles and rivers with her shovel and her pail. Every so often, she sprays the dozing adults with sand. She does so not out of mischief, but as a consequence of inadvertently standing up and brushing off her lap,*

*rearranging her beach towel, or emptying her pail. At regular inter-*
*vals the sunbathing parents cry out crossly, "Watch what you're doing!*
*Stop getting sand on me." Each time Lydia explains blandly, "I'm*
*just fixing my towel," or whatever it was she was doing. This doesn't*
*do the trick however, and every ten minutes more sand flies all over*
*the grown-ups. Eventually, Dad begins to feel like taking Lydia out*
*beyond the breakers and drowning her.*

What's missing here is an expert to tell Lydia how to fix her problem. No one has spent thirty seconds explaining to Lydia that this beach
sand is tricky stuff. Each time she stands up she needs *first* to back-up
two yards (show her how far) and *then* shake the sand off her towel.
Because Lydia is so little, her mind isn't geared to anticipate the properties of sand and adjust her behavior on her own.

The kind of nagging and objecting that adults offer Lydia is no help
because it occurs after the fact. As a result, she waves their remarks
away like so many gnats. The adult input, although loud and sincere,
does nothing to help Lydia be more sensitive to others. Indeed, it really
does the opposite, since it gets Lydia into the habit of dodging and
deflecting criticism rather than making constructive use of it. In this
moment she's being taught that the grown-ups think she's a pest; she's
not being taught the necessary lesson about sand that is required for
her to stop being a pest. She's being taught "not to listen," because the
message, though seemingly firm and clear, is over her head. Her problem is too hard for her to solve on her own. She needs someone to break
it down into smaller bits of concrete instruction.

The adults are supervising her body, but they are not, at the moment, really connected to her thoughts and feelings. Without a sensitive assessment of what notions the child is working with, adult "lessons" are easily lost as so much hot air. Parents may thus feel, "I've
told her a thousand times," without questioning for themselves even
once whether the message really is useful to the child—whether the
child can hang on to the message, absorb it, and live by it. *It requires*
*an active effort on the parent's part to understand not just the child's be-*
*havior, but the child's perspective, so that the parent knows what kind of*
*new wisdom to impart.*

## JUSTICE AND RULES

The nature of physical reality and the demands for socialized behavior among people can be understood and communicated by rules. Examples of this are the rule of gravity (i.e., things fall) or the Golden Rule (i.e., treat others as you wish to be treated). Society is built on the shared recognition of such rules, both physical and moral. They are impersonal, and this is the source of their magnificence: justice belongs to everybody. If you ignore the rules, bad things often happen. If you ignore the rules of gravity, things will hit the ground. If you ignore the Golden Rule, other people will not like you and you will not like yourself.

The impatient parent is often very eager to push rules onto his child and to punish him with rules. He does it in a way that emphasizes the head-on collision between the child's desire and the rule, rather than the beauty and universality and usefulness of the rule. By framing the rule in a punitive way, the parent invites the child to experience the frustration involved in the rule as a frustration inflicted by other people or by the parent, out of spite. This confuses everything. The child isn't sure where the problem is—he just wants to shake free of the whole thing.

Let's take the law of gravity, which is impersonal enough. Things fall. A wise parent sees a child with a teetering stack of plates and suggests compassionately (from his position of greater experience with plates) that they're going to fall mighty soon. The child can profit from this wisdom, and, hopefully, in time. This kind of interaction encourages the child to trust the parent as a positive guiding figure.

The irritable parent will add hostility to this message. From the beginning, he tends to see the child as "thoughtless" and "careless." The child is "going to be sorry." The parent can see, of course, that the child is not actually bashing the plates on purpose, but he cannot be free of the lurking suspicion that the child's carelessness is a personal affront to him. If the child "respected" the parent and all the money the parent had to spend on these plates he'd handle them more carefully! And the parent who feels chronically victimized by his child will take anything that breaks as a token of the child's "carelessness," even though it is not unheard of for plates to break even when handled with care. The parent takes the broken plates as confirmation of the child's lack of good faith.

Thus the law of gravity, which the parent didn't invent and certainly cannot personally enforce, has been mixed up in the child's mind with the parent's accusations of disloyalty. If the plates fall, which they're bound to do eventually, the parent can't resist saying, "I told you so. You wouldn't listen."

The grouchy parent has suggested that he and reality are on the same side, as it were, ganging up on the child. From the child's perspective, the parent's hostility, the child's resulting hostility, and the law of gravity are all jumbled together. What is communicated is that reality itself is his enemy, something the child wants to provoke. The child develops a habit of tempting fate and testing limits. Over time he tends to become what the parent all along has suggested that he is: a reckless and thoughtless person.

Parents who themselves harbor a resentment of authority set the stage for struggles around rules with their offspring. Such parents may submit to outside authorities because they see no alternative, but they do so sullenly. They resist the directives of the umpire at an athletic event or the boss at work. Teamwork is difficult for these parents because they tend to feel abused by group process rather than invigorated by it, and have trouble committing themselves to any collaborative purpose. Although not necessarily dishonest or antisocial, these parents lack the qualities of a good citizen that depend on mutuality, trust, and public-spiritedness. They have trouble pitching in for the common good. Problems with teamwork are often evident in their roles within the family, where there is typically difficulty with responsibility for feelings, ideas, and principles. The parent who resents authority is often a talebearer and manipulator, assigning the dirty work to someone else. Such a mother says, "Just wait till Daddy hears how bad you've been!" The parent who feels like a victim passes all of these patterns and attitudes on to his child, though unwittingly.

*A parent who has faith in his own personal authority raises his child in an atmosphere where reality is faced courageously, including the reality of loss and tragedy.* He teaches the child how to cope with reality, in all its bitterness and joys. The parent who feels like a helpless victim puts a twist on it—because he feels fundamentally cheated by life, he has a personal beef with reality. Reality is his pet peeve. Even the laws of the physical universe are suffered as a personal insult, an enemy whose purpose is to humiliate or obstruct him. He says, "Just my luck!" when things fall, break down, or don't behave as expected. This parent is a covert rebel; his is the position of passive gripes and grievances, rather than a mature acceptance of how things are. At the same time, he feels powerless to change anything. He sits on the sidelines complaining rather than engaging energetically in issues and taking positive action.

In this frame of mind, the parent who has experienced many hard disappointments in life often can't wait to inform his child that "he can't always have things his way." He is quick to punish the child so that he "learns" what he can't have. He may feel obligated to deprive the child, so that he'll "learn a lesson." This parent does not give reality much credit for teaching its own lessons, and he doesn't give the child much credit for learning them on his own. Yet all of the experiences of infancy and childhood are great teachers: solid floors and coffee-table corners, everything that looks interesting but is out of reach, conspire to teach babies that reality is *out there*; it is hard and unforgiving and does what it wants, not what the baby wants. The embittered parent isn't satisfied with this, however; he's convinced the child will have no possible inkling of reality if it weren't for the parent pushing his face into it.

Naturally, this invites the child to resist the laws of reality and to see them as hostile. Rather than helping the child understand and cope with these laws, the parent's attitude encourages him to escape, dodge, and dismiss the laws of reality. It inculcates in the child the very attitudes that the parent himself holds. It makes the child feel angry and helpless. It makes the child feel like a victim.

The parent who believes that no child *wants* to be conscientious, trustworthy, or considerate feels duty-bound to try to punish the child into it. The lesson is not lost on the child. He can see that the parent doesn't enjoy being any of those things himself. The parent is passing onto the child his own dim view of human nature and his own fundamental reluctance to be responsible and respectful of others. The more the parent tries to beat these lessons into the child's head through warnings and threats, the more the child is convinced that no one would want to act that way spontaneously.

One parent sees life as an opportunity for discovery, for personal expression, for devotion to loved persons and to humankind. He sees his child in terms of his joy in its unfolding potential. Another sees life as an obstacle course of duties and hardships raining from above, which need to be endured with martyrdom or evaded with mischief. A posture of chronic silent suffering is thus often intimately related to a chronically oppositional stance, although they seem on the surface to be miles apart. What they have in common is the position of victimization.

When this is the climate of the entire family, one may see the division of labor, so to speak, along gender or generational lines. The "saint–sinner" combination is often found in spouses, or parents and offspring. The hard-working victim has a shiftless victim for a spouse or child, and for the life of him, he cannot understand how this came about, since on the surface they seem as different as night and day. The onlooker can see, however, that the saintly parent has experienced the child (or the spouse) as one more hardship to be borne, and communicates this attitude in a thousand ways.

These are families where the child yelps, "That's not fair!" and the parent chimes in bitterly, "Well, life's not fair." This parent says, "Don't you let the teacher catch you doing that." He is in effect encouraging the child to break the rules behind the teacher's back. He's denigrating the child by implying that the child has no desire or capacity to refrain. And he discourages the child from having faith, trust, and belief in anything. This parent views rules as prison bars designed to frustrate him, rather than reasonable limits that ensure justice for everyone. The baleful parent complies with rules and authority out of a sense of duty, habit, and fear of retaliation—not because he really believes in the rules or respects them as safeguards of everyone's rights. This ruins his opportunity to reinforce the child's natural wish to follow rules; it encourages the child to mistrust and resent rules and the people and ideals behind them.

A cynical or embittered parent sees no justice anywhere; he cannot relate loyalty to the idea of justice. His is a dog-eat-dog world, empty of altruism, idealism, or high-mindedness. The issue, of course, is not whether life is or isn't fair, but that children need to feel that parents value fairness, that they *try* to be as fair as they can. *It is only through experiencing his parents' efforts to be fair that the child can acquire the strength to withstand the cruel disappointments that life can present.* Fate itself is not always fair, but honorable people always strive to be fair. Men and women of integrity carry on this valiant struggle everywhere— in the pages of our history books, in the examples of celebrated heroes, and in the lives of ordinary people in the child's community and in his very household.

The sensible parent sees a reasonable overall intent behind the authorities in society, although he may take issue with certain specifics. If he objects, he has avenues of redress open to him. The parent communicates his respect for due process and his faith in it. The parent's relationship with authority is realistic: it is a two-way street. This conveys to the child that authority is a good thing, and the child might want to have some of it himself one day. The parent's willingness to support the rules, even when they are personally inconvenient, helps the child to see the strength of rules and to respect them.

In this regard, the outside world has an important role to play in children's moral development. In situations where the local authorities fail to live up to their proper responsibilities, a parent will have a hard time conveying to his children that they ought to respect rules. All the public institutions the child experiences near at hand—the schools, the police, the health clinic—exert a positive force on children's character by being themselves trustworthy and effective. Wherever these institutions lack integrity, it follows that children will feel betrayed and neglected, and doubt will be cast on their faith in adult authority.

## DISCIPLINE

A parent who has confidence in his personal resources can respond flexibly to the child's need for safety, supervision, and guidance. He respects the uneven pace of the child's development. If the child fails to be totally "mature" on a particular occasion, the parent can accept it and deal with it cheerfully.

Some parents whose resources are inadequate to meet the child's immaturity halfway are tempted to think that discipline will fill the bill. They insist that the child act as he "should" all the time, since the parents can't afford it when the child doesn't. The parent may deny feeling angry; he may pride himself on being quite matter-of-fact or "cut and dried" about it. The child's development is stretched on a rack; he's allowed to take two steps forward, but not one step back. This is unfortunately not consistent with the nature of growth in real children. This child is made responsible for what is really the parent's problem, not his problem: the parent does not have enough resources to devote to the child.

Of course, discipline is an indispensable part of group activities like team sports, math class, or glee club. You certainly couldn't run an army without discipline, or a restaurant, or a cardiology department. Discipline is a wonderful thing. What it provides is an impersonal framework for coordinating the efforts of many unrelated individuals to maximize the integrity of the product—whether the product is singing on key, providing medical care, or learning algebra. The individual quirks of the participants need to be submerged and kept in line by those in administrative authority. Unfortunately, the rare individual who just won't fly right needs to be disciplined. Not every army recruit, math student, or horn player is going to make the grade. A decent-hearted band leader, math teacher, or department chairperson will do his best to respond to the problem individual with fair-mindedness, but eventually the show must go on.

However kind he may be as a private individual, the administrator cannot devote himself to understanding why every problem employee isn't doing his job; the administrator's role is to make sure the job gets done. The teacher has a class to teach and can't spend all day running after a particular child who escapes into the halls. The army sergeant needs to train the troops, and can't be bothered to "wipe runny noses." He's not there to provide therapy. Discipline applies equally to all, impersonally, in the interest of the group purpose. As any teacher or drill sergeant will tell you, discipline disintegrates the minute people become entangled on a personal level. *You can have discipline or you can have intimacy, but you cannot have both together.* The disciplinarian must not become emotionally involved, otherwise he'd allow the needs of the problem individual to interfere with the efficient achievement of the goals of the group activity.

There is sometimes a hope in the businesslike parent's mind that, by resorting to "discipline," he can avoid the dilemmas inherent in intimate relationships, and that by pretending to be impersonal with his child, he can somehow bypass the deep needs and confusion and inevitable conflicts that are always involved in close relationships. But the reason discipline cannot apply to families is that the real-life child is always the "problem individual," and the family is always emotionally involved. The real-life child is always needing special exceptions and flexibility, and—above all—demanding personal attention. The family does not produce some sort of "product" to which individual quirks are suppressed and subordinated. The family is devoted to the growth and well-being of the people in it, quirks and all. This is a good thing, because real children do not make very reliable troops or employees. They break down all the time. They collapse. They go to pieces.

When this happens, a disciplinary and administrative solution may, for the moment, push the child back on task, but it does not help him grow to be self-disciplined. For that he needs something personal, which involves deep emotion and the suspension of other agendas. At best, the development of self-discipline is a slow and uneven process that demands from the parent intimate love and personal flexibility. The imposition of discipline by a parent is an administrative act and the very opposite of these things.

A concern with discipline focuses on immediate behaviors that are out of line, whereas a concern with self-discipline focuses on the long-term process through which the child becomes responsibly oriented towards distant goals, genuine self-respect, and caring for other people. *A child achieves self-discipline as the product of his intense relationships with parents who are themselves self-disciplined personalities.* This is why the parent's authority cannot be delegated to anyone; it is a feature of the parent's own individual character, transformed by a profound love relationship into something that is genuinely part of the child.


## SCOLDING


Since the comedies of ancient Greece, it has been common wisdom that a scolding wife has a husband who never listens and never changes. There's a lesson in this for parents. Most parents can't control their irritation at all times because they are not saints; most parents scold their children, just as wives and husbands scold each other. Yet we must recognize that scolding never changes anything. It's automatic. It also breeds disrespect. Because it is ineffective, it contributes to the sense of isolation and impotence that people who scold often feel: "Good grief! Am I talking to the wall? You never listen!"

Nagging and scolding are common manifestations of a sense of victimhood. The one on the receiving end feels like a victim too. There is a kind of closeness, finally, since then everybody feels bad, but there is no real communication, sharing, or intimacy. It's two people feeling lonely and disappointed and miserable together. For some people, this is an overall approach to human relationships, a self-fulfilling expectation. It happens in their marriages and with their offspring. It's "fate."

Let's say a 12-year-old is asking to take the public bus across town to study with a friend. This is one of those parental decisions where what is permitted will depend on the parent, the child, and the many details involved. The wise parent decides, on the basis of all of this, that it's safe, or it isn't. The parent's authority rests upon his greater wisdom in assessing this kind of situation. He is an expert at it. He reads it the way the folks from the gas company read your meter. He examines the particulars and judges that it's permitted or it isn't.

The scolding parent cannot express the decision in terms of an outside reality, an impersonal quality of safety or danger inherent in the situation that he has soberly assessed. The scolding parent habitually frames the decision in personal terms of resentment. Riding the bus is a "privilege" the child hasn't "earned"; the parent reminds the child that "you haven't shown me that you can be trusted." What began as a plan to study with a friend has turned into an opportunity for the parent to enumerate the various ways the child has been disappointing. It is couched as a personal power struggle, inviting wrangling and argument. The child feels his honor is being attacked, so he jumps up to defend himself. The parent may be quite correct that the child is not safe on the bus. That decision is up to the parent and not under discussion here. Where the parent undermines his own authority is not in the content of the decision but in the attitude that frames it. He's not communicating, "Sorry, that's just not a good idea." He's communicating, "I won't let you because you never measure up."

In either case the child may go to pieces and rant and rave over his inalienable right to ride the bus. This only tells you that you are dealing with a child. It is naturally much more likely to happen, however, when the mean-spirited parent has implied, "I'm saying no because you've displeased me," than when the friendly parent has implied, "I'm saying no to keep you safe." In the first case, the parent has practically invited the child to challenge him with a tantrum; in the second, he has maintained his helpful stance of putting the child's best interest first.

## PUNISHMENT

Most people recognize that in extreme forms a parent's hostility can be frankly abusive. From time to time one observes this in certain mothers and their little ones in shopping malls. Mother turns her attention to the dress racks and some time thereafter the toddler wonders off. Soon the child's name rings out in blood-curdling tones, followed by a torrent of smacks, threats, and insults. It is strange how these children rarely cry. They take their lumps stoically and the process repeats itself in a few moments.

Here is a youngster exploring a terrain of experience that is bounded on all sides by the electric fence of his mother's rage. This is how mother was raised, probably not too many years ago; she is taking out on the child some of the burden of resentment she has carried ever since, while at the same time feeling very justified in so doing, because "he's got to learn."

What this child is actively learning, however, is a wary mistrust of his mother, as well as a deep disinclination to please her. His natural drive to discover the world is contaminated with the excitement of being "bad" and momentarily free of her. This is the absolute opposite of strong character development: instead of hanging on to the memory of a loving mother to give him courage in his explorations, he is motivated to escape her and memories of what she stands for. He is relieved to be free of her, but is also empty inside. This process impairs his capacity to learn about the world; it leaves him evasive, restless, and aggressive.

The troubled parent wants to punish the child because the child is in his hair. The child's behavior in the moment is an irritation even when it is innocent. The emphasis for this parent is often on the parent's needs rather than the child's. His tendency is to punish a child more severely for inadvertently breaking his expensive prescription eyeglasses than for breaking his cheap sunglasses, as if the child were more blameworthy just because the parent is more annoyed.

We recall that in other times and places it was considered routine and acceptable, if not indeed necessary, for a man to beat both his wife and his children. For us today, these patterns are under considerable criticism. Most professional persons who work with families see that nothing constructive comes from parents hitting their children, although spanking is still legal and not uncommon.

Naturally, most people endorse the idea that a parent's losing control is bad. What is often not addressed is the persistent belief that a thoughtful and deliberate intention to make the child experience pain of some sort is going to be helpful to the child. In this spirit, some parents who want the child to learn not to touch hot pots think that adding pain will accomplish this sooner. When the toddler reaches for the hot pot, the parent smacks the child's hand, saying, "I *told* you not to do that." As an ongoing approach this undermines the child's trust in the parent; it fills the child with a suspiciousness (of the parent, not of the pot) and a keen desire to hurt people himself. The child may think better of whacking the parent back right on the spot, but his hurt and anger are stored up somewhere. He is learning the lesson that human communication includes the strong hurting the weak whenever they feel like it. Sometimes this is the parent's worldview also, so it is not surprising that the child is being encouraged to share it.

Parents who are vigorously against hitting in any form may not recognize that they are not against deliberately hurting the child in other ways. They disapprove of inflicting pain on the child's body, but are firm believers in inflicting pain on his spirit. This is the essence of punishment. It is accomplished typically through depriving the child of enjoyment: the child is not allowed to have or do something he likes, something he would ordinarily be allowed to do if he were not, at this particular time, in the doghouse "being punished."

But let us examine this deliberate deprivation. It is an interesting thing that when husbands and wives do this to each other, we all agree it is deplorable. A woman who thinks she is going get her husband to help with the housework by punishing him, perhaps by refusing to have sex with him, would be considered silly if not outright pitiful. She would be told that her husband is not a show pony to be trained, but a human being with thoughts and feelings that need to be addressed with respect. Similarly, a man who thinks he will get his wife to keep the kitchen tidy by refusing to let her drive the family car or preventing her from listening to the radio would be considered a lout and a fool, if not some kind of monster. These approaches to communication are well recognized as undermining trust, intimacy, and real accountability.

Yet these same people may calmly deprive their 13-year-old of his favorite TV show because he has not cleaned his room, and some observers would think that they are being sensible, helpful, and constructive. They think what the parents are doing is necessary. The parent who thinks he's punishing his child in an "enlightened" way may take pride in being impersonal, bland, and matter-of-fact about it. The youngster is encouraged to accept the punishment in an equally bland, matter-of-fact way. This very effectively transforms the relationship with the child bit by bit into something detached and impersonal. These parents are often surprised later when their youngster fails to consider them an intimate source of inspiration. They are bewildered when he does not turn to them as a resource in matters of importance to him. He knows his parents are not bad people and that messy rooms are unpleasant to look at; he also has been taught that he cannot trust his parents with feelings that really matter to him.

Naturally it is sometimes the case that children deserve punishment. A youngster who purposefully and maliciously burns down his neighbor's garage will probably face impersonal administrative authorities who see to it that justice is done: they will demand that he pay monetary damages, or deprive him to some extent of his liberty. Within limits, children are socially accountable for their actions, just as adults are, and society has the right to punish individuals of any age who are proven guilty of wicked and antisocial deeds. And surely the parents of the youthful garage-burner ought to cooperate with the authorities, rather than undermine them. But the parents' responsibilities include *asking why* a youngster would burn down a garage, and obtaining proper treatment for the underlying problems.

Most of the everyday conflicts that tempt parents to punish their children are not crimes, however. They are the disappointments and frustrations that occur in every intimate relationship—failures to live up to expectations and the injured feelings that result. Normal parents are often frustrated by their offspring for the same reasons they are frustrated by their mates: they've been irresponsible, lazy, forgetful, disrespectful, selfish, obnoxious, impulsive, and careless. To commit these intimate offenses is human nature, and to want to inflict punishment in reaction to them is also human nature, but this reaction does not lead to justice, because it is personal.

The parent's legitimate goal is not for the child to "pay." The parent's goal is for the child to see the situation from the other person's point of view. What the parent so often complains of, fundamentally, is the child's lack of empathy for others. The child's capacity for empathy cannot grow when the parent approaches interpersonal conflicts as if they were legal violations. The child's empathy grows in proportion to the parent's faith in his ability to do better next time.

Parents who threaten and punish their children often have no awareness that there is any other way to care for children. They are incredulous to hear that children can be raised without the mentality of punishment. They cannot believe that all across America there are millions of children who grow up to be exceedingly hard-working, kind-hearted, well-mannered, and high-minded who have never been punished in their lives, not even once.

These days people generally tend to disapprove of punishing a child severely, whatever that means to them. But many decent people cling to the idea that punishment is a good idea in itself, or at least necessary. It has not occurred to them that they might be better off without the whole approach. It is a very remarkable thing how some families feel the need to carp at the children for every little thing, and some families never do. In some families children are made to behave; in others, they want to. Some children are constantly being punished; many are raised to upstanding adulthood without ever being punished. Each type of family can scarcely imagine that the other kind exists.

*The crux of the matter seems to be the strength of the parents' confidence that their children are, in the long term, eager to be responsible, loyal, generous, and loving, if only they can be shown how to do it, how it works.* Some parents can maintain this confidence even when a particular day is going very badly, when the child is falling apart and making everyone miserable. They can see on the face of their sister-in-law or a stranger sheer incredulity that they are not punishing the child for falling apart. But if you asked the parents why they are not punishing the child for being bad, they may answer that they have a different idea of what is happening. In the moment, of course, they might ardently regret that the child isn't holding it together better; they may feel like hanging themselves. But they remain confident that adding punishment to the picture is only going to complicate things in the long run. This is more like a broad outlook on the child, and perhaps on life itself, than a set of management tricks. That's why quick answers to questions like "What to do when your child won't _____ (fill in the blank)" tend to be in the long run unsatisfactory.

The punishing parent lacks a clear idea of how children learn to manage themselves. He thinks children learn because the parent reacts to the child's immaturity with frustration and hostility—that the parent's cross tone somehow corrects the child. The parent's hostility and deprivation does many things, but helping the child manage himself isn't one of them.

Most people recognize that one cannot learn to water-ski, to speak French, or to play the saxophone very well in the midst of an upsetting, humiliating, or painful emotional experience. Yet parents often think that they will "teach the child a lesson" just at those times that the child feels bad, by making him feel worse. They think the child only understands pain, or that inflicting pain somehow assists the learning process.

Of course every parent's frustration is natural and inevitable, as is his urge to retaliate. One might argue that no one knows the full depth or extent of his own rage until he's raised children. Parents have every right to experience anger at their children, and to express it. The child is hopping mad, and so are the grown-ups. *But parents need to keep in mind that there is no special authority in their anger just because it is the parent who is angry.* It's just two angry people, one big and one small. The parent's authority comes from his responsibility and his greater wisdom, both of which belong only to him and not to the child. But a sense of these legitimate sources of parental authority is just what so readily flies out the window when the parent feels like punishing the child.

Anger and impulses to make the other guy suffer are shared by everyone, part of the interaction. Rage is a great equalizer; it makes the playing field a free-for-all. *What the parent does in anger when he feels like punishing the child is thus invariably experienced by the child as something the parent gets away with only because he's bigger.* It may silence the child for the moment, but it detracts from his faith in the legitimate reasons why he ought to listen to the parent—that is, because the parent wants to protect and enlighten him. It's like telling the child to listen to the policeman because he has a nightstick rather than because he stands for our laws. This backfires because the principle of "the big protecting the weak" has been swallowed up by the idea of the big pushing around the weak.

The child understands that the angry parent is acting out of impulse, whim, and mood, which is the opposite of what is done "on principle." Of course, parents are entitled to their moods, and children know it. But the parent's authority is what lies underneath when his angry mood passes. If the child is punished, he can't help concluding that the parent's actions come from anger and the impulse to make the child experience a sense of hurt rather than from the better part of the parent's nature.

Punishment powerfully conveys the parent's lack of faith in the child's developing judgment. It communicates this message whether the parent is excited or calm, vengeful or matter-of-fact. This is the way all forms of punishment inflict the most fundamental damage: by declaring that the adult has lost faith in the child's struggle with his own imperfection. Above all, they hurt the child's feelings, as when the parent states he is disappointed in the child. This is often part of the parent's aim. Parents are not blameworthy because they feel like hurting their children; most normal parents feel like strangling their children pretty often, if one gets right down to it. That goes with the territory. What parents ought to think twice about is the belief that delivering hurt on purpose is going to do something constructive for the child's eventual character. They may do it because they just can't resist (and who hasn't?), but they shouldn't fool themselves that this is exerting authority.

Punishment is the assertion that the child's spirit is too coarse and too brutish to be reached by other means. It, in turn, coarsens the child's spirit. The child may be forced to comply this time, but not because he sees the wisdom of it. He hasn't learned to make the decision on his own, he's learned that might makes right. The child is inspired to respond to this with misbehavior. It is an *invitation* to misbehavior. It gives the child permission to do things even *he* knows he shouldn't because the parent's anger has communicated: "It's a war zone out there! Every man for himself."

Parental exasperation breeds an atmosphere of mutual suspicion. The child learns that it is the parent's goal to thwart, and his own role to see what he can get away with. Punishment blunts the child's perception of the very dangers and realities the parent is trying to warn him about. The parent confuses the goal of teaching the child that he must submit to reality with the goal of teaching him that he must submit to the parent. The punished child is advised to "think about what you've done." But, in truth, the child is busy thinking about the fun he is missing and how the parent is out to foil him. The suffering entailed in the punishment convinces the child that nothing could be further from his ambitions than being like the hated parent.

Thus the intended value of parental warnings is undercut by the threat of punishment. Punishment confuses the child about whether the thing to be feared is the outside danger or the parent's anger. It puts the emphasis not on avoiding something unwise but on getting caught. There is a strong tendency for the punished child to feel that if he isn't caught, he's home free. He got away with it this time. Punishment impedes the child's ability to make sound judgments about real dangers in the world and encourages him to be impulsive and reckless. It prevents him from learning to think ahead. Naturally, this is the opposite of what the parent hopes for.

The punished child is actually being cultivated *not* to be responsible. He is being carefully taught not to feel bad inside when he does something wrong, since the parent will make him feel bad soon enough when the parent finds out about it. The parent, by taking on the responsibility of making the child "regret" his deeds, has only succeeded in preventing the child from experiencing any *genuine* regret. He has caused the child to feel excited and triumphant at having outwitted the parent.

Now a child may enjoy balancing on a high rusty fence in the backyard, and the parent may cry out in dismay and alarm, "Get off that blasted fence this minute!" The child may *feel* punished because it's lots of fun to balance on the fence, and the parent is taking the opportunity away. But this isn't punishment because the parent isn't inflicting hurt for its own sake. His goal is not to deprive the child of fun. His goal is to keep him from breaking his neck. The child needs to find a safe way to enjoy himself.

If the child is utterly berserk and out-of-control (as small children so often are), the parent may need to extract the child from the overstimulating situation so that the child can calm down. This is sometimes called "taking a time out." It is not a punishment because it is not designed to make the child suffer, but to help him pull himself together.

Sometimes parents think of punishment as "consequences." Whether consequences are actually punishments depends on what they are and the spirit in which they follow. The consequence of playing on the fence may be that a busy mother cannot trust a small child to be safe in the backyard alone on a given afternoon; as a result, the child may need to spend several hours indoors, where it is far less amusing, because mother is unable to devote herself to watching him in the backyard. This is not her fault or his. He may be prevented from doing things he likes because he has given evidence that he can't yet manage himself safely while doing them. It can be most helpful and enlightening to the child if mother explains this logic to him kindly: she is not confining him to the house on purpose as a punishment, but the boredom he's bound to experience is a realistic consequence of his needing more supervision. This can inspire the child to demonstrate how well he can manage himself so that his sphere of pleasures is larger. Then he is eager to show mother he can stay off the fence and is proud of himself for doing so.

This constructive lesson is likely to be ruined if it is delivered in a certain typical annoyed sing-song tone that parents use when they want to sharpen the child's sense of disappointment over what "privilege" the child has "lost." This is part of the punishment mentality. It assesses what the child "deserves." No child is fooled by this language. He doesn't wonder what he deserves; he just wonders whether or not Mom is in a grouchy mood right now. The parent's annoyance has undermined her authority. It then becomes a question of manipulating Mom, or buttering her up, rather than a good-faith effort to do better. The parent's annoyance has allowed the meaning of the interaction to shift from learning about safety to learning about how to get on the parent's good side.

The point is not that parents should hesitate to step in helpfully whenever the child has gotten himself into a jam. The child needs them to do this; that's why there are parents. The point is that when the parent steps in coldly or smugly or angrily, with an intent to make the child "regret it," the parent has lost the authority that gives positive meaning to his intervention. He has lost the opportunity to contribute to the child's developing self-discipline. That's why parents who punish have children who misbehave. The more parents punish, the more misbehavior there is. The parent who often punishes has to step in all the time, because the child has very little self-discipline.

### *Clinical Considerations*

## Case

*Al was referred to treatment by the school at age 10 for fighting, nightmares, poor schoolwork, and running away. He had been placed on Ritalin at age 8 by his pediatrician for Attention Deficit Disorder, with moderate improvement in distractibility and impulse control; in the past year, however, his father was laid off, and subsequently relapsed into alcoholism. Father had left home. His departure coincided with Al's intensified symptoms, which did not respond to manipulations of medication dosage.*

*Both parents had a long history of substance abuse, including IV drugs; through rehabilitation programs they had achieved sobriety before Al's birth. There was also a 15-year-old sister at home.*

*Al's mother, Mrs. Chandler, had dealt with his escalating transgressions by grounding him and withdrawing privileges. On a few occasions she had whipped him (this precipitated his running away). Her attitude toward Al was scornful and withholding. In therapy, she was at first an extremely guarded, uncommunicative woman with little trust in the therapist. She was convinced that Al needed a man to discipline him more forcefully than she could herself. "But his father is just no good. Al's turning out just like him."*

Mrs. Chandler worked long hours as a waitress and Al was often unsupervised well into the evening. Father's whereabouts remained uncertain; a relative informed the family that he was living on the streets. The therapist recommended a partial hospital after-school program for Al, but the mother had a disagreement with the staff there during the evaluation phase and refused to enroll him. The therapist felt overwhelmed and frustrated by the stone wall of the mother's critical, punitive, and rigid posture towards her son and towards the professionals who tried to help her. Al, a sensitive and intelligent boy, was likewise unable to speak of any of the many issues before him, saying softly, "It doesn't matter," and shrugging off all queries and suggestions. The only account he could give was that he was wretchedly worried about his father, but mother had no patience for this preoccupation.

The therapist took the strategy of encouraging the mother to see what a fine boy Al was under it all and how the youngster needed her to be more affectively available. Al clearly needed someone to trust his inner goodness. Unfortunately, this approach backfired— mother accused the therapist of siding with Al against her. In her eyes, this discredited the therapy altogether, since the therapist had been taken in by Al; he had been "conned."

The despairing therapist sought consultation from a supervisor, who suggested that the initial goal of the therapy should be to reach down beneath the mother's surface complaints about her son into deeper layers of her personality, into her evident sense of betrayal and injury. He gave this a try. Mrs. Chandler was surprised and touched by the therapist's respectful interest in how courageously she had fought her own addiction and raised her children alone; she gradually began to lean on and trust the therapist with her own life story.

This rather paranoid, proud, and unbending woman then revealed atrocity-like experiences in her childhood at the hands of her stepfather, and a sense of being deserted by her mother, memories she had never articulated to anyone. Slowly she came to idealize the therapist as genuinely considerate, helpful, and kind, and finally accept *as meaningful the advice he gave about Al's need for warmth and compassion. The emphasis shifted from Al's bad behavior to his feelings about himself. His behavior subsequently improved and the family treatment (including the sister) went on to explore issues of loss, grief, and loneliness.*

Like many parents with authority-related complaints about their children, Al's mother had difficulties with her own hostility. Her anger at her parents and at her husband contaminated her response to Al, as did her underlying identification with the aggressor and resulting sadistic attitudes towards herself: she could not admit that she felt frightened and deserted by her husband's disappearance, and she lacked sympathy for Al's anxiety and sense of abandonment. Al thus took the rap for her childhood, her marriage, and her inner conflicts.

Al was caught in a vicious cycle, reacting to his mother's various displacements and projections with internalized symptoms of anxiety and depression as well as externalized signs such as destructiveness. These problems, as further narcissistic injuries to the mother, tended to stimulate her to feel even more hostile towards Al.

Parents with chronically low self-esteem, anger at unmet dependency needs, and attitudes of passive suffering are often prone to inject hostility into the realm of authority, with or without concurrent deficits in impulse control and/or substance abuse. Such personalities vary from the more-or-less normal through the spectrum of character disorders, including especially parents with overt antisocial, paranoid, sadistic, narcissistic, or borderline features. Adult children of alcoholics, survivors of sexual abuse, and those with mood disorders may also be prone to scapegoating their offspring as the bad object.

This dynamic commonly complicates treatment of otherwise straightforward biological diagnoses in the child. It accounts for a sizable proportion of those treatment arrangements where things do not seem to get any better, despite the "right pill." The therapeutic challenge is to help the parent identify some of the many sources of "badness," so that it has somewhere else to go besides the child. These are cases where it is very likely that "badness" will pop up in the transference, often leading to a negative countertransference, which is typically a clue to this phenomenon.

The therapist provides a holding environment for the parent, modeling the empathic authority the parent may have missed in his own childhood, and allowing the parent to identify with the wise and patient therapist. The parent is thus able to become more empathic and therapeutic with the child. One might take this a step further and observe that it was in this spirit that the supervisor listened compassionately to the therapist's frustration ("This is a bad case! This is a bad mother!") and conveyed faith in his therapeutic skills and in the long-term outcome.

# 5

## ✌

# From Collapsing to Coping

$\mathcal{A}$ major consideration that parents must take into account as they respond to the developing child is that *psychological development is not fixed*. The growth of the child's skeleton moves in the forward direction only: once a shoe is outgrown we can be well assured that the child will not wear it again. In contrast, the growth of personality is fluid. Children revert to babyishness all the time. A child's character moves backwards and forwards, often within five minutes—a feature that often catches parents unaware and that can cause great dismay. Understanding the nature of this "to and fro" movement releases the parent from blaming himself or the child when the child does not "act his age" at all times.

## THE CHILD WHO FALLS APART

It is part of our modern vision of the ideal family that children are always cheerful and independent. The majority of new parents are therefore astounded and appalled to discover how frequently their own children collapse and fall apart. They had no idea it was going to be like this and they are afraid to let anyone else in on the secret. There is a veritable conspiracy of silence on the subject of children falling apart. It never happens on TV. The parent feels abandoned and helpless when the real-life child—reasonable and charming just a moment before—goes completely to pieces and stays that way for what feels like an eternity.

Is this not the story of parenthood? The child goes to the zoo in good spirits with Grandma or the parent of a friend. With his own parent, however, the child mysteriously refuses to go; once he's there he mysteriously refuses to leave; he has a fit of terror at the sight of the zookeeper's uniform; he throws up; he drops his retainer in the pond. There are certain children who cannot tolerate any special experience without, as one might say, ruining everything.

To further complicate matters, parents often cannot clearly identify that the resistive child has fallen apart. It is easy to spot it in a toddler who has a full-blown tantrum—shrieking, kicking, biting, and holding his breath with rage. In fact, once we recognize it for what it is, it's a bit of a relief. "It's just a tantrum," says the parent, smiling in embarrassment, trying to salvage his pride under the cool appraisal of onlookers.

It is harder to recognize the manifestations of collapsing and falling apart in another child, where the episode may be more subtle. It expresses itself in carrying on, sulking, pickiness, fussiness, inconsolability, aggression, demandingness, argument, whining, inattention, dawdling, helplessness—indeed in any of the so-called negative behaviors that parents recognize as the immature and dependent part of the child's personality. This morning he was great; now he's terrible.

Yet when we stop to consider the nature of childhood, it should not surprise us that children are not very skilled at managing themselves, at controlling their frustration and despair. This is part of development. Children are not very good at controlling grape juice at first when they are learning to pour. The knack of managing all of these things consistently and reliably comes slowly.

Thus it is that all children fall apart. Each falls apart in his own individual pattern, which may undergo change at different ages. Many children fall apart when fatigued, when hungry, or when overexcited. Some are touched off by their timidity, others by their intolerance of delay. One of the most universal triggers to a child's falling apart is having his feelings hurt, an assault on his self-respect, or an injury to his pride. This may happen because the parent has been cross with the child. The parent's expression of impatience and disapproval, however understandable and however ridiculously minor, shatters the child's whole world like a sheet of glass.

Some children fall apart frequently and with great intensity, others rarely. Some recover quickly, others take hours. Children with certain neurological or psychiatric disorders may fall apart especially easily, but *falling apart is not an illness and it is not caused by illness. Its cause is childhood itself.*

At some point it may perhaps be observed that grown-ups fall apart too, and more often than we'd like to admit. Indeed one of the commonest triggers of an adult's going to pieces is dealing with a child who is in the process of collapsing—it's contagious.

The parent becomes upset with the child who is falling apart for many reasons, but prominent among them is the common idea that children properly handled shouldn't collapse. When the child goes to pieces the parent feels deeply inadequate about his ability to provide for what the child needs. The parent concludes there must be something wrong with the parent himself, with the child, or with both of them. The parent sees the child's falling apart as a defect, a stigma of failure.

There are powerful social forces that encourage parents to be intolerant of the collapsing child. Prominent among these is the "administrative" approach to parenthood, which is closely related to the commercialization of family life and an emphasis on concrete achievements accomplished on schedule. Our modern expectation of rapid independence leads us to admire and value the child who accomplishes independent tasks like a miniature adult. The child who is falling apart is anything but independent, that's for sure! Just look at him: he's flung himself on the floor bawling like a baby!

Many parents, to be sure, have arranged their lives in a way that requires the child to function quite independently. If he doesn't, it creates a management crisis. When the child falls apart, the parent hears the clock ticking. Other obligations and commitments call out to the parent: "I have to get to the bank, to the dentist, to the carpool. I have to get to work." The child who has fallen apart presses his babyishness right into the parent's face. "But there's no time for this," the parent mutters in a panic. At this moment, the parent is sorely tempted to demand, shame, bargain, threaten, plead, or coerce the child into "not being a baby."

There are certain rushed modern parents who would like to believe they can "make" the child's independence come sooner if they use the right techniques. They would like to believe that children can be made to behave in age-appropriate ways. The consequence of this is that many parents have come to expect and insist that the child do so in order for the parent to get through the day on schedule.

The busy parent has been encouraged to see himself as accomplishing tasks with his child so that the child can also accomplish tasks unaided as soon as possible. Such is the power of the institutional metaphor in modern life, where the "job" of parenthood is likened to an administrator in industry or a sergeant in the military. This is the mentality of impersonal discipline, timetables, punishments and rewards.

The great limitations of this impersonal frame of mind become obvious when we apply these ideas to other deeply intimate relationships. Who on earth would talk about courtship and romance, for example, in terms of tasks, rewards, and punishments? A person who saw romantic love as an administrative agenda would miss the joy, passion, rage, tenderness, and absurdity of it. Such a person would have missed the very essence of the experience, which is about *emotion*. But just so: the parent and child are after all in a love relationship, not enlisted or employed.

The administrative pressure on the child to be independent confuses demanding that the child be independent in completing a concrete task with encouraging the child's eventual independence of spirit, which is a very different enterprise. In fact, from the vantage point of the child's eventual initiative, his curiosity, and his courage, the question is not how quickly he can be made independent of his parents' attention, but how richly he can make use of his dependence on this attention. The giraffe has a long neck; human beings have a long childhood. Dependence is put there by the forces of evolution so that children can receive a legacy from their parents, and that includes values, ideals, culture, and a sense of meaning. The small child's craving for the parent's company as he puts on his socks or cleans up his toys provides a brief window of opportunity for the parent to nurture his soul and spirit. It is the child's healthy insistence on this as his birthright that makes him liable to whine and fuss and fall apart when made to do these things alone.

Parenting is after all not simply a bunch of tasks, or simply making the child accomplish tasks. It is the *process* of being with the child, on the road getting there, that leads to the child's ultimate character. In particular, the essence of parenting is often what takes place when the task *doesn't* move forward smoothly the way it must in a factory or in an army. That's when parenting happens. It is the story of the parent's special presence at the moments when the child needs the parent in order to grow.

*Parents can experience great relief in understanding that the child's falling apart, his "back-and-forthness," is only a sign that the child is alive and developing.* Collapsing and falling apart is the child's way of attempting to reorganize his inner life to be richer and more capable next time. It is exhausting to the parent because it is a feature of the child's unique and profound bond with the parent.

The child at these times is, in a sense, drawing out of the parent and into himself the very resources that will make him more independent tomorrow. This is why the parent feels temporarily empty and depleted—sucked dry—by these experiences. The parent often feels wrung out like a dishrag under the best of circumstances, even if he has all the time in the world. It is an arduous experience even for the parent who does not suffer from self-doubt about the rightness of his approach.

This is the reason it is so much harder to be the parent at home with small children than to be the baby-sitter in the same home with the same children. The children do not go to pieces with the baby-sitter in quite the same way. This is not because the baby-sitter is a more effective disciplinarian, although a smug baby-sitter or an insecure parent may think so. It's because the child does not have the same intimate attachment to the baby-sitter that he does to the parent. The baby-sitter cannot meet his intimate needs. Being sociable, being friendly, and being affectionate are not the same as being intimate.

A parent can be confident that these taxing episodes can represent his finest hour. The child makes use of the special relationship he shares with the parent at these times to move forward in the process of managing himself. Anyone can take a child to the zoo when it goes smoothly.

Only a parent can do it when the child falls apart. These are the parent's opportunities to contribute to the child's inner resources and character. Although our modern life encourages us to be intolerant of the fluidity of the child's self-management, these episodes are not a sign of pathology or a lack of appropriate technique; they are an aspect of child care that only the parent can do.

### Vignette

*Max, age 4, and his mother chat through the backyard fence with their neighbor when suddenly the neighbor's dog bounds toward them. The dog is loud, active, and friendly. Everything happens quickly. The dog runs up to the fence trying to lick Max, yelping furiously. Max is at first frozen in fright, then retreats shrieking into his mother's arms. Between his wails, he says something about the dog biting him. (There is no sign of his having been bitten, actually.)*

What we see in Max is typical of the child collapsing. His personality, including his body, slides back into the functioning of infancy. Instead of walking, he kicks and stomps; he needs to be carried; sobbing and howling replace words. There's no reasoning with him now. His management of his arms and legs, speech, thought processes, and feelings have moved backward in time.

The child who has gone to pieces cannot readily put himself back together again. He cannot recognize the actual facts of the matter, although they are plain to his mother: he was not really bitten, he was only surprised and frightened; he's perfectly safe now. The child cannot absorb these useful facts because *the upset child thinks chaotically*.

The child needs the parent to meet him at the level where he can begin to make use of what the parent can offer. Often, this too must go back in time to the very beginning, to a prolonged embrace in which the parent's soothing and crooning and the child's outraged wailing together form a kind of music that envelops them both. They become one.

Only then can speech and thought gradually return to the child, and we notice that at first a kind of berserk, magical, primitive thinking dominates over logic. Max says, "Daddy will get a gun and shoot that bad dog!" Max starts to talk, but what he says is not reasonable. Rather than reacting to these wild remarks at face value, mother lets them ride. She may point out the reality without forcing it on him.

To let this process take its own time is the hallmark of an empathic parent. By doing so, the parent does not cause the child to be babyish. The parent simply acknowledges that the child *is*, at that moment, babyish—and works with the material from there. The wise parent waits it out with the child as he pulls himself back together.

Part of giving comfort is labeling the distress in words, so that mother's soothing crooning may as well be accompanied by the words, "The doggie scared you," as with "There, there." To label a feeling not at its height (when the child isn't listening) but later in its retreat gives the child a preparation for similar experiences with dogs and fright next time. This preparation, the understanding of what he had felt, is linked in his mind with the parent's intent, which is to soothe.

*The parent's mission is to assist the child's emerging capacity to recognize the outer reality for what it is and to recognize the inner reality (that is, his own emotion) for what it is also.* This difficult and time-consuming process can only take place in the context of the child's being dependent on the parent, *leaning on* the parent often physically as well as figuratively.

The human infant is full of feelings, but only through the intimate relationship with devoted parents can they be sorted out, recognized, and managed. The most fundamental coping mechanism is the parent's lap and the loving comfort available there. The newborn's feelings are strongly connected to physical needs (food, the proper temperature, and support against falling). But the provision of bodily comforts becomes psychological, social, and spiritual, right from the start. The child's physical satisfaction is the result of milk and warmth; his emotional satisfaction—a sense of comfort and security—has come with the milk but is not the same as milk, because it is personal. (In this context, the difference between breast and bottled milk is not only a question of the antibodies in mother's milk, but the emotional differences between the experiences.)

The baby needs the intimate human relationship as well as the milk; his relationship with the parent very quickly becomes much more than the milk. The baby's active expectation and evocation of comfort, soothing, and relief of distress from the parent is the avenue through which love is expressed and accepted, and the avenue through which the parent helps the child grow on his path toward greater maturity. The child's yearning to be close to the parents, comforted, indeed enclosed by them is what gives them their special wisdom and authority. That is why he will listen to the parent, but not a stranger. It is within this intimacy that learning takes place, so that the child can take over, bit by bit and with endless movement back and forth, the monumental enterprise of managing himself.

## GIVING IN

It is for this reason that when a child has gone to pieces over some trivial desire—something the parent can fix—there is no reason to fear that the parent's giving in will undermine the child's growth. Parents do not always have confidence in this. They often are reluctant to give in. Of course, they cannot give in if the child is asking for something unreasonable, inconvenient, or harmful; by definition, giving in refers only to those issues where the parent might reasonably take either position, where the question of doing what the child wants is actually debatable.

Sometimes parents won't give in because they have lost patience with the child and feel like punishing him by withholding the desired thing. But often they long with all their hearts to give in because they feel bad to see the child upset, and because they have a good hunch that giving in will prevent the child from falling apart (these are both excellent reasons). Yet they dig in their heels and refuse because they believe that this will encourage the child to make a fuss next time, to become spoiled, to remain babyish. These anxieties are not really justified.

### Vignette

*Sam and his family are at the State Fair, at the end of a long day. Everyone is tired and heading for the car. Sam suddenly remembers the ponies, getting excited and then hysterical over "one last pony ride." The parents look at one another with panic—the boy is crazy about horses and his sobbing and screeching are unnerving. What to do?*

Mom and Dad feel a jumble of impulses—they don't like seeing Sam suffer, and they are not in truth so exhausted that they couldn't take him for one last ride. But should they? Is this good for him? Doesn't this make them seem inconsistent? Will this just encourage him to act like a baby to get his way?

If the parents say "No," then the child's mind stays glued on the missed pony ride, with sadness and anger. There is the memory of the parents saying "No" to something he wanted just then so very badly, a negative feeling over everything.

If the parents give in, the child is relieved of the great agony of the missed pony ride. The child knows the parents gave in because of their compassionate attitude towards his sense of loss. This disposes Sam to feel grateful, relieved, and appreciative.

Of course, if they give in bitterly, then he is disposed to feel isolated and lonely in his triumph. If the parents' attitude is one of being victimized by a wailing child and forced to capitulate, then Sam has good reason to feel he can manipulate them. He has succeeded in making them give him what he wants, rather than discovering that in their hearts they really want to give him what he wants. If the parents give in with the implication that they were blackmailed by the child's howling, then surely the child's faith in the parents' goodness is spoiled. By giving in peevishly, the parents ruin it; it's as if the child can have the pony or the parents' good graces, but not both.

If the parents give in with tenderness, the fact that the child is acting awful isn't being rewarded. The fact that the child is grieving and angry is being relieved. Of course, he *is* acting awful. It is very likely that even Sam has an inkling that he is acting awful. Thus he is all the more surprised that his parents gave in; it helps him realize that he is loved in spite of acting awful. This is especially valuable because it is in this context that the child begins to be mortified about acting awful when his parents are so kind. This gives Sam plenty to think over. It causes a child to wonder if he is worthy of such wonderful parents and to vow to be better next time. He begins to look for avenues to express regret for his babyishness and appreciation for his parents' kindness.

A small child isn't going to announce all of this in a big after-dinner speech. It's just the beginning of ideas and emotions that need continuous reinforcement. Yet this is an important step in the process of becoming a generous and tender-hearted person himself, and his wanting to thank his parents rather than torture them. In particular, it is an awakening of his awareness of his desire to torture them and an awareness of remorse for this.

He can't always have his way. The thousand things that a child wishes for, yet cannot possibly have, teach him that he cannot always have his way. *No child thinks he always gets his way because he lives in reality with all of its disappointments, especially the profound frustrations involved in being a child, in being little and helpless when one wants to be big and powerful.* The parent of the child who is falling apart is prone to feel that the child is tyrannical because meeting the needs of the distressed child requires so much time, attention, energy, and self-discipline. The role of parenthood itself exerts a kind of tyranny over the parent because it demands so much. But this does not make the *child* a tyrant.

The things a child needs from parents are empathy, respect, leadership, tenderness, and support. He always wants them and always deserves them. It is not possible to give too much of these things—all human beings always want more of them, no matter how well they are treated; this is human nature. Parents need not fear that they can spoil their children by being too kind or too considerate. It will not ruin them for the hard world out there—on the contrary, it will fortify them for it. A parent cannot stifle a child's independence by being tender and loving and empathic towards the child's feelings. A parent undermines a child's independence by attempts to control the child's will, not by attempts to relieve the child's distress and give pleasure.

*A child becomes "spoiled" when his craving for the parent's sincere interest, attention, respect, and devotion are habitually and consistently displaced onto other things that the parent offers as a distraction or substitute.* The child is indulged with material things or permitted to misbehave as a consolation for not getting what is needed: the parent's intimate connection to the child. Parents who often neglect a child's real feelings may try to buy the child off, so to speak, with material things that the child then comes to expect and demand. In extreme situations, the child may conclude that no one is genuinely interested in his feelings, and he himself may thus become insensitive to the feelings of others. In the end, this tends to make a child rather cunning and exploitative; it encourages him later in life to look for soothing not in human beings—but in money, food, alcohol, personal power, glamour, or other similarly self-centered stimulations.

The permissive parent, on the other hand, lacks the organization and self-discipline to pay close attention to his child, although he may have good intentions of doing so. The parent's communication with his child is constantly derailed and distracted because the parent is always functioning in the midst of chaos. His attention is unreliable. His children yell, interrupt, and walk all over the sofa—not because they are falling apart but as a regular thing. They do it not because they are overwhelmed by distress but because it's fun. They act awful and grin about it. The parent lets them. He permits misbehavior because he feels a little guilty inside about not providing the children with more structure, supervision, and intimate listening. The children are spoiled but they have not necessarily given up hope in human beings.

Sometimes parents hesitate to give in after they've said "no" for fear it will make them seem inconsistent. It does not. We observe that in real life, sensible people often change their minds. In fact, a rigid person who cannot do so is hampered in his human relationships. It is a sign of maturity, flexibility, and intelligence to be able to revise one's previous opinions and positions on the basis of new information. Here the parent is faced with plenty of new information: he sees the full strength of the upsetting effect on the child of being deprived of one more pony ride. The parent need not apologize to anyone for having changed his mind. He has a perfect right to do so. The kind of inconsistency that has a very negative effect on children is *moral* inconsistency—applying a shifting standard of ethics from one situation to the next. The parent who gives in to the pony ride has his values straight—he is acting in his child's long-term best interest. Just because an evolving situation looks different to him now than it did five minutes ago doesn't mean the parent isn't being true to his values.

## AVOIDING POWER STRUGGLES

But let us say that the parents reach a quick consensus that one more pony ride is just out of the question. Dad has a bad knee that is beginning to hurt and Sam's older brother is anxious to go home. Here the parents have to deliver the bad news: "We just can't have one more pony ride." The more soothing and tender their sympathy for Sam's sorrow and disappointment, the more the child can express his sense of grief. Often this progresses into a kind of prolonged sobbing mantra—"But I want to ride the pony!" "Yes, I know how much you want to," with endless repetition on both sides as the family trudges towards the car.

The parents' willingness to tolerate Sam's disappointment binds up the child's hurt with the parents' ongoing love, which is there to console him despite all. The parents have astutely shifted the emphasis from the potential idea "I won't let you ride that pony," to "We just can't ride that pony." It is a grief issue, not a power issue, since the parents' decision not to go for one last pony ride is expressed as a piece of outside reality. *The parent's empathy encourages the child to be angry at the reality, not the parent.*

The parent's decision is an acknowledgment of that reality, a reality of arthritic dads and the needs of other siblings, as well as rush-hour traffic and a dozen additional factors that play into their decision. The parent need not feel obligated to enumerate these factors to the child, or argue their cogency. The parent need not feel on the defensive for making the decision, as if the child were a dangerous enemy. The parent may choose to enlighten the child about the reasons for the decision if he thinks this is going to be productive, or choose not to do so. In other words, the parent has the authority to assess adult realities and make decisions on them. He has this authority not because his body is bigger, but because his overview of the context is bigger. He has wisdom about reality.

The parent reports on the outside reality: "We're just *not able* to go on that last pony ride." He accepts the child's bitter protests and seemingly inexhaustible expression of grief. The parent has maintained a bond of loving closeness with the child that supports the child through the grief and also through the child's shame (which may be hidden at the moment) of falling apart and acting like a baby. The parent has preserved the intimacy with the child—what is impersonal is the fact that the pony ride is just not feasible. This is an external fact, up to the parent to determine with that special expertise that makes parents parents and separates them from children.

The fact that the pony ride is not feasible is outside, up there in the sky. Parents can assess the fact that the pony ride is impossible with a special telescope that is the right and privilege of grown-ups to use. The fact that adults see farther than children, and the fact that adults make decisions and children have to live with them, are themselves pieces of outside reality that can be railed against (and of course, *will* be), but cannot be debated. Parents are authorities on when pony rides become unfeasible, children aren't. That's why when children say "No, no! The pony ride is feasible," their judgments may be overridden.

## NAMING EMOTIONS

It is not the parents' intent to cause pain to Sam. It is their humble intent to go home. However, insofar as going home without the last pony ride clearly causes Sam pain, and insofar as he is a child falling apart, there is a strong tendency for the child's unrealistic thinking to suggest to him that his parents *want* him to feel pain. He feels deprived and punished. He gets, as all children do normally when they fall apart, a little bit paranoid. He attacks his parents because he believes that he has been attacked, just as Max who was frightened by the dog also mistakenly believed that he was attacked. This is again the kind of magical thinking that comes naturally to children. A year-old baby learning to walk falls against something hard and glares at it suspiciously. It attacked me! Mother may even join in this view of the world playfully as part of her empathy with the child: "Bad coffee table! Don't you hurt my baby!" But mother's willingness to share in the child's magical thoughts cannot stop the powerful forward march of the child's growing realism. He learns soon enough that coffee tables are not alive and have no intent to hurt him. Yet in moments of collapse, older children and indeed adults return to magical ideas of attack: someone's hurting me on purpose!

The child whose thinking is chaotic takes major strides forward when he is able to bind his strong feelings into words rather than acts that involve the whole body. The parent can help tremendously here—first, by containing the body (usually in a lap if the child will fit there), and then by collaborating with the child to find the right words to express his feelings. *All soothing begins in an embrace, and soothing oneself involves the memory, however distant, of an embrace.* The parent needs to help the child piece together the words expressing the child's version of the situation. The parent may as well anticipate from the outset that this version is likely to differ quite vividly from the way the adult sees it.

It is not necessary that the parent participate in a lie by telling the child that he agrees with the child's version of the story. All he must do is agree that it is the child's view and that the child has a right to hold this view. A parent can say, "Ah yes—you feel like all day long everyone else has had all the fun and no one has let you do what you want to do. You feel like we've ignored you and been mean to you." The parent's view might in truth be quite the contrary (and, naturally, it often is). The parent's view might be considerably closer to the objective truth—that this is a fussy youngster whom everyone has gone out of his way to please on this particular day. And all for naught it seems, because the child fell apart anyhow.

At this moment the parent is often faced with two incompatible goals. One is to make the child acknowledge the legitimacy of the adult's objective (or at least, more objective) truth, so that the child sees the error of his ways, with the hope that this will cause him to shape up on the spot. The other goal is to help the child articulate his own point of view so that the child's ability to manage strong negative feelings can grow. This is like developing a muscle with use; the muscle here is the child's recognition of his own emotion and the capacity to bind it up in language rather than in action. This means that the next time the collapse can be less physical and more verbal, making self-knowledge, intimacy, and negotiation more likely to happen in the future.

Sometimes a parent is reluctant to help the child put his distress into words because he doesn't want to focus on the negative. What this parent ignores is that the negative—which is out-of-focus—is just as much present, although it is present chaotically rather than comprehensibly. It is present in a way that seeks to express itself in action rather than words. A child with strong emotions and no words to name them lives under a perpetual itch to act. He is driven by his emotions rather than owning them and being accountable for them. With time, the habit of acting instead of thinking and verbalizing can come to have its own gratifications and rewards—such as the pleasure of exploding, the relief of not containing oneself. It is typical of such personalities to be genuinely innocent of their inner lives—they just don't know how they feel about anything until they've gone and done something about it! This tendency interferes with the exercise of mature judgment.

The problem for many parents is that in their eagerness to get the child to "admit" the adult's objective truth, they pass over the opportunity to help the child gain understanding and mastery over his own perspective. The parent is in a rush to get the child to see things the parent's way. But this only helps the child find words for the parent's feelings, not his own.

Parents may worry at times that they do damage to the child's sense of justice by engaging in dialogue where the child is allowed to carry on about how dreadfully he is being picked on when to all appearances the very opposite is the case. There is no danger of this, first because the child's real sense of justice can only grow from his genuine experience of what is fair, not from some words the parent makes him say. But most important, the parent is not suggesting to the child that he *is* picked on, he is only suggesting words to fit the emotion the child already has. The parent listens in a neutral way, without "leading the witness." If the child agitates for Mommy to do something about his sense of injustice (i.e., punish Daddy for picking on him), Mommy need not comply with this. The parent can be a passive listener. There need be no objective injustice, there is only the child's subjective sense of injustice. This is itself a valid thing, although a different thing from objective injustice.

## HURT FEELINGS

If the child's capacity for discourse is still babyish, he may shriek and rant and rave and call his father the worst thing he can think of—"a big fat dummy!" If even in his rage he is still cute, his parents may need to stifle their amusement. But if the child is a shrewd and observant little fellow, he may in his wild tantrum hit upon an insult or hateful remark that is not amusing at all. At the end of the day it is by no means unusual for a child who wants to hurt a grown-up's feelings to be quite successful at it. The fact that the child falls apart in itself can hurt a parent's feelings.

*The entry of hostility into the picture—Sam's and his parents'—easily undermines the parents' capacity to provide Sam with what is needed.* After all, the parents' decision did inflict pain, both because of the loss of the pony ride itself and because of the humiliation when Sam's passionate wish was overridden. That's why this is an occasion for tact and tenderness. But it is hard for a parent who feels attacked and unappreciated to feel much like being tactful.

This is where parents can begin to fall apart somewhat themselves. They can easily react not as adults but as children do, with retaliation. Their urge to hurt the child may be strongest when the child is falling apart—that is, when he has begun to act like a much younger child, when he has become physical, self-centered, and unreasonable. He has become babyish, only not cute. The child is flooded with the impulse to hurt and often does inflict pain. This meltdown has an extraordinary capacity to induce the very same processes in parents. It's catching! The parent experiences a powerful downward pull, so to speak, to react in immature modalities himself. Everything the parent has done to *give* to the child, to prepare him for maturity, seems to crumble in front of his eyes. All that effort ruined! No wonder the parent feels like yelling and smashing something.

Here the impersonal necessity of going home and overriding the child's wishes easily gets mixed up with the parent's personal element of spite. In this frame of mind, the parent is liable to say, "No, don't you hear me? I'm *not* taking you on one more pony ride!" This just invites the child to cry, "Yes, you have to!" "No, I don't!" "Why not?" "Because I said so!" and on and on, like two children in a sandbox. The parent has abandoned his position of greater wisdom and has become caught up with his own anger and disappointment in the child. This only reinforces the child's tendency to feel attacked because the child cannot understand the parent's motivation when it is presented as a muddle of impersonal reasons and the parent's personal anger. The parent whose hostility gets in the way when it's time to deprive his child of something is liable to reinforce the child's view that the parent gets his way only because he's bigger.

The child who has lost control of himself is likely to be quite painful to be with because he feels hurt, he thinks you are hurting him, and he wants to hurt you back. Now no sensible parent will allow a child to hurt anyone physically. It is hard, however, to know how to handle the child's wish to hurt people's feelings. Children can be good at this. Children, like adults, say things they do not mean when they have fallen apart. It is not unusual for children to tell their parents, "I hope you die." Remarks that convey this level of hatred can be intimidating, depressing, and infuriating. They can be quite shocking. A vengeful youngster with a dramatic streak can make it seem as though he means this literally and has been hoping it all along every day of his life.

Parents have feelings too, and it is inevitable that a child at times will hurt his parents' feelings when he is upset. For parents to pretend that they don't have feelings, or that they are immune to the child's attempt to hurt their feelings is itself an effort to deny the existence of intimacy in order to get back at the child. It is indeed very useful for parents to inform their children that parents do have feelings and these feelings can be hurt. This wisdom usually goes further when it is said quietly rather than at a roar, and when it is said at a time when the child can make sense of it.

*The essential nature of the child who has fallen apart is that he is not listening and not thinking clearly even if he seems to be listening.* Thus it is a hopeless moment to try to explain to the child that he is not displaying good manners. Of course he's not displaying good manners— he's trying to hurt your feelings! He's beyond good manners. He is, as it were, not himself at the moment.

The parent who must react to all of this by insisting that the child show good manners will say, "I won't stand for it, I won't have it!" This is the context where doors slam and parents wash children's mouths out with soap. But if the parent hopes that the child's experience of hate and his wish to hurt the parent will actually disappear because the parent has insisted on it, the parent is fooling himself. The child's emotions that are denied immediate expression most assuredly go somewhere. The parent who will not tolerate hearing about these emotions directly in words will hear about them later and indirectly through some other route—through the child's lack of trust in the parent and in the ideas the parent stands for.

Briefly sending a shrieking child into time-out until he can regain his composure may be helpful; sometimes a (young) child will march to his room hollering and weeping and return three minutes later smiling. But punishing a child who has fallen apart for the terrible things he says never works. Sending the child to his room is banishment, leading the child to feel that the parent lacks the strength to endure him. The parent has relinquished an opportunity to contain the whole child because the parent has not contained the destructive part of the child. The child says terrible things because he has not yet learned how to understand his destructive feelings for what they are, and to express these feelings in way that is effective and at least marginally socially acceptable. He can't yet manage these things. The parent who cannot listen to whatever terrible things the child has to say not only doesn't provide his child with any help in overcoming these feelings, but also causes him to feel punished and disappointed in some additional new way. This does not further the goal of self-management. It doesn't "teach him a lesson" (other than teaching him that angry parents will retaliate, hurt for hurt).

To teach a lesson, the parent must be in a friendly mood and the child must be in a listening mood. If these things are wanting, lessons need to be postponed. A child who has fallen apart needs to be tolerated, enclosed, soothed, and protected. Adding further hostility and excitement to the situation (which parents are liable to do if their feelings are hurt) only prolongs it.

The child who has fallen apart is in, as the lawyers would say, a state of diminished capacity. He is not responsible for himself in quite the same way he is at other times, and his mind is not working logically. The child may have a very foggy recollection of events that took place when he is in this condition, like a fever dream. Reminding the child how unreasonable he was yesterday is pointless, as is demanding an apology.

The child's ability to manage himself and to cope with reality develops along an upward growing edge; he continuously adds to the most mature part of his personality through the natural force of life within him and the love relationship with his parents. The everyday babyish reactions are relinquished bit by bit as his more complex ways of responding to the world become habit, second nature, and a part of the child. But it is always possible to find babyish reactions in every child, just as one can in every adult under the right circumstances. It is not possible to extinguish the potential for these reactions by adding to them punishment, hurt feelings, and hostility. Parents naturally often feel that the child who has fallen apart is behaving in ways that are not acceptable. Well, of course! Where parents make their own job so much harder is in their aim to fix that problem *then and there*, by battling it out with the child while he's fallen apart. This just makes for a head-on collision.

## REINFORCING SELF-MASTERY

The wise parent is willing to write off a particular episode of falling apart as a lost cause. He tries to minimize damages all around, but has no ambition to correct the child at that moment, change his behavior, or intervene in any way other than to provide comfort and safety and gentle encouragement to get off square one and on to the next thing. He offers the steadying presence of a kind, self-reliant, and self-disciplined adult. He puts his faith in the ongoing long-term process of self-mastery, which takes place not only during the child's backward-looking moments of misery, but through inspiring moments of learning, feeling, thinking, and sharing with his child. He knows that his relationship with his child is based not upon the mean things they both say when they're mad, but upon the genuine tenderness and respect and mutual concern they share with one another over the long haul. *It is the continual reinforcement of the child's developing character by these positive elements in the relationship with the parent that become, in time, self-mastery.*

The qualities within the child that contribute to his ability to manage himself are diverse, and include his understanding of the way the world operates, his ability to express his thoughts and feelings in words, and his capacity to recognize the rights of other people. It is easy to see how small children, whose development in all of these areas is incomplete, so easily fall apart. Someone who doesn't understand how the world works is constantly frustrated by its unpredictability. Someone who cannot communicate in language is likewise readily overwhelmed with feelings of chaos, and someone who cannot yet put himself in another person's place is bound at times to be quite vexing to be with. Without thinking about these particular matters, parents see to it that their children grow in each of these areas, just through the ordinary activities they share with their child.

### *Vignette*

*Denise and her mother are cooking a turkey dinner for Thanksgiving. Denise is 4, and already keyed-up by the relatives staying in the house. She keeps asking mother if the turkey is cooked, but it is not ready. Denise begins to go to pieces with excitement and frustration, but mother helps her not to fall apart. "Let's take a peek into the oven—Nope, not ready." The observation that the turkey is not fully cooked and the reality that you simply can't eat it that way are given as facts. It's not as if mother had the intent to deprive Denise of the turkey. Mother is not the villain, it's that blasted reality again, spoiling everything! Mother uses her intimacy with Denise to help her deal with her disappointment: we can help mother put sugar on the sweet potatoes; we can have a cookie to tide us over; we can discuss the story of Thanksgiving.*

One cannot always have what one wants, but that fact builds character only when parents supply to the child *something else to build with*, something in place of what one wanted. The parent needs to supply the building materials, be they a physical thing (a cookie), an act of imagination (a Thanksgiving story), or simply the love relationship (mother's lap). Character is the active use the child makes of the parent's comforting intimacy as he travels the long road of learning to cope with his own needs without collapsing, of becoming one day truly independent.

### *Clinical Considerations*

#### Case

*Johanna at 14 suffered an adolescent "breakdown." With no evident precipitating event, she began to be withdrawn and preoccupied. She stayed home from school for vague complaints for weeks at a stretch until she was spending most of her time in bed. She was unable to make the simplest decision, taking half an hour determining what clothes to wear, or deciding whether to take a bath or eat breakfast. Her parents reported that she described to them her conviction that her classmates at school gossiped that she was a lesbian.*

*Johanna had three older sisters, all highly successful in varied academic or professional fields. Johanna herself had experienced a significant hearing impairment since birth and wore hearing aids at all times. In contrast to her sisters, Johanna had always needed to struggle perfectionistically to keep up in regular classes. There was no family history of mental disturbance and no evidence of drug or alcohol abuse. Her mother's mother had been killed in a skiing accident when the mother was 12.*

*Initially the family sought care from a psychologist who, after a few visits, decided that the gravity of Johanna's symptoms required treatment by a child psychiatrist. This delay, as well as lengthy subsequent confusion regarding her insurance, caused several weeks to go by before Johanna was referred to the psychiatrist. Fortunately, and rather ironically, she was by this time considerably improved, already back attending school, and no longer suspicious of her classmates.*

*When seen by the psychiatrist, Johanna was a pleasant, cheerful, but somewhat matter-of-fact and unimaginative youngster. She was able to participate in normal conversation with little evidence of hearing impairment and did not seem self-conscious on this account. She had only the vaguest memories of her recent illness and seemed unable to describe it. She could not imagine why she had been concerned that her classmates had thought she was gay, since she previously had never given the possibility any thought and currently perceived herself as a heterosexual.*

*For months, her preoccupation in treatment centered anxiously and concretely on the schoolwork she had missed during her illness, and lengthy specific negotiations with each teacher regarding how she would be making up these deficiencies. She repeatedly denied feeling upset. Although cooperative and talkative, she skated carefully around any subject that might have suggested the dark side of human nature. This did not give the impression of guardedness or evasion so much as a lack of awareness that selfishness, anger, envy, or demandingness could play a role in her life or in the life of anyone around her.*

*Father was an exceedingly tender and sensitive individual and he and Johanna were very close. His work as a freelance consultant allowed him to spend much of his time at home. It was father who had taken Johanna to the many doctors and specialists involved in treating her hearing loss. A high-level executive, mother was less often available both for the therapy and for Johanna, owing to the demands of her professional life. At work and elsewhere, mother was conscientious, hard-working, rigid, and self-critical.*

*Intellectually, both parents recognized that Johanna had been in the grip of a mental illness. Emotionally, however, mother remained at all times rather detached and disapproving, given to remarks such as, "Well, I'd like to spend all day in bed lounging around too, if I could!" She stated that she had been determined not to spoil Johanna simply because of her hearing impairment. At one point, she made the observation that the sudden loss of her own mother had rendered her impatient with people who complained about "every little thing." There was a clear gulf between the father's tender compassion for Johanna and the mother's brisk demands for performance. Measuring up, of course, was especially taxing for Johanna because of her limited hearing and the presence of three older sisters with whom she could unfavorably compare herself.*

*The psychiatrist surmised that the mother had never acknowledged to herself her painful anger at the loss of her own mother, or accepted her childhood self as helpless, needy, and devastated. The mother's bootstraps approach to emotion had caused her to view with cold disdain the part of herself that was weak, soft, and babyish. As mother could not respond to regressive wishes within herself, she had little patience with them in her children. Johanna, as the child with a physical disability, could reasonably be expected to need more. But mother seemed to respond to Johanna by distancing herself even further from her needs, perhaps in response to a sense of guilt over the child's imperfection. The strength of mother's own wish to regress and corresponding punitive superego resistance to indulging in this regressive wish was a struggle readily projected onto the child.*

*Johanna's breakdown, the psychiatrist believed, came at a time when her adolescent sexuality stirred up conflicting impulses towards both parents, particularly unconscious romantic wishes with regard to her beloved father and fears of retaliation by a mother perceived as sadistic. A retreat from this dilemma into a homosexual position was equally unacceptable to her and projected onto her classmates.*

*All of this had rather mysteriously sealed over on its own with symptomatic improvement, a development that can be viewed as a flight into health or, perhaps more optimistically, a spontaneous cure. Because Johanna felt "fine," she and her family were not motivated to continue therapy. Neither Johanna nor her family appeared very psychological-minded, and their vigorous disinclination to look inside themselves was both a solution to their conflicts and a resistance to an "uncovering" psychotherapy.*

*As a result, the psychiatrist's hypothesis about Johanna's deeper issues could not be confirmed—the treatment remained both brief and superficial. Johanna had reconstituted herself (at least for the moment) as the obedient, tidy, asexual little schoolgirl, and with heartfelt congratulations to the mystified psychiatrist, the family took leave of treatment.*

A longer therapy might have helped Johanna consciously identify a greater fund of emotion, perhaps including her self-blame for being unable to find the key to her mother's heart, or fear of her mother's jealous wrath if she should lay claim to her father's love. As it appeared, the mother kept herself and her daughter on a tight rein at all times; regression was not tolerated. Johanna was thus left without words to describe and understand her states of inner excitement, rivalry, or anger—all the affective experiences her mother had no use for. The result was a youngster rendered prim, bland, and inhibited.

Johanna could not identify or tolerate in herself those aspects of inner experience that her mother could not acknowledge. Yet the regression burst forth nonetheless. In the form of a psychotic fragmentation of the ego, the regression had the quality of a visitation from outer space, alien to Johanna and unconnected to anything experienced as genuine within her.

We must bear in mind that regression in the service of the ego is a necessary feature of many experiences that make life worth living; we let ourselves go in a limited way when we suspend disbelief and weep at the movies, or fall in love, or undergo inspirational "rebirth." Regression is a feature of commitment and creativity, apparent when we throw ourselves totally into any experience.

Thus the treatment situation can be viewed as a place permitting collapse, where the need for partial regression is legitimized. Commonly indeed, people seek help either for their children or for themselves because they've reached a point where they say, "I can't handle it! I give up!" The patient's intellectualized request for information often disguises an equally profound need for compassionate listening and comfort, representing a partial acquiescence to dependency. The clinician is not, of course, a parent, but within the structure of the therapeutic session, he takes on certain features of the parent: listening nonjudgmentally to the patient's perceptions and helping the patient find words for emotions of which the patient may be only dimly aware. This is the axiomatic technique of talk therapy: to help the patient bind his feelings into words, rather than to symptoms and acting out, so that his actions are less unconsciously driven and he experiences more freedom of choice (S. Freud 1917).

The sensitive parent does this for his child in the course of an ordinary day, not because the child is in therapy with the parent, but because the parent aims to enclose the whole child (his babyishness and growing maturity) in his love. The therapist, by similarly accepting the whole patient, allows him to become better integrated. This is both an affective and intellectual experience for both parties. It is also an opportunity for internalization of the supportive relationship, for modeling the process by which this takes place. The dependent aspect of treatment, however, can itself be experienced as a temptation and seduction into a state of need. Like any seduction, this is not always welcomed, and for certain personalities may carry an unbearable unconscious weight of yearning and anxiety.

# 6

## The Struggle to Be Nice

### DEVELOPING CONSCIENCE

Every parent is delighted to see his child struggle to be conscientious, generous, and forgiving. Parents know that these qualities do not come easily to anyone, because they struggle within themselves at times to be patient, empathic, and respectful when they are tempted to be otherwise. Inner struggle is indeed the very hallmark of character and its growth that occurs throughout life. The battle to resist temptation and seek the higher ground of principle is one of the human interest stories with the most profound and universal appeal.

Loyalty, responsibility, honesty, hard work, and commitment are all somewhat *difficult*, and part of us would always prefer an easy out. Hollywood movies show this so well: the average Joe, torn between doing the cheap, pleasant Wrong Thing and doing the difficult Right Thing, goes through inner doubts and contortions (egged on by the female lead, who dumps him in disgust while he dallies in temptation in reel three, where we're all afraid he'll do the Wrong Thing). Eventually, he comes through, does the Right Thing, and is embraced by the female lead who has been eagerly and anxiously watching this battle from the sidelines, just like Mom and Dad used to do.

It is easy to see that toddlers, who are so typically of two minds about almost everything, battle within themselves between temptation and virtue. They often proclaim out loud their inner drama of impulse and restraint as if there were two people talking: "I'll take this cookie! No, no—can't have it now."

The parent's understandable wish to see his child *be nice* is sometimes complicated by the parent trying to "make him be nice"—and jumping right into the child's struggle with himself, so that the child and parent end up struggling with each other. This tends to backfire because the child experiences the struggle as between himself and the parent rather than between two contrary pulls *within* himself. He sees no reason to struggle with himself since the parent does it for him. The parent may jump in this way because he has been taught that this is his job, because he is in a rush to make the child grow up, because he lacks faith that the child will experience an inner struggle on his own, or perhaps because he is convinced that no one—including himself— really feels like being nice.

Immediately there is a contradiction visible in the struggling parent who asks: "How can I make my child be nice? How can I make him be sorry? How can I make him share?" This parent is barking up the wrong tree, since no one can *make* a child share, be sorry, or feel any of these things. The parent can be so misled by his preoccupation with surface behavior that he overlooks the fact that the child has thoughts, feelings, and an inner life. The surface behavior certainly is that the child does not share. He has twenty cookies on his plate, and he doesn't look the least bit friendly when his little sister reaches for one of them. In this moment perhaps one cannot make him share. One can make him relinquish some of the cookies, and probably this would be sensible. But that is not sharing. Before the child can share, he has to feel like sharing. He has to want to. This is a long-term project—not something the parent can make happen on the spot.

The wise parent knows how to stay out of the cross-fire. He invites the child to see the disappointments and demands of reality *as features of the nature of things*, not deliberate frustrations imposed by the parent himself. Likewise, the wise parent locates the ambition to be a nice person and all that this involves *within the child*, not as external demands imposed by the parent. These approaches on the parent's part are an implicit communication of his respect for the child's separate psychological existence; they are effective techniques because they build, molecule by molecule, upon the child's sense of his own existential separateness and self-reliance. By not invading, managing, interfering, controlling, prying, manipulating (or the body-related images experienced in the child's unconscious fantasy: violating, mutilating, raping, and castrating), the parent protects the child's sense of his own integrity and wholeness.

## PRIMITIVE GREED, RAGE, AND FEAR

It is a good thing, after all, that a part of the child is out for himself and no one else. Passionate selfishness is the sign of an infant's readiness for living: his demanding howl is the keynote of his insistence on thriving. If that part were not vigorous and lusty, he would never have had the strength to take the first breath of life, or cry until he was fed, or learn to walk, or run and grab things and absorb greedily and with gusto as much as he can of human experience. This powerful zeal to be alive itself has the effect of bringing about intense bonds with the people taking care of him. His feelings, once all-important, begin to operate in an orbit where there are other people and their feelings, as well as his. There is his will, but there are other wills. And there are frustrations associated with other people, even in the absence of their intent to frustrate. There is plenty of opportunity for love and hate, for joy and destructiveness and despair.

The child's natural impulses to hurt and destroy, impulses that are so universal and inevitable, are part of his impulse to live and to love in a world with people in it. A child who is tenderly loved and treated with the utmost respect and devotion will hardly be free of these impulses, but he will begin to feel a struggle with them within himself based on love. He will feel emerging regret and concern about his own wish to inflict hurt on his parents, because he loves them. The small child takes on the parents' role, just as he plays dress-up in their clothes, by being tender and solicitous to the parents and concerned about his hostility towards them. *The kinder the parents are, the more likely the child is to feel the prick of this concern, which is the voice of conscience.*

A toddler is angry, and throws his socks at Mommy. Because he is little and naive, he is still unsure of the difference between socks and rocks, and uncertain whether he might injure Mommy by throwing socks, or perhaps drive her away forever. In his anger of the moment, he often does even these things in his thoughts, but soon feels frightened, alone, and small. In this mood, a rustling curtain or creaking door is certainly a monster who will devour him, since he deserves it. All children who love their mothers will experience this.

When the child is feeling angry and hateful toward the parent, he is likely to think the parent feels the same way. In a fit of rage, the small child wants to annihilate everyone who stands in the path of his wishes—a few hours later, at bedtime, the same child is, for some reason, suddenly anxious that someone is out to annihilate him. The fears of monsters, burglars, bogeymen, the bad thing under the bed—the universal fright of being attacked that all children experience—is the fear of the potential for attack that they experience within their love relationships. It is the child's wish to attack the parent and the child's imaginative presumption of the parent's wish to retaliate. The angry child wishes the parent would go away forever; the next moment he fears he will be punished by the unavailability of the precious and loved parent. It is the other side of the coin, the fulfillment of the wish and the punishment for the wish.

This forms the basis of eternal myths, folklore, and literature, where the bad witches and evil stepmothers seek to destroy and devour their children, who invariably escape in the end into the arms of the rescuing and loving parent. The witch, the bad things under the bed or in the closet are the aspects of the child's emotional tie with his parents that he is too little to recognize realistically and manage. The monster is the child's view of himself when he is being "bad," and his view of the parent's reaction to this "badness." It is also his view of his own reaction to the "bad" part of himself. It is an inner struggle that he cannot yet contain, which has spilled out under the bed and into the closet.

A minor frightening experience in the child's actual life—the sight of the parents' ordinary exasperation, or perhaps a scary movie—may reinforce the child's tendency to fear what lies under the bed. But it does not cause it; the cause is his great childish love and his great childish hate and his inability to deal with them both together. *The wise parent is aware of the child's inner struggle with his own rage and makes use of this awareness to provide reassurance and suggest solutions.* Teaching the child to manage himself is the sum of these reassurances and solutions, and includes the rules of how people get along with one another despite their inevitable conflicts and moments of being at cross-purposes, both with others and with themselves.

## BACKING UP THE CHILD'S SELF-CONTROL

The greatest reassurance to the small child is the parent's indication that the child's selfish, destructive impulses are recognized, the feelings are validated, and the destructive acts are not going to take place. The parent consoles the child for having to submit to the impersonal laws of behavior. This is just like the parent's consolation to the child who ran into the laws of the physical universe, "There, there, that bad coffee table gave you a nasty bump when you fell. Maybe it would be better not to run in the living room." The parent comforts the child who has run into reality and, crestfallen, comes to the parent for solace. This is when the child is ripe for advice. The parent articulates the rules of behavior to which people adhere, while commiserating with the child on the great difficulty involved at times in following the rules, "Yes, I know how much you'd like to tear your brother limb from limb right now, but we can't hit him. When people are angry, they *tell* the other person what made them mad." The parent provides a sense of security for the child, who is himself anxious about his overpowering desire to dismember his brother, whom at other moments he is proud of and loves. His anger is contained through its being acknowledged, with only the action being prevented. The parent does not insist that the child cannot feel angry (even if there seems no real justification for it), he only insists that the child cannot hit.

If the child's inner resources of self-containment are not winning the battle just yet, the parent may need to contain the child physically so that he does not hit. The parent does everything possible to locate the battle for self-control *within the child*, by encouraging him to recall that the child himself knows hitting isn't allowed. In this way the parent stays, as much as possible, a genuine ally of the child's better judgment. In a moment of emotion this is not so easy to do naturally; the parent is tempted to say, "You know better than that!" contemptuously, scornfully, or condescendingly, or in some tone that indicates the parent's impatience and disappointment. *The wise parent understands he cannot speak for the child's conscience, he can only speak for reality; the child's conscience has to grow on its own.* The child's conscience is intensely personal; it is part of his essence as a separate human being, however dependent and small.

## GUILT

The conscience of the small child is weak, insofar as it cannot do the job reliably. At the same time, it is typically overly severe, rigid, and literal-minded. In every sphere, of course, children think simplistically, and their approach to the rules of conduct is thus very simplistic. The small child is like a dry sponge, trying to soak up the characteristics of his parents, including their ideas about what is and isn't done, while interpreting adult behaviors concretely and inflexibly. A little boy loves to put on Daddy's shoes and eyeglasses, and march around proudly. He is enthralled with lists of what men do—the boys do this, the girls do that. "The man is the doctor, the lady is the nurse," he proclaims to his mother's amusement (she is a surgeon). The child is only taking the pattern that he sees, and making a rigid rule out of it—he thinks in inflexible stereotypes because he is 3 years old and just learning to organize his world. His rules are iron and unforgiving.

A small child's ideas of punishment are similarly rigid. He believes concretely in the law of an eye for an eye. He does not distinguish very clearly between the wish to annihilate people he loves and the act itself; therefore his guilt over this wish is immense. *The small child thus needs a great deal of reassurance because he is so hard on himself.* The more tender and respectful his parents are towards him, the harder on himself he is likely to be and the more concerned he will be with being "bad." He needs to be informed that his parents understand that he hates them sometimes, and that nonetheless they still love him, all the time.

The child who feels very bad about what he has said or done has a wonderful surprise in store for him, news that the parents can deliver.

The concept of *apology* has been invented for just this occasion. When a person says he's sorry, the bad feeling goes away. The other person, by accepting the apology, acknowledges the badness and weaves it into the broad context of things, saying magnanimously, "Oh, it's okay." The parent's suggestion to "Say you're sorry," is thus a ray of sunshine into the bleak landscape of the small child who has recently been angry and has hated everybody, and who is now anxiously convinced that everyone rightly hates him. The beauty of saying that one is sorry is that the love relationship then has a fresh start.

If a child can say with regret, "I forgot," then he shows the beginning of remorse, of knowing he could have done differently. If the child indicates that he "forgot himself," then he is acquiring an ability to regulate future action. Of course, the parent can ruin it by laying on a scolding; then the child's impulse is to defend himself and disown any self-criticism. The parent need not jump with both feet onto the bandwagon of the child's remorse; his role is more effective as an empathic witness to the child's inner struggle, suggesting ways that the child can relieve himself of the pangs of guilt through reparation, without demanding that he do so. Naturally, sending a child to his room "until he's sorry" doesn't do much to acquaint the child with feelings of remorse. It usually means waiting it out until the child is so bored that in order to escape he is willing to undergo the humiliation of saying something he doesn't mean. The parent thinks he's making remorse come faster by adding punishment, but he's really making authentic remorse less likely to happen. The child's destructive feelings get swallowed without meeting up with remorse.

### Vignette

*Rochelle, 12, does her homework in the den while mother prepares dinner. Rochelle is a perfectionistic, timid, dutiful girl, and she has been slaving away for hours on her math. She asks for mother to come help her; mother says with a certain irritation, "No, Sweetie, I can't help you right now. In fact, dinner is ready. Go get Daddy and your sister."*

*Rochelle's feelings are hurt because she feels overwhelmed by her anxiety about the math exam tomorrow, and because in this moment of need, her mother's tone struck her as rejecting and unsympathetic. In response, she sits sadly over her math; she does not round up her sister and her father as requested, and indeed does not come to dinner herself. Mother, of course, has collected the rest of the family in the interim and has hollered to Rochelle half a dozen times to come to dinner. By this time, mother is positively stewing, feeling hurt and angry because Rochelle had refused to help her when she had her hands full.*

*Mother is sorely tempted to handle this problem the way her own sister would—marching into the den and demanding that Rochelle obey and come to the table. At the same time, she is well aware of having made a conscious vow never to react to her children the way her sister does (in truth, Rochelle is far more anxious to please and sensitive to criticism than her mischievous cousins, who see life as a game of what they can get away with behind their mother's back).*

*Mother knows she would be well within her rights to demand obedience. Yet, in her heart of hearts, she sees nothing constructive in forcing a showdown. At the same time, she feels let down by her daughter, whose help at the moment she needed, and is feeling quite sorry for herself. Dad and sister implore mother to go in and apologize. But mother is too annoyed, too proud, and too stubborn to do so. Their dinner is finished and Rochelle is still at her math. Mother has resisted acting directly on her anger (by scolding), but she expresses it passively in a compromise (by not apologizing and letting Rochelle's dinner get cold).*

*After dinner, mother comes into the den. For an endless period, Rochelle stares miserably into her homework, not speaking; eventually she asks why mother refused to help her with her math. "If you had just helped me, then I would have gotten Daddy," Rochelle explains. Mother confesses that this hadn't occurred to her. Mother says she's sorry, as indeed, she is—with dinner finally over, mother realizes that she had been feeling tense and short-tempered, and that the poor child was only trying to do her schoolwork, for Pete's sake. "I'm so sorry," mother says, with genuine remorse. Rochelle's eyes fill with tears, "No, no, Mommy. I should have helped you. You were right." They then embrace, and mother warms up Rochelle's dinner.*

*Later in the evening, Rochelle spontaneously observes to her mother that it was not the mother's apology but simply the passage of time that she needed before "feeling sorry."*

Here a mother and daughter—both hardworking and overly sensitive personalities—have gotten into a typical family tiff. In the end, both parties felt guilty. The episode strengthened their characters and their tenderness towards each other, rather than eroding these things through a show of force. It takes a certain faith in the child to allow the child's heartfelt apology to take its own time, but nothing the parent does can rush it. That is, many things can rush the words to be said, but nothing can rush the genuine emotion. Parents are often tempted to extract the right words, either because they are out-of-sorts and impatient or because they haven't considered an alternative.

But a child who holds himself to high inner standards is especially likely to react badly when the parent reminds him what he should have done. The reason is that *the child himself knows what he should have done*; he didn't succeed in doing it because (like most people) he is not a saint or a paragon at every moment, not because he is ignorant of what should have been done. The parent, by artlessly enumerating what was expected, often makes matters worse—it insults the child's ethical intelligence by implying that the child doesn't know any better. Then the child feels even less in tune with the parent.

Very often the parent, who is irritated at the child (because the parent, too, is not a saint at all times), uses this opportunity to inflict subtle suffering on the child—by reminding him, he's really informing the child what a low opinion he has of the child's ethics and common sense. The judgmental, condescending tone becomes an avenue by which the parent discharges some of his hostility. It is an especially sly way to do it, too, because on the surface (i.e., the words), the parent is right. Typically, the hostility is not lost on the child and causes him to fight back. The child doesn't have the sophistication to put his finger on the distinction: the offensive part is not what the parent says, but the fact that the parent says it.

But the parent then can claim he doesn't want any back talk. The child just has to stuff it. This will work well if the goal is for everyone to eat dinner efficiently. The child is made to swallow his anger along with the dinner; this does not turn the child into an ax-murderer, but it definitely coarsens his emotions. He develops a thick skin. Then the parent has to lay on the verbal lash even harder to keep the child in line. The real casualty is the emotional sensitivity, the intimacy between parent and child, and the child's capacity to empathize with the parent and others. What gets lost is the child's genuine wish to be a better person.

## SOCIAL NICETIES

There is nothing wrong with teaching very small tots to say "please," "thank you," and "excuse me" at the appropriate moments. What is trouble for a child is to be told to say the polite thing as if it were the *only* thing, as if the child's feelings underneath did not exist. The parent helps the child understand that it is important at times to say that one is sorry even when one feels it was the other guy's fault—when you don't feel sorry at all. This is a piece of important wisdom. However, a child can only learn this useful lesson once he is already secure in the knowledge of when he is really sorry and when he isn't. One can only come to terms with the language of social rituals once one is at home in the language of genuine feelings.

But parents make the acquisition of this more sophisticated wisdom possible when it is taught to the child *after* the child has had an opportunity to experience and develop a sense of authentic concern, authentic remorse, and authentic gratefulness, based upon love relationships. Then it does not damage his sense of integrity to participate in the little white lies that social life demands.

Of course, both the short-term and long-term aims are real and both are necessary. We must learn to behave as others behave, to follow convention, and squelch some of our inner desires—this is necessary in order to participate in a socialized situation such as nursery school or the working world or the family itself. There will be times later when a child will need to say he's sorry when in truth he is not the least bit sorry, because it is socially expected. The child eventually will have to learn that living with and getting along with other people involves a certain hypocrisy at times. The world of good manners demands this of all of us. A person who only shared or apologized when he really felt like it would be pretty intolerable company whether he was 4 years old or 40. Parents are there to make sure that the birthday girl or boy doesn't eat the whole cake himself just because he feels like it.

The wise parent understands, however, that behaving according to the rules of birthday decorum and experiencing authentic generosity are two different things. The parent helps the child learn when hypocrisy is necessary because this is how people behave in social situations. At the same time, the parent's intimate love for the child, the joy he takes in the child's emotional life, creates the stimulus for the child's growing capacity for being truly "big," for wanting to be altruistic, which gives depth and sincerity to the otherwise empty words and deeds. The social and the genuine are never really the same, although they often coincide.

## THE GOOD SPORT

Being able to congratulate one's rival—*being* a good sport as well as showing good sportsmanship—is an example of maturity of character and the culmination of a long process. The child who has been able to discuss his feelings of disappointment and loss in all areas of living is the child who can handle these feelings with dignity. It hurts, but it passes. He knows this because someone has listened sympathetically to the endless disappointments involved in being 3 and 4 and 5 and let him complain about them, and helped ease their bitterness through patience and empathy. These experiences helped the child contain losses and disappointments at 6 and 7 for himself. He knows that what he is feeling is temporary and that it is not the end of the world. When he is faced with an organized kind of rivalry, such as athletics or competitive school events, he is ready to be taught the additional wisdom of good sportsmanship. He may observe the good sportsmanship of older athletes in action, or be informed by a wise parent, teacher, or coach. Someone points out to him that the loser actually congratulates the winner. Young children are likely to do this grudgingly at first. It is a sign of greater maturity to do so with genuine friendliness and enthusiasm, and say, "I'm happy for you!"—although one might have been even happier for oneself. It takes a truly grown-up spirit to be able to take joy in passing the baton to someone once smaller and weaker, who is now more grand and capable than you are. But of course this is what each family will do for its progeny, as it hands over its authority and power to the next generation.

The parent who sees himself as a perpetual victim may have no patience with this developmental sequence. No one helped *him* with his feelings! This parent is often in a great rush to "make" his child conform to what is polite. His envy of the child makes him rip everything out of the child's hands and destroy it. If the child has won, he ruins his primitive whoop of victory by glaring at him and saying, "That's not good manners." If the child is defeated, he says smugly, "Get used to it." The child's sense of the authenticity of either his joy or his suffering is equally undermined by the parent whose own approach to life is that of the sore loser.

## EMPATHY

"Being nice" involves the child's capacity to recognize the rights and feelings of others and to use this recognition to inhibit acts that are otherwise appealing. This entails many steps in development. Of course glimmers of generosity are there from the beginning. Even children too young to talk will show great sensitivity *at times* to the feelings of others, perhaps looking concerned if the parent is unexpectedly sad. The sensitive parent recognizes that even in earliest infancy there is an impulse to share, which is part of the impulse to love. The parent observes that the infant holds out food for the parents while he is being fed and pats the parent comfortingly.

Naturally, this intuitive emotional empathy doesn't go very far in the real world; the next minute the child needs something for himself and starts to fuss. *Only very slowly does the child begin to understand in a sustained way that other people are truly entitled to feel things, to believe things, and to want things that are different from his own feelings, beliefs, and desires.* It is fair to say that even a good many adults do not really understand these matters. This involves accepting the fact that other people are truly separate and independent and have mysterious and sometimes surprising goings-on inside their heads. It also requires the recognition that the self is only one among many; our consciousness of our personal existence always dictates that each of us is the very center of the universe. Maturity requires submission to the contrary idea, that one is only a single participant in a *shared* reality of laws and principles that apply to all—and this is a lofty and rather difficult idea to accept.

Thus it is that much of the time the infant and child carry the banner "Me first!"; slowly and gradually the immature person enlarges his capacity for sharing, waiting, and giving, so that others may have their due. This transformation is not an easy one. One might say it is not psychologically complete until the very moment of death, when the individual comes to terms with relinquishing his hold on the earthly world to those with the vigor to make use of it—when one accepts that one has already taken one's turn at living, and acknowledges the satisfactions one has had with gratefulness, despite the fact that they were imperfect.

A parent who sees this process as a lifelong agenda for the child can be patient when the child of 2 or of 12 shows that his development in this area is not complete. Of course, a child of 12 has an awareness of his own behavior when he goes to pieces because his little sister has entered his room and made a mess of his toys. He is furious at the invasion but also ashamed of being furious. He has one foot in babyhood, where anyone who messes with his toys deserves instant annihilation; he has the other foot in the adult world, which disapproves of babyishness in a boy of 12.

## SIBLINGS

When there is more than one child it is easy for parents to constantly feel a need to admonish each child to be nice to the other. Many parents are shocked and dismayed at the intensity of hostility that breaks out between brothers and sisters. It causes parents pain to see this because it is their dearest hope that the children will be friends later in life, especially when the parents are gone. The unabashed hatred between siblings that often erupts makes the parents wonder how the children will ever look back on their childhoods as happy ones, or recall that there was love and closeness there.

A small child who magically thought like a mature adult would recognize that there is enough love for everyone in his home. He would be patient waiting his turn because he trusted the grown-ups to see to it that he was not cheated out of it. He would have come to terms with the fact that other loved persons may have a private relationship between themselves that excludes him, without diminishing the love they have for him. Such a child would have recognized that all other individuals have their own ideas and wishes, which may inconveniently collide with his own. He would have come to see himself as a generous big person, who takes pride in giving to and caring for the small, the weak, and the needy. And not least, he would have given up the babyish idea that the strength of his own wants should control traffic and stop the sun in its march across the heavens.

Although every child has certain moments of experiencing relationships in this mature and magnanimous way, no child sustains this perspective for very long. Even adults have trouble doing so. Indeed the way children's minds are put together inclines them to the very opposite. Small children cannot even conceptualize partial or delayed satisfactions—they feel that they need everything *now*, and to possess it all to themselves. Anything that stands in the way of this is shoved roughly aside. From this very fundamental perspective, one can see how the sibling (whether older or younger) is the embodiment of everything that is hard to swallow about reality. The very existence of the sibling is the result of some vague and jealous notion of what Mommy and Daddy did together, laughing, when one's back was turned. The sibling's eager face is right there whenever it is time to wait, to share, to be frustrated. And often the sibling's face at these moments reflects his own triumph.

It sometimes helps parents to realize that the child may need help in directing his feelings of rage onto the true culprits—the parents themselves. The sibling is, after all, only there because the parents wanted him. The fundamental outrage is committed by the parent, who appears to be giving more to the sibling. The situation of rivalry existed before the arrival of the sibling because even then the child had to share each parent with the other. No child ever has the parent all to himself.

He has, at best, a major proportion of the parent's time and devotion. The new sibling realistically shrinks the parent's availability still further, but it is still a problem between the child and the parent. It is the parent who makes the decision to divide his time, and the parent needs to take responsibility for this. But the jealousy of the parent was disguised and balanced by the child's close bond with this rival. The child is not dependent upon the sibling as he is on the parent, so he is freer to resent him openly.

Most parents try to be reasonably fair to each child, but they will invariably fail to be perceived as such during the course of childrearing. There is a natural tendency to palm off the responsibility for the resulting anger onto the sibling, rather than for the parent to take the heat himself. The problem with this is that there is little negotiating room between siblings since that anger is only a deflection of the child's more troublesome emotion of disappointment in the parent.

From time to time one sees parents who have trouble accepting responsibility for the jealous child's anger. The evasive parent plays the role of helpless innocent bystander as the two siblings slug it out. This can become a permanent stance adopted by a parent who remains everyone's nice guy while the siblings are embroiled in unresolvable conflict. The parent who cannot tolerate being confronted directly and honestly may somehow generate situations where siblings are constantly at each other's throats. This often underlies lifelong complaints about siblings who "just don't get along." The problem goes back to the parent, who may not have been capable of genuine intimacy with either sibling, but who conveniently allowed each to believe that the other was really to blame for it.

Similarly, a parent who sees life in terms of victimization is likely to experience his children as victimizing both him and each other. The ordinary squabbling between children is felt as a public advertisement of the parents' failure. The victimized parent may see the interaction between the siblings in terms of a chronic winner and loser, of one who is "always" picking on the other "for no reason." The sibling situation is ripe for induction of these roles by a parent who has needs to deflect responsibility, to be helpless, or to be martyred.

A parent who is satisfied with the big picture—observing that his children march ahead overall as time passes—will bring equanimity to the inevitable rows and uproar that dot the path. The parent recognizes that the functioning of the jealous child has moved backwards in time, so that the more mature abilities—to share, to cooperate, and to see things from the other person's point of view—momentarily break down. A child who is excited and upset can only see things from his own point of view. What is important is that the trend shows, year after year, the child's greater participation with others on a mature level. A parent who has the ambition to prevent all conflict and distress among siblings, or among the child and others, is bound to fail in this goal.

The parent's greatest resource in aiding this developmental process is the child's natural inner push to do what the grown-ups do. This extends to the caring, giving, and sharing that the adults display with the child and with each other in the course of ordinary living. The eternal situation of parent and baby continues to be a preoccupation for the child, but he begins to feel more and more like taking on the parent's role in this twosome, rather than the baby's. Learning to be an effective caregiver, in fact, is a great consolation to the child, a way of making something positive and active out of the losses involved in relinquishing babyhood. The parent encourages this process by involving the older sibling in gratifying caretaking activities with the younger one. The wise parent sets the tone so that the older youngster feels proud and appreciated. This helps the older sibling become tender towards the little one and towards the weak and helpless in general. The little one, soon enough, will be able to be the big one from time to time. Not infrequently, we see homes where a brittle and intense older child is regularly indulged and nurtured by a more sunny-natured younger one.

There are limits to the caretaking a child can perform. Some youngsters have been thrust into too much parenting prematurely, being made to baby-sit or watch or care for younger brothers and sisters as an actual job because there are no parents to provide it on an ongoing basis. Such a child develops unevenly: he has certain skills of a person beyond his years but remains immature in other ways. He has been robbed of a portion of his own childhood by tending to the childhoods of others. This can even kill the older child's interest in caring for other people or for raising children of his own. As an adult, he feels he has already paid his dues. Now that he is free and on his own, he brooks no interference in putting himself first.

## RESPECTING THE CHILD'S TIMETABLE

The wise parent expects and anticipates the child's loving-kindness, solicitousness, and concern for others, and builds on these experiences. It should not surprise parents that a child grows appreciative, respectful, and considerate of the feelings of others to the degree that the parent appreciates, respects, and considers the child's feelings. The parents provide a model and a stimulus. The parent is not perfect in this regard because he is human and because he lives in the real world where there are many interferences. The child is not perfect either for the same reasons, and for the additional reason that he is not very mature at managing himself. The small child rides a bicycle with unevenness and sudden lurches; the small child writes his name with crude irregular letters. The productions of the immature person are in general, lumpy, imperfect, and poorly controlled. The efforts of the small child to be dignified and gracious, to maintain his mood and his concern for others, are likewise primitive. He falls off course in these aims just as he falls off his bicycle, even when he's trying hard.

The patient and optimistic parent accepts that as children grow, they naturally become more generous-spirited toward others. A parent who feels victimized has no faith that this can happen—maybe it does on Mars, but not here on Earth. He himself does not feel moved by generosity very often. His sense of having been cheated by life interferes with his taking much joy in sharing, giving, and caring for others. He does these things because he feels bound by the chains of duty or ashamed to seem otherwise. He doesn't expect that his children should *want* to share, only that he should battle to make them do so. He is tempted to batter the child with demands that are out of step with the child's development. For this parent, the long-term goal of encouraging his children to want to make a contribution to their family, their country, or to mankind is just a bunch of words. What counts is the only thing that is real to him, that his children shape up right now.

The parent who does not respect the timetable of the child's unfolding development in these areas makes trouble for himself by aggressively insisting the child be nice, be grateful, be sorry, or be generous when the child doesn't feel any of these emotions in a genuine way. Indeed, the parent is likely to insist that the child "be nice" just at those moments when the child feels least like doing so spontaneously. The child is introduced to the word "share" just when he's hoarding something, so that it has to be pried away from him. This child has little opportunity to discover the personal meaning of fairness, or generosity, or respect for other people because the child's primary goal is to evade the parent and escape the struggles the parent is always generating. This produces a child who is motivated to evade and to escape, and, moreover, one with little genuine awareness of the feelings of others.

We sometimes see the development of conscience undergo mishaps when a child's love attachments have been unreliable. Then the child's destructive feelings tend to take a path independent from his feelings of guilt. The sense of remorse may occur, but it occurs too late to prevent action. This makes for an ineffective conscience. The conscience may express itself belatedly in acts of self-punishment that come after the impulsive behavior, rather than in self-restraint. This often results in a chaotic personality, where blaming others and blaming oneself occur in alternating and disconnected states of mind. This is sometimes seen in persons with addictions, who seesaw between indulgence and repentance, or in persons who commit domestic violence, where vengeful abuse alternates with remorse. Love and hate are experienced, but not together.

It is very plain that "making the child be sorry" (or "making him feel guilty") as some parents aim to do, is an ambition that is bound to fail. One cannot "make" a person fall in love, and for the very same reason: falling in love and feeling sorry are emotional experiences that have to start from the inside of a living human being where motivation is authentic.

The child who is constantly pushed to feel something that he doesn't feel may in extreme cases lose the ability to experience genuine feelings. Compliant children who are relentlessly badgered to "be nice" ahead of their inner schedule may become adults who feel mechanical and empty inside. They do all the right things without really feeling alive. They go through the motions without a sense of possessing true emotion of their own. This person is nice for others but feels futile for himself.

A child with a more aggressive temperament might react to the same pressure with resistance. He doesn't buy into it at all. The child feels pushed around; he doesn't feel the least bit sorry. He sees nothing in it for him personally in *appearing* to be sorry either. This child is then free to act on his greed and hostility in any way he likes. Later he may learn to *seem* sorry in order to get his way more effectively. This person feels for himself but not for others.

## Clinical Considerations

The following observations of a schizophrenic youngster illustrate in a particularly dramatic way the issue of mental representations that lack stable boundaries, and that cannot fully integrate "good" and "bad."

### Case

*Willy, a bright but very disorganized 6-year-old boy, was in a special school and individual treatment. He was an only child in a religious and firmly structured home. The parents were kindhearted older people. Father was an accountant. Mother, a sensible and intelligent woman, worked part-time as a librarian. Father's mother was described as a withdrawn and "odd" personality. She had had a lively relationship with "ghosts" throughout her adult life and rarely left her own house.*

*Willy was less than a year old when his mother complained to the pediatrician that he did not seem "connected" to her or to the world, but her observations met with reassurances that Willy was normal. His speech developed as musical echoes of phrases spoken to him. He was exceedingly inconsistent in following directions, and his lack of judgment made him a menace at home unless he was closely supervised at all times.*

*When Willy was first seen in therapy, he was a large, handsome, lively boy who made poor eye contact. His drawings and handwriting were sophisticated for his age, but his social relatedness and language were bizarre. His speech had a peculiar chanting rhythm, like a child skipping rope. As he walked down the hall, he announced cheerfully to no one in particular, "Dr. Cooper is a nice lady, a nice lady. We put turtle oil and Worcester sauce on it! And then he comes home. Um. Um. Um. (something unintelligible) . . . It goes right through to the bottom before you have to change it. Mix it. Shine it all up."*

*Being with Willy gave one the sense of glimpsing parts of many people and situations in fragments, as in a dream. One had difficulty understanding whether he was describing something in the room or in his mind. Despite all this confusion, there was much that was endearing and seductive about Willy.*

*The aim of therapy was to tie together bit by bit these disconnected pieces into feelings and ideas that meant something coherent. Willy spent many sessions connecting one wall of the office to the other with festoons of cellophane tape, constructing a web that veritably glued the office together; the space was quite filled up with these attachments.*

*As the therapist and Willy defined a "little world" together in her office, the sense of a shared reality grew. One day, Willy was examining a ceramic coffee mug of particular sentimental value to the therapist. Willy carefully set the cup in thin air, as if there were an imaginary shelf underneath, and then withdrew his hand. The mug fell and shattered on the floor.*

*"Willy!" the therapist cried with genuine pain and outrage. Their eyes met for a long and terrible instant. Willy's face expressed regret, yearning, and fright. The therapist then said with kindness and insincerity that the broken mug did not matter, a foolish statement since it was abundantly clear to both of them that it did. In the therapist's anger was a kernel of useful truth—something in Willy acquiesced to his disorganization, got pleasure from it, and used it as a vehicle for achieving magical satisfactions without having to take reality into account.*

*This moment of intense closeness—a meeting of the minds, one might say—marked the beginning of a period in which Willy made rapid gains in clarifying the boundaries between cause and effect, between his mind and the world, and between himself and other people.*

*Some months later the therapist was preparing for a vacation. Willy did not seem to hear the explanations, but wandered excitedly about, mumbling. Finally, he peered out of the window and said, worriedly, "Bad . . . " The therapist remarked, "Yes. That's what's bad.*

*I'm making you angry by going away." Willy stopped in his tracks and looked the therapist squarely in the eye. He then suggested with a conspiratorial grin, "We'll just sweep the badness right here, under the desk."*

Despite his intelligence, it was hard for Willy to form a coherent idea of any sort. He did not seem to recognize where he left off and other people began. All manner of simple distinctions were lost on him; categories and boundaries that separate yesterday from now, Mommy from me, and cause from effect, all ran together in his mind like a watercolor left out in the rain.

These disturbances of ego—impairments of thinking, feeling, and relating—are characteristic of persons with schizophrenia (Kraepelin 1919). These deficits prevented Willy from building a reliable psychic structure based on internalizations. One might say this is a fundamental problem in schizophrenia, a feature of thought disorder (Bleuler 1911).

Thus the lack of a stable "parent" inside Willy did not reflect a lack on the part of the environment—the actual parents were resourceful and compassionate persons—but the child's biological handicap in registering, organizing, and hanging on to its image (Bender 1947).

These ego problems led to superego difficulties. This did not mean that "good" and "bad" had no meaning for Willy, but that he was in the habit of dealing with these entities concretely and magically. He did not locate them as realistic attributes inherent in himself and others. For Willy, the problem of "badness" could be approached concretely. One might, for example, solve it with a broom.

Motivation also entered the picture because Willy had more faith in magical solutions (which are easy) than realistic ones (which require effort). His defensive operations relied primarily on the primitive, magical mechanisms of introjection and projection, in which the child imagines himself part of what he values and spits out what offends him (Winnicott 1956).

Willy's pathologically concrete approach to morality was not only a deficit; it also served the defensive purpose of preserving unsullied the image of the perfect therapist, free from reprehensible vacations and Willy's own anger—all of which could be grandiosely swept away. This is a particularly literal-minded example of splitting, the resistance to integration of both good and bad aspects of the self and other, in order to protect the idealized inner relationship from being annihilated altogether by aggressive impulses (Kernberg 1975).

From the perspective of his character growth, Willy was accomplishing laboriously and incompletely at the age of 6 the developmental tasks ordinarily well consolidated in toddlerhood. In particular, we see how Willy's sense of personal responsibility and his capacity to hold others accountable for their own behavior were being acquired slowly and with great difficulty. He did not want to be bad, and he did not want the beloved therapist to be bad. Indeed, he offered to collaborate with her in the mischief of splitting. In his magnanimous and witty suggestion that the therapist disown responsibility for causing him distress, this psychotic but nonetheless tenderhearted youngster held forth a kind of generosity and concern for her, despite all.

# 7

## The Emphasis on People

### AN APPETITE FOR THINGS

Most parents are dismayed when they see economic forces at work behind their child's values and ideas. It depresses them to hear their children announce boldly that a toy or an article of clothing is no good because it is inexpensive, or that another youngster doesn't count for much because his family is poor. Parents want to encourage their children to reject materialism. This concern is often connected to the parent's desire for the child to learn to be thrifty, farsighted, and self-disciplined with regard to money. The parent wants the child to understand that money doesn't grow on trees. This often reflects as well the hope that the child will develop concern about family finances and consideration for other people in the family who need things too. The parents are mortified when the child scorns the poor and the needy. Because from an adult perspective these matters seem to be about possessions and money, parents easily overlook the fact that from the perspective of the child's development, these are really questions of the child's *being nice*: being generous and grateful, sharing, being thoughtful of others, and valuing human attachments. The parent thinks he's teaching the child about cash, but the child is really learning about intimate relationships.

The issue of materialism is a particular challenge for parents whose choice of lifestyle involves constant rush and consequent emotional depletion. Much of the rush itself is generated by pressure parents feel to keep up financially and the modern emphasis on the things that money can buy. And yet, the same parents are concerned about the consequences of this lifestyle and the tendency of their children to be focused on money, toys, clothing, and other purchases, rather than on values that revolve around higher human aspirations and needs. Many parents look at the great degree of commercialization of all phases of our society and wonder how they can raise a child to be more than a soulless consumer of goods and services.

The parent is understandably dismayed at the greed in the world and may respond with a vigorous campaign against what he perceives as the child's greed. A tempting strategy for many parents is to try to rigidly control the child's access to commercial purchases and to money. Unfortunately, one can predict that the child becomes only more greedy with this approach, rather than less so. The parent's worst fear is that the child is insatiable—"He's never satisfied!" The parent establishes a tone, however, that constantly reminds the child that he can't have everything he wants. Rather than providing as many experiences as the parent can that give the child a genuine sense of satisfaction, the parent *convinces* the child that he is insatiable by focusing on it, complaining about it, and trying to cure him of it.

The parent is tempted to withhold something fairly modest that the child wants because he doesn't want to encourage the child's greed. Now if he simply provided the desired thing without any great ado, the child would experience the joy at having it, and gratefulness to the parent. Furthermore, by letting the child have the thing, the child gains the important lesson of satiety: after a certain amount of enthusiastic consumption of something, one feels full of it and ready for a different kind of experience. This also would provide pleasure to the parent— so much so at times, that this itself is a reason the parent feels that something must be wrong with it.

If the parent forbids the child to have the thing, however, one can guarantee that the yearned-for thing will look even more attractive to the child than ever before and the parent will look less so. The parent standing between the child and something the child wants is bound to set the stage for preoccupation with it, envy of those who have it, and disappointment in the parent who withheld it when the wish was genuine.

When repeated over and over in a joyless mood, *this approach conveys to the child that his appetites are a source of discord, rather than a source of enjoyment and of feeling alive.* This has relevance to other areas such as food and sexuality as well as money. Every child understands that he cannot have everything he wants. The ordinary difficulties presented by the physical world provide endless opportunity for children to understand that their own wishes do not control reality. The shoe that won't go on because the laces are tied, the hard floor that wallops the toddler learning to run—all of these small everyday disappointments and unpleasant surprises help a child understand that reality is *out there* to be grappled with. That beloved people come and go, that the child's parents will die, and that the individual himself also will one day die are further evidence of realities to which each human being must submit. Strangely, parents do not feel guilty about their inability to produce for the child things that are inherently impossible. The parent explains kindly and calmly that wishing will not cause living people to drop dead, or bring the dead back to life. Parents have no difficulty explaining to children that they cannot have a pet zebra, or a real helicopter.

All the same, some parents are greatly concerned that they must, through opposing and frustrating the child, *teach* the child that he cannot always have the material things that he wants. Yet life itself teaches this, and the parent's job is simply to make these lessons comprehensible and less bitter than they would be otherwise. The parent does not have to be the world for the child. Fortunately, the world already exists. The parent's task is merely to assist the child's understanding of the world and facilitate its mastery.

The parent often fears that by giving things to the child he will produce a demanding, spoiled little person who is unconcerned with the feelings of others. But the only way for parents to ensure that their child is eventually a kind, tender, and generous person is for them to be kind, tender, and generous to the child—not only on special occasions, but on all occasions.

What often hardens the child's heart and makes for an exploitative personality in the long run is a mean-spirited atmosphere where there is a permanent effort on the child's part to get something out of the parent and a permanent effort on the parent's part to withhold it. This doesn't teach the child that he can't have everything he wants, it teaches him that the parent doesn't want the child to have satisfaction, which is very different.

Of course, a parent who feels victimized will experience his child's healthy greed for things as especially bitter; he is eager to show the child that life is not fair and not fun and that everything has a price. The parent reacts to the child's demands—one by one, inch by inch— as attacks. Faced with a parent unwilling to give joyously, the child has little alternative but whining, demanding, sulking, or even stealing. This makes the parent miserable but in some way justifies his approach because it shows how greedy the child really is.

When money in the family is very tight, the child's innocent nagging for various purchases can cause decent parents great pain. Fundamentally, the parent feels angry and hurt that the child can't have what he wants. This makes the parent feel helpless and guilty. If the parent had at that moment extraordinary resources of wisdom and self-discipline, he'd explain kindly that he would love to be able to provide the child with what he craves, but unfortunately, he just can't do so right now. This, by the way, would go a long way toward satisfying the child because the parent is communicating that he would like to give the child what the child wants, if only he could.

What sometimes happens, however, is that the parent is upset by the child's requests; the more reasonable the request the more it makes the parent feel inadequate and ashamed to have to say no. A common reaction at this point is to bite the child's head off, because the parent can't stand to listen to the child's pleas: "I told you no already! I'm not wasting money on that thing." This makes the child feel like it's all his fault; the child feels hurt and ashamed too. This may silence him, but it only makes him feel sad and isolated. It's easy then for the child to conclude that the reason he doesn't get what he wants is because he doesn't deserve it; he made the parent angry. Sometimes the parent is so upset about his financial problems that he prefers for the child to think he's being punished rather than for the child to know the truth. This may be better for the parent's pride but not for the child's feelings.

## THE CHILD'S OWN MONEY

Parents often translate their anxiety about their child's greed into a scheme that creates the fiction of the child having his own money. From time to time, this works out well, as when the child amasses what seems to him an impressive lump sum of birthday gifts and feels rich, powerful, and loved. There is a kind of healthy grandeur a child experiences because of Grandpa's generosity and the total of his friends' presents. This is refreshing for the child because it permits, as a special occasion, the bypassing of his parents' usual role of gatekeeper for every cent.

Some children take delight in the concept of an allowance for purchasing necessities or saving up for a cherished goal. The child for whom this works well is often an obedient little personality who accepts things at face value and gets pleasure out of discovering the lines of life so that he can color neatly within them. It's also good for children to feel they can earn a bit of their own money by baby-sitting, paper routes, and other legitimate paid work. The older youngster who is actually earning a substantial amount of money in competition with working adults is, of course, another matter. Here the youngster is involved in an impersonal business relationship with employers that bypasses the parents, not only in fantasy, but in fact.

Often, however, no matter how much lip service parents pay to the concept of the child's own money, the fact remains that both the quantity of it that the child owns and the things he is allowed to purchase with it are completely under the parent's thumb. This does not make it wrong, but it puts the focus where it really lies: on the interpersonal relationship between the child and the parent. Handling small amounts of money in this context doesn't do much to prepare the child for future relationships with money, but it does a lot to prepare the child for future relationships with people. It sets the stage for how he expects to get what he wants from other people, including the degree of mutual honesty and generosity involved.

The allowance is supposed to simplify the parent's dialogue with the child about what he can and can't purchase, but it often just makes it more complicated. The parent still prevents the child from buying something totally inappropriate, even if the child can pay for it; conversely the parent sees to it that the things the child really needs get purchased anyhow. The child is never really budgeting for expenses the way the adult does—he's only involved in a complicated effort to get the things he wants, things that it seems to him the parents somehow don't want to give him directly. Many children understand that the admonition to save up their allowance is a euphemism for the parent who is saying underneath, "I don't want to give this to you." Furthermore, the timid child is befuddled by the businesslike trappings; the child is misdirected away from his genuine question, "Why don't you want me to have this?" and from getting a genuine answer.

The allowance system works well for some families, but for others it provokes endless argument. The conflict is endless because the subject stays at the level of money and belongings, rather than at the level of human relationships and emotion, where resolution is possible. The aggressive-spirited child may shrewdly see through the sham of his "own" money. He grasps the issue: it's the parents who are calling the shots about what he can and cannot have. Such a child is in danger of becoming a tireless negotiator, demander, and arguer. Often a parent feels more than a little intimidated by an intense and relentless youngster who is fixed on obtaining a certain item. This child knows perfectly well that what he gets is dependent above all on his parent's mood, and that this mood fluctuates. That's why he asks for the same thing over and over, hoping that the wind has shifted. His demand, we observe, is never for something utterly unrealistic (an elephant, a trip to Paris); it is the sort of demand that the child understands perfectly well the parent *might* realistically cave in to.

The key to this kind of interaction is the underlying negative emotional tone in the dialogue between parent and child. The unpleasant tone is what keeps the mechanism going for both parties. The parent is exasperated by the child, who refuses to take "No" for an answer. The child does not understand that the parent finds the child's greed offensive and depressing, especially the way he keeps it up. The child thinks concretely; he's fixed on the object he wants to purchase. The parent contributes to the child's confusion because he harps on why the child really doesn't need the item, its various disadvantages, and the fact that the child hasn't patiently saved up enough of his "own" money.

It is not at all unlikely that if the parent felt somehow especially tender toward the child—bursting with pride because the child had suddenly demonstrated great patience, selflessness, and consideration for others—he would be only too happy to purchase the blasted thing for the child. And deep inside, they both know this. *What the child wants above all is not the toy, but for the parent to want to give it to him.*

If the child felt more secure in his parent's respect, he would have less craving for the thing. It is indeed chiefly because the thing only represents the parent's wish to give pleasure to the child that the gift really satisfies. It is the child who is not convinced that the parent has his heart in the gift who wants another and another and another.

## THE PARENT'S GENEROSITY

When there is chronic pulling and tugging around the issue of money, purchases, and things, it is often overlooked that what the child wants and needs is not the parent's cash but the parent's generosity. A youngster's intense need for things is often a disguised craving for reassurance that the adult really feels like giving him pleasure. This is the moment that spoiling enters the picture: when a child accepts what money can buy as a substitute for what money cannot buy. *A child who wants companionship, tenderness, humor, respect, and authenticity in his relationship with his parents but cannot have these things can readily be persuaded that there are many things he desperately wants at the mall.* The youngster has neither the insight that he wants something intangible, nor the vocabulary with which to express this want because these are capacities for intimate expression that children acquire through deep emotional closeness, and it is this kind of closeness that is lacking. The child is restless, endlessly craving stimulation and admiration and easily bored. These traits seek an outlet in things rather than in human relationships.

The parent who says bitterly of his child, "He's never satisfied," is always right. What would satisfy the child is the parent's joy, rather than his bitterness. In the absence of that, the child seeks satisfaction from empty things that need continuously to be replaced. The issue of the demanding child is often tied up not only with the parent's money but also with the parent's time and tenderness. Human beings do not come into this world biologically hard-wired to need cash. They come into this world needing (and giving) love and attention. Human beings gradually become mercenary to the degree that their capacity for loving intimacy has been stifled and the capacity for acquiring cash has grown in its place as a substitute. People who are truly nice—generous, loyal, responsible, and caring—primarily orient themselves around love relationships and see cash as a subsidiary thing, useful and necessary but only as a means to an end. The end is life with other people.

On the road to this worthy goal, one often sees these days a parent who puts so much of himself into the process of earning money that his own personality is empty of resources at the end of the day, just when his children are looking for his appreciation, interest, tenderness, and intimacy. This parent has these things to give when he is rested, when his mind and spirit are clear. At the end of the workday however, the parent is dog-tired and himself in need of nurturance. Having given everything he's got to the job, he's in no frame of mind to exercise the kind of self-discipline and judgment it takes to respond richly to his children. His personal resources are temporarily impoverished.

This parent loves his children, but he can't avoid giving their needs for closeness a bit of the brush-off. It is easy for these needs to be deflected to some other avenue for fulfillment, most of which cost money. The parent is in a jam. Perhaps his job depends on his willingness to put out every ounce of energy he has into the workplace. The parent has a vague feeling that his children are developing into inscrutable strangers, and this makes him feel guilty. Answering their loud demands for material things makes him feel less guilty, both because these are demands he can actually meet, and because it allows him the relief of feeling exasperated: "These little hedonists. All they want are material things. That's how kids are these days."

*Parents need to be reassured that their children's eventual well-being in life may be better served by spending more time with the child and less time at work, even if this means less money.* It takes a courageous parent to make the active choice to reduce his family's material standard of living somewhat in order to upgrade its psychological standard of living. It takes perhaps above all a deep conviction that the child who has easy access to his parent's intimate attention, tenderness, and responsiveness has the greatest riches of all. It takes the conviction that the child who grows to be responsible, kind-hearted, and loyal is his parent's greatest treasure. It would be hard to find a parent anywhere who did not agree in the abstract with these values. What is troubling is that a rushed and consumer-oriented lifestyle often undermines these ideals, so that it is not at all difficult to find parents who deep down believe in them, and yet do not live by them.

Parents do not commonly recognize that they lend pleasure and excitement to the idea of money when they use it as an expression of love. It is a habit for many parents to give money to a child at birthdays, at holidays, or as a sign of acknowledging a job well done (taking out the garbage, getting good grades). However, it is not necessary to use cash or purchases as a way of making special times emotionally meaningful. Giving a child money for grades may deliver a mixed message. It may transfer the kind of concern that the child ought to have about his grades and what grades mean to a concern about the dollar. There is nothing terrible about celebrating the end of the term and a wonderful report card by sharing a special treat with a child (with the emphasis on *celebrating*). A child who is doing badly in school will need far more than the bargain "Five dollars if you pass science"—although one might argue that anything that improves motivation is worth trying. A child may be even more delighted to get his bicycle when he discovers he really wants one, rather than having to wait until his birthday. Parents need not teach children to wait; life does this by making children wait until they are adults for much of what they desire. On the child's birthday, his specialness can be celebrated through being the center of everyone's attention—with homemade gifts and favorite foods. It is not that spending a lot of money on a child's birthday is in itself bad (if the family has the money to spend); it's the *focus* on money, rather than on emotions, that lessens the child's involvement with people. By making a great fuss and issue of money, and doling it out as a reward in a morality play, parents encourage the child to take money very seriously and to see it as an end in itself.

Parents should aim to put more of the burden onto the child of deciding whether the child ought to indulge himself in some item that he craves, but which seems to the parent like a waste of money. If the child begs and pleads whenever he has a whim to buy something, and the parent hems and haws in reaction to the plea, the child has no opportunity to weigh for himself the value of the purchase in the context of the greater family good. The child will not struggle within himself if the parent provides him with a ready-made struggle. The child who is in a perpetual tug-of-war with his parents sees the object of the game as getting as much rope as he can by pulling against the parents' resistance. This child is unlikely to take note that some other family member hardly ever buys anything for himself. When the burden is on the child, the more generous the parents are, the more genuine is the child's growing sense of concern and responsibility for the family as a whole. Of course, generosity in this sense does not mean spending the largest dollar amount; it means spending whatever one has judged to be a realistic amount in a spirit of joy and sharing, so that the child feels touched.

## BEING USEFUL

The essence of paying an allowance in exchange for chores is often an attempt on the parent's part to make the parent's decision-making about the child's work and the child's pleasure more impersonal and businesslike. The allowance is based on the salary system, a miniature wage for a miniature worker, and became popular in America with the decline of farming as a dominant way of life (or at least as a dominant metaphor for our way of life). Children on the farm did real work. This was necessary for the survival of the family, as it still is for some families. There was a great deal of hardship for many families struggling at a subsistence level, but the hardship was imposed by life, not the parent; good parents did what they could to sweeten this hardship. The child's labor was valued because the work it accomplished was real and the child felt valued. In this way, there was a psychological fulfillment in direct useful labor, which provided parents an opportunity to be legitimately grateful and appreciative of the youngster's contribution.

This kind of usefulness strengthens the bond between parent and child and builds character in a most fundamental and traditional way. This arrangement stimulates the child's natural wish to help and allows him to work off his sense of indebtedness to his parents for having given him life, nurturing, and love. Such an experience provides a transition for the child from dreamer to doer, from being the center of helpless need to being a dependable resource capable of meeting others' needs. It prepares a youngster for taking on the role of a responsible adult in his own family-to-be and as a public-spirited member of his community.

All children need to feel useful to their parents. In the old days, when the family was truly battling to survive, it was easier for this to happen in a straightforward way because the survival value of the child's effort was obvious. Today the child's help is more likely to be convenient rather than crucial to survival. But even here, *what builds character is a home atmosphere of flexible mutual cooperation, so that the child feels the impulse to pitch in and is appreciated for doing so.*

The modernized concept of chores is often linked to the allowance for this purpose, but often with a certain shift in the feelings. The addition of money and the expectation of a fixed routine has a tendency to subtly change the human relationship. A parent who hands the child some cash for cleaning the birdcage or hauling out the trash cans is less likely to think of expressing his debt of gratitude and appreciation to the child in human terms, since "he's already been paid."

The regular allowance for regularly performed chores has a tendency thus to dilute rather than strengthen the child's desire to help out; the interaction has moved a step or two away from the arena of intimate personal devotion toward the administration of the personnel department. If the adult wants to be businesslike about it, he shouldn't be surprised if the child does too, and takes the mercenary position of being out for whatever he can get. A parent who doesn't think his child would help out at home if he weren't paid doesn't have much confidence in his bond with his child. Of course, the dry cleaner doesn't press your suit because he loves you, but then you didn't stay up all night with the dry cleaner when he had a fever.

The parent might bear in mind that the more mechanical the assigned chores (a list of things to do each day: fold the clothes, walk the dog, water the garden) the further the youngster's experience of them will be from the genuine impulse to give, genuine appreciation of his parents, and genuine gratefulness to them. This does not make mechanical chores bad, but it underscores the fact that mechanical chores in themselves don't do much to encourage a child to feel grateful to his parents and eager to help them out in return. One thing has to do with intimate feelings and spontaneous wishes to pitch in, the other has to do with accepting institutional rules and regulations blandly because one has little choice in the matter or because it is a ticket to something one wants for oneself.

The life of a child has plenty of work built into it. School, properly approached, is exceedingly demanding (or should be). It takes an enormous amount of effort, leaving the child pretty much worn out. If a child is really working to his limit at school, there is no need for him to be put to work in other areas just for the principle of the thing. The child and his parents are both already toiling together toward the same goal: "breaking their backs" for the child's future.

Of course, being generally respectful at home means being alert to what needs to be done, and there is plenty that needs doing in most homes: cooking, cleaning, shopping, child care, laundry, straightening up. All this doing is hard work, whether someone is paid for it or not. That people do it together with a sense of personal involvement, of common purpose, and of cheerful and willing collaboration is what makes this a home and not a collection of transients on the same hotel floor. Small children love to help when they observe that contributing to the household's common effort is an important part of what makes a person really count and that the grown-ups' attitude toward one another is truly helpful and appreciative (no martyrdom here!). These experiences lay the groundwork for a child to be, in time, a considerate spouse, and to support teamwork in every area. Furthermore, they inculcate the values of effort, achievement, and self-sufficiency, and connect them to a personal sense of security and well-being.

## THE PEOPLE-CENTERED HOME

To grow up to be responsible, generous, and concerned, the child needs to feel that his parents respect human beings and put human priorities first. This begins with the child and his needs, but is balanced by the laws of reality and the claims of other individuals' needs. Of course, parents may structure these priorities with rules, but a child can only learn to respect other people's thoughts and feelings if he can observe *the genuine ongoing interest in people's thoughts and feelings that lies behind the rules.*

Children who come from a home where people really are *interested* in other people—how others think and what they feel, how they got to be who they are, their goals and values and dreams—are nice to be with. They have learned that intimate communication is a two-way street; they are great talkers but also respectful and good listeners. They become shrewd observers of human nature and keen judges of character. Nice children come from the richest kind of homes, where what is valued is the human spirit, its needs for love and respect, for solitude, for beauty, and for challenge and accomplishment. In these homes, the progress of each member of the household in all of these dimensions is itself a drama of great interest to the others. The varied choices people make, both in and outside of the house—friends and public figures—are the subject of lively speculation and scrutiny.

In a home that considers people first, one can have great fun with a 5-year-old for very little money by gluing uncooked macaroni on cardboard—making houses, rainbows, space stations. Here the best sort of play is often creative and group-based, using very simple raw materials: paper, scraps of cloth, crayons, salt-and-flour mixtures, or clay. Children produce masks, newspapers, talent shows, and gifts for loved persons. For these families, the greatest theater is the theater of living; children in these families are rarely bored. At the same time, they are not isolated—the lively involvement of other people creates a situation where one may air one's troubles and upsets in an atmosphere of trust, and may appeal to others for advice, support, and encouragement.

It takes a parent's vigorous presence within the home to set the stage for this kind of family life, which brings out sharing, a concern for others, and real thoughtfulness. Parents who provide this for their children need not worry greatly about money, since they are providing their children with the most valuable thing of all—*a sense of meaning*. The meaningfulness of life is not something that can be preached, it can only be passed on by the parent in proximity to the child, in a way that includes the child.

One should point out that it takes no special talents or training for parents to place the emphasis at home on the human beings in it. It does take, however, the recognition that this is what one is after. Parents whose major goals in life are to make and spend money will pursue something else, either because hardship forces them to do so, or because their values and habits of mind suggest it.

It is the home's orientation around human beings that stimulates the child to vivid emotions, including love and hate, concern, jealousy, triumph, and despair. His feelings are not given the brush-off as inconvenient or unattractive. There is the constant presence of living models who demonstrate how more mature personalities deal with emotions in a way that is expressive, productive, and responsible. The fact that the group functions with each person's best interest at heart, with an emphasis on consideration and respect, leads toward resolution of inevitable conflict. The values of loyalty, commitment, and generosity may not be preached, but they are embedded in behavior.

This is a home that supports with interest and pride the achievements and activities of the young child, and cheers on the adolescent's steps toward real independence. Such a home is not child centered; it is centered on the human being in all phases of life. It is not in competition with the outside world, but is a source of stability and coherence that the developing youngster can take with him, inside, when he leaves home for good.

When the child is thus deeply respected as an individual, he naturally comes to have respect for others. Initially this includes foremost the people the child loves and those with whom he is familiar. As the child matures, this respect grows to include all human beings, including people who are unknown, who are different, and eventually even those who are in direct conflict with him. It is easy to be tolerant of someone who agrees with you. The hard part is to extend the same tolerance to someone who doesn't agree with you, or to be tolerant of people and ideas of which you don't approve.

Much of the child's understanding of tolerance grows out of simple experiences at home. Parents should inform children that one may love someone dearly and yet hate some of his ideas. Parents need to demonstrate in ordinary home life that grown-up talk can be an exchange of views, *without* the need for the victor to convince, silence, or humiliate the vanquished. This may be hard for some families, where someone needs to come out on top of every dialogue; in these homes, the tendency is to shout down the opponent, or avoid altogether any discussion that involves a conflict of viewpoint. But real respect for others depends on children outgrowing their natural tendency to interrupt and dismiss the ideas of others, and learning instead how to say, "How interesting! I completely disagree with you," with equanimity and friendliness. The parent may need to direct traffic in dinner-table debate, so that the timid, soft-spoken person is not drowned out by the loud and feisty one; the parent need not regulate the conversation like a committee meeting, but he can see to it that everyone has his say.

Parents who are eager to make their children mirror their own cherished beliefs may have trouble showing respect for the child's opinions, particularly if the child's ideas are pretty silly. What easily gets lost is a valuable opportunity to teach the child how to participate in a discourse that acknowledges divergence of opinion and leaves room for differences.

## BROAD-MINDEDNESS

For children to learn that other people have thoughts and feelings will be a lifetime project in fair-mindedness. The divisions in our larger world that foster "us versus them" tensions between groups can be challenging for parents who want the child to be proud of what he is, yet able to respect other persons who may, likewise, be proud of being something else. The best way for parents to achieve this is by introducing the child to positive features of his own heritage well in advance of the sad day that the child becomes aware that there is bigotry and disrespect in the world. Parents must make efforts to help children understand that the persecution of various groups has a long history on this planet, and that his family is eager to resist participating in any form of discrimination. For a child to believe in fairness and justice, his parents must show that they do so.

If the parents have a strong sense of group identity, they must understand that supporting the values of the child as an individual and as an American may come into conflict with pressure they feel to remain loyal to their particular group. Insinuating that the child should not form friendships (or later, should not fall in love) with anyone outside the group will prejudice the even-handedness of the child's outlook on others and lead him to the depressing conclusion that other people's parents have warned them similarly not to become friendly with him. This does not further the child's self-respect. The history of the world is such that many parents want their children to stick to members of their own group. Parents cannot be blamed for having this feeling, but they must recognize that placing this constraint on their child acts to diminish his capacity to experience the world and his place within it in his own way, rather than in their way. If a child grows to attach great importance to his own heritage and arranges his life to include active involvement in this heritage, he is likely to gravitate to similar individuals for his close involvements. This is completely different from a child's avoiding potential relationships with persons from other backgrounds because he fears his parents will disapprove.

To encourage our children to be truly nice people and truly respectful, we must indicate that they must react to each person on the basis of his individual qualities. The consequence of this is that the child eventually becomes a person with deep independence of spirit. The parent cannot control or dictate where this spirit will lead.

Acts of selfishness and destructiveness are natural in small children; they are the behavioral expressions of their feelings of anger, envy, and hate, which are also natural. The child slowly comes to terms with his anger, envy, and hate by developing concern for others and a faith in and understanding of the rules of fair play. He begins to express his anger in ways that are more mature and effective, as he observes the grown-ups do. We notice that the raw aggression comes first, and the wisdom to channel it usefully comes much later, and only after a lengthy period of deep, reliable emotional intimacy with parents.

Adult destructiveness, so apparent in hatred, crime, and war, is in general related to a failure of the process by which the child feels securely loved and thus understands and takes responsibility for his own primitive feelings of hate and envy. In populations where there is much general social deprivation and instability, it is always easy for authoritarian leaders to stir up enthusiasm for attacking another group that is perceived as possessing envied advantages. The alarming success of hate-mongering around the world is the result of skillful manipulation on a public scale of deep individual emotions of resentment and inferiority. Personalities who have been allowed to experience security and satisfaction in childhood bring these feelings into adulthood. They are less vulnerable to propaganda and more willing to see members of other groups as individuals, and as having rights, too. In this way, every loving and respectful parent can do something not just for his own child but for humankind.

## Clinical Considerations

### Clinical Case

*Melanie, age 15, was brought to treatment after she forged a check. Her parents were particularly offended by the forgery—it was a slap in the face. She already had everything one could ask for. Melanie was an only child, an average student of allegedly superior ability, who had a history—according to her parents—of resentful, rebellious, and devious behavior. They did not like her boyfriend. The father, a salesman, had been seeing a psychiatrist for panic attacks, and it was this psychiatrist who had referred Melanie to a child therapist.*

*The therapist met with the parents. Father did most of the talking, calling on his wife from time to time to endorse his views. The mother compliantly followed suit and in general appeared to cater to her husband's opinions, if rather mechanically and joylessly. The family had grounded Melanie for three weeks when the check with the forged signature was discovered. The father was especially angry that Melanie did not seem contrite. He had always believed that honesty was very important in life. The therapist noted that all the same there was an element of satisfaction in the father's tone.*

*Melanie herself was a thin girl with a disagreeable expression who looked a good deal like her mother. She was superficially chilly and sarcastic and claimed that she had no personal difficulties apart from her parents and their stupid problems. She would be fine if they only would leave her alone. She dismissed as trivial the brou-ha-ha about the forged check (which was, to the therapist's surprise, for the amount of twelve dollars).*

*The most impressive feature of her presentation was her scornful mistrust of therapy and her apparent conviction that there was nothing about it that might be of benefit to her. "Why don't you try it on my parents?" she said coolly. Despite her cynicism, the therapist observed that she was not actually disrespectful to him as a person; it was the treatment enterprise itself that she mocked.*

*The therapist met over a period of weeks with Melanie and her parents, both separately and together. There was much discussion of Melanie's mediocre grades, her boyfriend, and her unwillingness to "give" the father what he felt entitled to have: her trust, her gratefulness, and her admiration. Throughout, the therapist dreaded the arrival of this family; there was a suspicious number of cancellations, suggesting that the feelings were mutual. The therapist had an uneasy feeling that this was somehow a "phantom" therapy, that he was going through the motions without having real leverage on the central problem.*

*One night, during winter vacation, the therapist was awakened by a phone call and was informed that Melanie had taken an overdose of her father's pills; she was being hospitalized. Unsettled, the therapist sought supervision from an older colleague regarding how to proceed with this troubling case—he felt sure that he was "missing something."*

*The supervisor focused on what seemed to the therapist an extraneous detail: the father's treatment with the referring psychiatrist. "But isn't that a separate issue?" asked the therapist. The supervisor agreed that on the surface it surely appeared so, but reminded the therapist that it was his own complaint that he was "missing something." He was missing information. The treatment of this family was taking place not only in his office but in someone else's office—an arrangement about which he knew nothing. Might there not be something important there?*

*Taking stock of these words, the therapist met with the family as soon as Melanie was discharged from the hospital to explain his need to have all the cards on the table. At first, the father refused to give consent for the therapist to have this personal and confidential material. The therapist, however, held his ground, stating that he could* not provide meaningful treatment without free collaboration with all other practitioners; he had tried it and it had failed. It had proved dangerous to Melanie. He could not help Melanie with his hands tied.

At this point, the father became angry and rather self-righteous. "You can't just fire us," he complained. "You'd be abandoning your patient." As with Melanie's forged check, father's attitude conveyed a certain pleasure, as if he had caught the therapist in wrongdoing. But the therapist was not to be made guilty. "I'm not abandoning you," he said with dignity, "and I will happily help you find some-one else who is willing to provide further therapy under your limit-ing conditions. I need to make clear to you, however, that I person-ally am not able to continue to take responsibility for Melanie's safety under your conditions because I feel these conditions undermine treatment."

The therapist could hear his heart pound heavily as a frigid si-lence ensued. It was Melanie who broke the silence. "Gee, Dad," she said slyly, "do we have anything to hide?" The father then laughed, and abruptly reversed himself. He remarked breezily, "Well, this is silly. I don't care if you have any of my records. Go ahead." He dis-missed the therapist's query as to why he had not wanted to give con-sent and he signed the forms with a smile.

That afternoon, the therapist spoke at length by telephone to the father's psychiatrist and sought a copy of the admission and discharge summary of Melanie's hospitalization. The father's treatment, it appeared, had in fact revolved around his several-year-long love af-fair with a co-worker. Evidently, the father was under chronic pres-sure from this lady to leave his wife; he was unwilling to do so. His panic attacks occurred especially in the context of the excitements and anxieties generated by this ongoing romantic triangle.

In the notes made by the social worker at hospital admission, the therapist discovered that Melanie revealed having had sex with her boyfriend on several occasions over the last year. When Melanie had told him that she wanted to stop this, the boyfriend had threatened to leave her. This had prompted her overdose. Alas, this useful chart entry had not been heeded by the hospital staff upstairs. By the time *she had been installed on the inpatient unit, Melanie had changed her story. She said she overdosed because of a family fight. The diagnostic assessment on the discharge summary was that her suicide attempt was "situational," yet the nature of the particular situation that prompted her actions was far from clear.*

*Greatly edified, the therapist had a sudden joyous sense that he was beginning to understand this case for the first time. He had the framework of a hypothesis. Melanie was caught in the treacherous waters of her parents' marriage, in which there was a chronic fundamental dishonesty. He suspected that Melanie must have known the truth, or at least was responding to a pervasive sense of inauthenticity.*

*She feared to be like her mother, who could not "hold on" to a man. Melanie wanted something from her mother that she could not get; instead, she took a check. She saw her mother, with some justification, as a helpless doormat. Renouncing this identification, she modeled herself on her father's problematic behavior: she exploited and demeaned the mother (in forging her signature) and acted out sexually. She had her own secret. She chose to participate in sex with a self-centered boyfriend, who (like her father) was not fully committed to his partner.*

*At the same time, Melanie was besieged by her father, who criticized her for his own flaws: she was dishonest, she was not genuine, and she was not grateful. Melanie could not trust her parents, making it hard for her to trust in anything. She bravely set herself apart from them and from trusting the therapist, but she was too unfinished and needy to go it alone. She reached out to a boyfriend who in the end did not have her best interest at heart. That had been the last straw.*

*In the next family session, the therapist pointedly encouraged the family to communicate more openly—the father made a minimal reference to his once having "strayed"; the mother said that she had been aware of it. Melanie rolled her eyes at the ceiling and said, "I really don't need to hear this."*

*Following this session, Melanie was able to establish a more useful individual treatment relationship with the therapist in which she was able to detach herself from her parents' follies and pursue her own goals. The parents were seen from time to time as a couple around parenting issues. They appeared unwilling to examine further the question of their marriage and its meaning for Melanie. The father continued his affair with his co-worker, but his relationship with his daughter was less hostile.*

This case illustrates the need for parents themselves to behave honorably in order for children to develop a healthy sense of conscience. This father, although not overtly abusive, displayed many traits of narcissistic characters; he was basically disrespectful of both his wife and daughter and vented considerable covert aggression at home, untempered by concern for other people's feelings. From his perspective, other people's feelings appeared to exist chiefly in order to supply him with gratifications and rewards. The family secret, his infidelity, was of course only a symptom of personal tendencies that appeared elsewhere in his close relationships.

Melanie's capacity for object relations was itself undermined by her resulting narcissistic deficits and identification with both the exploitative father and the correspondingly masochistic mother. Since her parents were so bitterly disappointing, she too felt entitled to break the rules, to get what she could.

Like Melanie, a disillusioned youngster may put up a brave front of believing in nothing, but in the end, he can't believe in himself. The prematurely cynical young person may blandly neglect the superficial rules (as here, in forging a signature); at the same time, he is vulnerable to archaic and grandiose inner demands for perfection, with consequent depressive reactions. ("If I were a perfect daughter, Daddy would not leave us.")

The lack of honesty and integrity in the relationships within the family is often mirrored in the treatment situation, where the therapist may be barred access to significant information. Blatant examples of this arise in cases of overtly antisocial personalities who may simply lie to the therapist to conceal important facts. More commonplace, perhaps, are subtle and unconscious efforts on the part of the patient or family to distribute information in diverse sites; no single therapeutic pair of hands holds the full deck of cards.

The household in which more than one mental-health professional has a therapeutic interest is at risk for unconsciously exploiting this situation as a resistance to therapy. A diffusion of emotional impact results when one family member is in talk-therapy with Clinician A, but a spouse or parent is in treatment with Clinician B. Countertransference distortions, economic dependency on referral arrangements, professional jealousies, or rigid adherence to various therapy models may lead clinicians to collude with this compartmentalizing of affect and ideas, to the detriment of the best interests of those in treatment.

# 8

## Citizenship in School

### SCHOOL DISCIPLINE

For generations, American public schools have concerned themselves with teaching two broad areas—the "three Rs" (reading, writing, and 'rithmetic), and citizenship. Success in these areas, both the child's mastery of the material and his mastery of the personal tools of democracy, depends on the child's character. At the same time, success at school contributes to his character and is vitally important to its growth.

Nursery schools might like you to think they make a business of teaching, but they cannot really teach any discipline because the preschool child is not ready for disciplined learning. He is ready for people, creativity, and interesting experiences, but not for the institution of education. The preschool child is just *there*, in the present tense. He's not working on getting somewhere in the future. He's busy *being*, not putting forth an active effort to become something else one day. Nursery school should not be a struggle for a child, but grammar school should always be a struggle. It's work. Real school should be hard work and it should pay off over time.

It follows that a child needs to be ready for school before he can get anything out of it, and that this readiness involves his sense of his own future, his personal hopefulness, and his willingness to exert effort. The capacity for work is always related to one's conscience; it means giving up something that is more fun. It requires an inner struggle. It implies recognizing a duty to one's self. These attitudes come from within the child; they form his character as it has developed thus far in life. A good school will encourage and reinforce these attitudes, but the school cannot "teach" them unless they are there within the child to begin with.

It is only after a child has consolidated these inner qualities that he can be taught to work at any specific discipline: how to do arithmetic or build a bridge, how to read or upholster a chair. There is some variation here in timing: occasionally one sees a violin prodigy at 4 years of age, or a more or less normal child who cannot read until 10. Some little children learn to read very early because it's fun. If it had been real work, they couldn't have done it. The child's personality, on the average, is not ready for the effort of true education until about age 6 or 7, and no fancy tricks can rush it. He cannot acquire specific work habits until he is ready for work in general.

A kindergarten child might sit down to do a bit of homework, but this is largely a play-acting performance in the spirit of wearing mother's high heels. A school-age child at 8 or 10, however, begins to say to himself and to his friends, on a regular basis and without prompting, "I can't play right now; I have a lot of homework." It is in this moment of renunciation that the child shows the stuff of which he is made. His expression may reflect the regret at the fun he will miss, but it is not hard to see his seriousness and quiet pride underneath. *Giving up fun in order to do schoolwork is something the child owes himself because of the importance he places on his future.* It is a sign of his self-respect, and insofar as it then contributes to his success at school, it will also add to his self-respect. This self-discipline provides a deep sense of meaningfulness to the child.

It is an excellent thing if a child is so interested in a subject that he pursues mastering it for its own sake, and this happens sometimes. By and large, though, the youngster is interested in his classwork because he believes that doing a good job in the fifth grade will prepare him to do a good job in the sixth grade, and that this process will enable him to eventually make use of his own potential and what society has to offer in a satisfying way. Such a person believes in himself.

The satisfaction of school is the child's sense of getting somewhere on the road of his own life. It may not mean he's chosen a career, but it means he has the ambition to get somewhere, to be someone. He wants to account for something in this world, and just about every child knows that to do this you need to read, write, and do math, as well as behave responsibly. Children recognize the simple truth that a person who cannot do these things is unprepared for adulthood.

A child's sense of self-worth is tied strongly to school success. Almost any child who is not doing well in school feels mortified and anxious, even if he covers it up with clowning, bravado, and defiance. Other children are surprisingly keen observers of their classmates' personal adequacy in this regard; they pity and disapprove of the child who isn't with the program, whose attention wanders.

The child's attention is focused on the stuff on the blackboard and what the teacher is saying because he is motivated from within. This is not primarily because he is being entertained, or because he loves the past participle; it is not because he wants to avoid getting in trouble. It is because he sees his own self-interest in learning and the teacher's interest in teaching as progressing in the same direction. He knows that the teacher is teaching him not alone but among others and that he has no special claim on the teacher's devotion. The teacher is concerned with each child in a relatively impersonal way. The teacher aims to be fair, but the bond between the teacher and student is not necessarily intimate. This is another aspect of the discipline involved in education.

## THE TEACHER'S ROLE

A teacher can only build on the character that the child exhibits. If the child is not oriented towards personal achievement from the inside, there is little a teacher can do. The child's body is there but his mind isn't. It is in this area that some parents make the demand that school must be fun. But education itself is, generally, not heaps of fun, especially at first. The parent who insists that school be fun has missed the whole meaning of work; he views the child as a tyrannical infant needing to be entertained at all times. This is a type of spoiling. Such a parent has no faith in his child's character. This approach is bound to fail because studying irregular verbs or the exports of Spain can never compete in entertainment value with the latest TV show or with a simple game of catch. It cannot compete with daydreaming.

Although the best teachers care about their students and have tenderness and humor in their hearts, the basic process of grade-school education presupposes that the child already knows why he is there. The child is conscientious and industrious because he takes his future seriously. An exceptional teacher may be hugely entertaining, but many fine teachers are quite dry and dull. This was true when we dwelt in the forest, learning how to make a canoe of bark, and it is true now.

Children often adore a rather quiet and serious-minded teacher, precisely because the class atmosphere speaks to their yearning to move ahead with proficiency, dignity, and respect—without the seductions of personality or gimmicks. Children have trouble putting into words why they like this teacher; often they say lamely, "because she's strict," when they really mean, "because she's high-minded." It's the discipline they value. A child who loves school is deeply invested in this process. It is a different thing from a true love of learning for its own sake, which often does not make its appearance until adolescence or adulthood. *Loving school is the reflection in a child's sense of well-being that comes from applying himself diligently and being successful.*

Naturally, even the most responsible of grammar-school students still shows only intermittent passion for schoolwork. He still needs constant support and structure from parents, reinforcing his investment in himself at all levels and maintaining a friendly partnership with the school. And, of course, there is a limit to what parents can do.

A tragedy takes place when a child attends a school that is not up to the task. In many rural and urban settings, public schools in America lack the resources to offer adequate learning. This is a national disgrace, not only because many of their students will lack academic skills, but because many of their students will, as a result, lack faith in themselves as people. In some ways, attending a terrible school is more destructive to a child's spirit than not attending school at all. A terrible school reminds the child every day of all the things that he will miss out on in life, and is a deep betrayal of his hope and trust.

The maintenance of firm classroom discipline is a manifestation of our American values of free speech, fairness, and justice for all.

This does not mean that everyone shouts all at once—on the contrary, it means that everyone listens quietly with respect and open-mindedness to the opinions of others. A truly fine teacher is concerned not only with communicating those ideas (i.e., facts) that are beyond dispute, but with communicating the important concept that many of our most significant ideas are, and always have been, the subject of vigorous dispute.

A fine teacher opens a child's mind to the ways in which human beings in different times and places have had views both remarkably similar and remarkably different from ours; the teacher emphasizes the importance of trying to understand the real meaning of viewpoints that seem at face value to be foreign or ridiculous. This moves the child forward from the natural reaction of intellectual immaturity—laughing at strange customs and ideas—to the reaction of intellectual discipline and curiosity, a respectful wish to understand things that seem new and confusing.

A wise teacher paints the world in its true shades of gray, rather than in the dogmatic black and white that characterize childish thought. This leads the student in the direction of understanding how great men and women could have been quite imperfect in many ways, and how past generations could have held dear, and heroically defended, many ideals which we today consider utterly wicked. This approach does not cause young people to become cynical; it introduces them to the sobering notion that the answers to the great moral questions that have faced each age were by no means so transparently obvious as they appear to us in retrospect. It promotes a healthy humility in the face of the complexity of human conflict and engenders skepticism in the face of sweeping generalizations. A wise teacher stimulates students to adopt a posture of thoughtfulness and considered judgment, and to mistrust facile emotionality, whether in schoolyard gossip, the nightly news report, or the pronouncements of nations.

A good teacher engenders respect in his students for the fact that wisdom does not come cheaply. He demonstrates how snap judgments are often faulty ones, and applies a brake on the childish tendency to rush towards quick and easy conclusions. The teacher stands for the value of *process* in all things: the process of critical thinking on an individual level, and the process of group discourse, upon which civic devotion to due process depends. To carry forth their responsibilities within a democracy successfully, our children must not only be able to read, but to respond dispassionately to what they read—to see things not just superficially, but in their wider implications for the individual and for the group.

The relationship between the child and the teacher, and the child and the youngster sitting next to him, is the perfect laboratory for these issues. These are aspects of citizenship. A capable teacher controls the class so that everyone has a fair opportunity to express his own viewpoint. The teacher structures the discussion so that the children learn to disagree with each other and with the teacher himself in an energetic and constructive spirit. The teacher makes it plain that toleration of another's ideas and choices does not necessarily imply agreement. This means one may attack an idea without attacking the person who holds it. The teacher enhances the student's self-regard by insisting that each voice be heard with respect. In this way the classroom becomes safe from the bullying, ridiculing tendencies of the mob mentality that occur so readily among children. The teacher's authority makes it safe. At the same time, when the teacher calls for a consensus, the mechanism of democracy is put into action.

Through all of these activities, the teacher teaches American values—both as facts (e.g., The Bill of Rights) and as principles of personal consideration and intellectual freedom. This builds character in each student by interrelating the child's intellectual growth, the dynamics of classroom decorum, and the history and ideals of our country. It prepares the child to approach any decision with a certain gravity, and to weigh his wishful impulses against realistic pros and cons. The implications for the child in all spheres of living—as an educated citizen, and as a potential spouse and parent—are profound.

In addition to this, a particular teacher may provide a transforming experience for a particular child. The child transfers some of the magic he might feel for his parents onto the teacher, who is then idealized and adored. In this way the child's love and the business of schoolwork come together and combine in a new way. The teacher becomes his muse and inspiration. Many adults can remember feeling this emotion towards a certain teacher. This may fill a deep need in a child at a crucial time, rescuing a lost youngster from loneliness and self-doubt; it may play a lifelong role, evoking an abiding interest in a particular field or approach to life. Sometimes this love affair exists only in the heart of the child, and the teacher is unaware of it.

## Clinical Considerations

### Clinical Case

*Brad, age 7, was brought to evaluation because of his inability to follow classroom rules. The school had recommended a special education class, a recommendation that the family could not understand. Brad was an adopted child brought to the United States from a wartorn European country at the age of 26 months. Some of the parents' forebears had, generations ago, emigrated from the same country, and although the parents had little involvement with their ethnic roots, the fact that the child shared this geographic link had made the adoption seem especially fitting to both parents.*

*These parents, Mr. and Mrs. Koblenz, had married very young, and shortly thereafter borne a child, a beloved daughter, who was now married herself. Thereafter Mrs. Koblenz had been unable to conceive another child. Having come from big families, the parents yearned for a house full of children. They welcomed Brad into their home when Mrs. Koblenz was 35. Father ran a hardware store; mother had once been a cashier but did not work outside the home.*

*Brad had been medically evaluated at 26 months and found to be normal. Nevertheless, Mr. and Mrs. Koblenz had some suspicion that he had been abused in his homeland; Brad never displayed the lively interest in other people, the energy, or the high spirits, that had characterized their daughter as a child. He was alternately aloof and clingy, intense and peculiar.*

*His development had been marked in all areas by a great reluctance to relinquish earlier behavior patterns in favor of more mature ones. He dragged around a ragged blanket to this day. He had not been fully toilet-trained until he was 5. He still frequently crawled under furniture and made humming noises to himself for hours at a time. He was slow to talk, and had a very limited vocabulary.*

*Brad had a number of behavioral oddities: he liked to lick windows and mirrors and had an inexplicable fear of anything burning—candles, matches, the stove. Most nights, mother lay next to him on his bed until he fell asleep, at which point she tiptoed out of his room. Otherwise Brad would wander about the house, sleep in strange places, or call out to mother fretfully. He had fears of certain foods and insisted on a rigid diet. Mother had seen to it that the pediatrician did not object, and then prepared the foods Brad wished.*

*Much of the time, mother described, she could not "shake free of him." He would not willingly separate from her at the neighborhood playground, grocery store, or even at the homes of neighbors and friends. Here, too, mother adapted to his need for physical closeness, since he seemed to "space out" when necessity imposed a separation.*

*Brad did not mix well with other children; he tended to invite bullying, which he suffered passively. Once, out of the blue, he had struck another boy over the head with a glass bottle.*

*Brad had attended a small nursery school, which had made many adjustments to his disorganization. The assistant had spent a considerable portion of her classroom time with Brad on her lap. He similarly survived kindergarten with much attention from a kindly teacher; this teacher had suggested that he repeat kindergarten. The parents, however, had wanted Brad, already older than most of his classmates, to move ahead with his peers.*

*It was in the first grade that Brad was deemed unable to function. He would drift around the classroom, fail to perform required tasks with the group, and busy himself with drawing faint wavy pencil lines all over tables, schoolbooks, and his own skin. The teacher had met with Brad's mother and informed her that he was emotionally ill. These words had pierced her like a dagger. Was it true?*

*The school then made an evaluation, which revealed a full scale IQ of 86, with somewhat stronger skills in nonverbal areas. There was evidence of mild organic visual-motor deficits. Problems were noted in the areas of attention and peer relationships. A special education class was recommended.*

*The parents felt bewildered by this process and sought an independent evaluation from a clinician. It was his opinion that the mother, due to deep underlying ambivalence about this child, was stifling his efforts to become independent and was overindulging him in ways inappropriate to his chronological age. She was overinvolved. The clinician did not express these ideas directly, but implied that it was Mrs. Koblenz's responses to Brad that kept him enmeshed with her in primitive ways.*

*Mrs. Koblenz did not like this therapist. She left every session feeling more anxious and baffled than when she walked in. After half a dozen sessions, her husband suggested that this clinician was not the only fish in the sea, and encouraged her to ask him for a second opinion. This request only confirmed the therapist's convictions: she was doctor shopping until she found someone who would tell her what she wanted to hear.*

*A second clinician was consulted to evaluate Brad. He observed Brad to be an awkward-looking youngster who sat in the waiting room leaning against his mother's shoulder. Brad entered the office mechanically and sat down passively in the chair. He spoke softly, with a speech impediment. When specifically asked about hearing voices, Brad admitted to frequent auditory hallucinations from shadowy figures. They came from "The Disappear World." He knew these voices were not real and that other people did not experience them. They were not pleasant, but not frightening. They were part of him. Brad's reality testing was otherwise intact and his thinking logical throughout.*

*This clinician assessed Brad as suffering from diffuse ego deficits, probably related to early environmental failures and perhaps organic insults that occurred during his first 26 months of life. Brad's image of himself, of others, and of the world was not coherent, but haunted by residues from this chaotic period, a world that disappeared. Consequently, Brad could not manage himself; he was inordinately dependent upon his mother or substitute figures. Having less structure inside, he needed more from the environment. An inevitable crisis had ensued when the public school system put demands upon Brad that he could not meet.*

*The parents, on their part, believed that loving-kindness would help Brad overcome whatever he had lacked in early childhood; their devotion would eventually erase these losses. He would surely catch up with other children in time.*

*This clinician saw that where these parents needed help was in conceptualizing the child's limitations and in grieving over the losses that this new concept of the child involved. He informed the parents about some of the typical sequelae of early trauma and deprivation; over time, he helped them recognize the true length and breadth of their willingness to adapt to and to fill in for Brad's deficits.*

*At last, the parents experienced much relief at being understood. Feeling allied with a professional, they were then able to renegotiate with the school the issue of Brad's education placement. A suitable compromise was reached with part of Brad's day taking place in a support room and part in a regular class. His family continued in treatment where he made slow but substantial progress.*

Where these parents needed particular help was coming to terms with their recognition that Brad was not like other children—that his needs exceeded what the ordinary classroom could provide. The parents' issue was largely one of grief, relinquishing their fantasy of an ordinary boy and accepting that he would need more—not only from them (which they personally were able to provide) but from other everyday institutions, which were less flexible. Their need to see Brad as more capable than he was had led to a lack of insight into the position of the school system—that a regular class could not meet his needs.

The second therapist saw the parents' "denial" as a complication of their love for Brad, their deep wish to see him perfect and whole, and their resistance to accepting that these cherished hopes and dreams for him might be unattainable. Their denial, of course, was unhelpful, insofar as it got in the way of their collaboration with the school. The second therapist recognized, however, that the parents were adapting to the child's deficits without any particular secondary gain, without needing the child to have deficits in order to resolve their own inner conflicts, to repeat some problematic feature of their past or present, or to fulfill some other pathological agenda.

This is an important distinction for a therapist to make and one easily overlooked, because, on the surface, the parent often looks like part of the problem. The child is missing something, something intangible (such as an ego function). This missing thing is required in order for the child to march forward at the pace of other children. The devoted parent compensates for the missing function, and remains involved with the child on a level that was once natural when the child was smaller, but is now increasingly out-of-step with his peers. The child and parent remain bound to one another in a curious dance, frustrated because they find one another so frequently underfoot, and prone in this stressful closeness to ordinary reactions of despair and anger.

The parent knows that something is wrong, but does not know how to express it. The picture often gives the impression of intense neurotic suffering on the part of everyone concerned. This state of affairs is often taken to be evidence of the parent's symbiotic needs, but this is not necessarily the case. The parent's dearest wish may be to be free of the child's enormous needs, a feat that the parent simply does not know how to accomplish. Of course, the existing arrangement may not be ideal; the goals of treatment may be to identify what ego function the child is missing and compensate for it in some other way, such as psychotherapy, an educational plan, or medication.

In these cases, it is an error to assume without confirmatory data that the responsibility for the child's deficit lies with the parent. The intellectual history of child therapy in the twentieth century indeed provides many sad examples of just this mistake, in which hypothesized parental rejection, ambivalence, overinvolvement, engulfment, and so on were presumed to cause many syndromes now recognized as primarily due to biochemical, brain structural, or hereditary disorders.

There are, of course, some rejecting, ambivalent, and engulfing parents, and as a result of these problems their children often develop symptoms. But one cannot work backwards from the existence of a child's symptoms as the sole evidence of the parents' rejection or overinvolvement. There needs to be *other* evidence that the parents are rejecting or overinvolved. A thorough examination of the parents usually reveals compelling evidence of these personality trends, when they are to be found, in several areas of living—and often in every area of living. These tendencies are often quite visible in a parent's behavior towards the therapist.

The well-intentioned parent of any disturbed child is, however, exceedingly vulnerable to blame because the good parent always feels guilt in the presence of his child's suffering. The parent's willingness to be blamed can be mistaken for evidence confirming his role in causing the child's deficit. Likewise, the parent's resistance to recognizing the seriousness of the child's problems is often misinterpreted as the parent's need for the child to continue to have these problems. But many times these parents resist recognizing the child's deficits because of their great reluctance to let go of the fantasy of the normal child and to undergo a painful process of grieving. Yet the suffering involved in relinquishing the beloved image of the normal child is not pathological, although it may appear so.

Left to their own devices, parents have a tendency to grieve chaotically for their disturbed child—despairing one day and hoping again the next, as the inescapable unevenness of living first raises and then dashes their hopes. On their own, parents cannot arrive at the understanding that their child is one of a group of children with such-and-such syndrome, which carries such-and-such prognostic implications, for whom it is realistic to expect certain kinds of future events and unrealistic to expect others. Parents cannot spontaneously know whether the child suffers from a poorly understood condition whose outcome is exceedingly variable. But for parents to hear even this can be a great relief, because while it is indeterminate, it is nonetheless objective. Thus it is that the professional assessment of utter uncertainty is very different from the parent's own personal uncertainty, because the professional uncertainty can be confronted as a given, mourned, and in time accepted.

# 9

## The Floundering Student

### MOTIVATION

Most nursery school and kindergarten children will listen with rapt attention to the teacher, although perhaps only for brief periods. The child will be genuinely fascinated and open-mouthed. With every passing year, the number of children who tune in to the teacher's voice with this kind of alert interest falls. By junior high, many children in America are not active participants in their education. They are passive. These children are not calling attention to themselves. They are invisible. Their behavior is more or less adequate and their grades are more or less passing. It is their learning that is not adequate. Such a student may not be a problem in relation to the group; he is only a problem in relation to his own character and his own future.

Because the qualities of self-discipline and pride in one's work are quite vulnerable in childhood and adolescence, troubled students are commonplace. Anything that causes upset and preoccupation to a youngster—physical illness, family discord, divorce, moving to a new neighborhood, death of a loved person—can interfere significantly with his sense of purpose and confidence in himself at school. In addition, there are often subtle biological limitations, and commonly there is a mixture of reasons. Even for children with a biological diagnosis that

impairs learning (one might say *especially* for these children), the issue of character remains extremely important to the child's eventual
success; that is, success in school is highly dependent on individual
effort, attitude, motivation, and conscientiousness. And naturally, success in turn tends to improve one's level of motivation, just as failure
lowers it.

It is easy to squash the elementary school child's motivation because
the child is easily lost and doesn't know what to do about it. For many
children, it is difficult to pinpoint the precise cause of their school
difficulty. The common denominator is that the child has lost some
degree of hopefulness regarding his own future. He has lost touch with
the eagerness for the work and with the seriousness he once brought
to it. His mission for being there, his sense of duty to himself, erodes.
A child is demoralized by schoolwork that is momentarily asking too
much of him, which is bound to happen at times since the child and
the curriculum may march forward at different rates. This is especially
likely for children who are weak in organizational skills or reading comprehension—the child sits down to a sea of assignments, each a mass
of incompletely understood instructions, losing one page, doing Part
II instead of Part IV on another, missing the point on a third. The child
puts forth a lot of time and effort, but it is wasted because he hasn't
caught on to the main idea. The child is not stupid; he just doesn't have
the tools right now to work efficiently on his own because of his uneven development.

A sensitive teacher in a supportive school environment may be alert
to this child's difficulty and give him the individual attention he needs,
but the confused child who is not disruptive easily gets lost in the
shuffle. Such a youngster sits in class understanding some of what is
going on but not all of it. If this persists, the process gathers steam
and can be extremely destructive to the child's pride and conscientiousness. Few children can bear for very long the anxiety of trying
hard and still feeling baffled. Eventually the child has to run away
from the discomfort and panic that effort in the classroom produces.
He develops an attitude of letting it slide. Rather than watching the
teacher like a hawk and madly waving his hand for help the minute
he's confused, the child becomes passive. The teacher drones on and
on. The youngster daydreams, sketches on the covers of his book,

winks at the fellow behind him. Once he's given up meticulous conscientious attention, a great deal of the potential value of his education is lost. Learning then becomes something that happens in spite of himself rather than because he owes it to himself. Attention is impossible without motivation, especially the very focused, careful, and serious kind of attention required for school.

Success in school is a measure of a child's having accomplished to a good degree a long process of self-mastery and self-discipline. The child has, *inside*, the courage and good judgment that has developed in his love relationship with parents, and these qualities are further refined and expanded by the educational experience.

When a child is not doing well in school, this failure has an unfortunate tendency to spread and to undermine his character growth in other areas. The poor school performance erodes the child's relationship with his parents, his sense of being lovable and valuable in their eyes. The parents may communicate disappointment, but the child himself often feels he has failed to live up to their standards even if they do not. This makes the child feel lonely and isolated from his parents; when concurrent with puberty, this state of affairs typically leads to a false assertion of independence: the child makes a wild lunge at the rights and privileges of grown-ups—not the kinds of effortful achievements that betoken real maturity, alas, but the superficial evidence of adulthood.

The peer relationships of the poor student typically suffer. Once a child ceases to feel deeply involved with the material being taught, the experience of sitting in class quickly becomes sheer torture. The teacher and those students who are working hard have no patience for this youngster, who is present only as so much deadweight, and they usually make their irritation known. Then the youngster has no one to turn to but peers in similar straits. These peers offer a kind of support and comradeship but tend naturally to discourage each other from getting back to business. The reason is simple: if such a student managed to break out of the doldrums and to reorient himself towards success, his low-functioning chums would be left behind in the dust.

This is the essence of peer pressure: the mutual effect (always bad) that a group of children who are not making it have upon each other. Peer pressure is pressure to engage in something self-destructive in order to prove one is a member in good standing of the group and to prove one is definitely not feeling hopeless or inadequate. Vulnerability to peer pressure is generally a sign of feelings of hopelessness and inadequacy. When children spur one another on to acts of courage, talent, ambition, or honor—which of course young people frequently do—we do not call it peer pressure.

The whole conglomerate of antisocial developments is especially irresistible to the poor student because the youngster feels he is locked out of the wholesome future that is the inspiration to envied luckier youngsters. He lives in a nightmare, a continuous present that is never followed by a tomorrow. He experiences with anger and shame and grief the death of the good little child inside, who long ago had naïve and touching hopes for the future. Like a condemned man, the student without a future looks ahead no further than to the bittersweet taste of one last cigarette.

One hears this story frequently from adolescents who make poor choices for themselves. They are, at bottom, almost always anxious about their ability to succeed competitively in school and in life, and are almost always in some sort of academic pickle even if they happen to be very intelligent. Often the sense of missing the boat in school goes back many years, to a point where the child lost confidence in the ability of his own hard work to master material. Being in school was transformed into a game of escaping hot water, rather than growing wiser and more capable. This was the difference between knowing a subject well enough not to get a *D* or an *F*, and knowing it cold.

Troubled teens almost always get lousy grades. The teachers and parents may say, "He can *do* the work. He's just not trying." They mean "can do" in the absolute sense, that the child has the native ability to do it. What grown-ups often don't understand—although the student is often painfully aware of this point—is that the work has become *too hard* in view of the youngster's having failed to consolidate the study skills and the basic information that were being taught the year before (when he got a *D*) and the year before that (when he got a *C*), and has lost the confidence in his own work that is the product of success in early grades. The youngster really *can't* do the work. He can't do any kind of work.

Frequently the floundering student describes the following: at intervals, he makes a sincere effort to turn over a new leaf and tries to do an assignment on his own. He is quickly frightened by the realization that success in this subject is not going to happen (that is, immediate pleasurable success). The bitterness of this disappointment—in himself because of the revealed inadequacy, and in adults who fail to rescue him when he's depending on them—is easily transformed into an attitude of indifference or defiance. He takes on a posture, "Who's trying, anyhow?" Such youngsters are easily discouraged because they have had little exposure to the process of slowly acquiring mastery of a challenge and have no confidence in it or in themselves. It is a vicious cycle, especially mortifying to teenagers who want to feel independent. It takes on a catastrophic, black-and-white quality as well, because of their immaturity of judgment. The lack of self-discipline and low self-esteem are really two sides of the same coin.

It is easy to call these students lazy or presume that they are too busy having a good time to do schoolwork. A few airheads may actually manage to have a good time for a while. But most junior high and high school students who neglect or skip school are in for an experience even more boring and depressing than the geometry class they avoided. The apathy and hopelessness of an endless mid-morning needs to relieved by excitement, which is easily obtained though risking danger of some kind—sex, shoplifting, drugs. Puritanically we read this turn of events as the tremendous allure of having unprotected sex with someone you really don't like very much or stealing a sweater you don't need as *pulling* the weak person out of geometry class. To combat this, we point out what the teen is already aware of—shoplifting is wrong and the sexual escapade was pretty much of a drag. Even the cigarettes give you cancer. This is approaching the issue backwards.

Teenagers who skip school and hang out in this manner *can't begin* to tell you how completely miserable they are. The day isn't long enough to tell you. They are often quite puritanical themselves and, with surprising regularity, wax moralistic about their inability to resist cutting class and participating in hooliganism, all the while despising themselves and their peers. But what really motivates these youngsters is not the strength of these irresistible temptations but the strength of their hopelessness.

Such youngsters may have attained considerable skill in some other area: dance, athletics, or art. Unfortunately, the feeling of virtuosity does not generalize because the special skill was usually acquired well in the past and was based on some degree of natural talent and a real love of the activity. The concept of slowly gaining proficiency in an academic area where the youngster initially lacks both any specific gifts and any genuine interest is alien to him. He has reached a point where gaining new skills is impossible.

The successful rehabilitation of these youngsters once they are embedded in chronic problems is a multifaceted affair, perhaps including drug and alcohol treatment, sex education, legal sanctions, family therapy, and proper identification and treatment of an underlying psychiatric disorder. The issue relevant to this discussion is the teenager's school failure, which is sometimes tacked on to the portrait as a kind of afterthought, whereas from the point of view of the youngster's spirit, his character, his hopes, and his dreams for himself, his school failure is quite central. It is the cardinal sign of his lack of healthy investment in his own future, and therefore sets the stage for other self-destructive pursuits.

All of this is not to suggest that school failure itself is the *sole cause* of a long list of complex problems that include drug addiction, unwanted pregnancy, crime, or mental illness. *School failure is, however, a powerful and subtle predictor of such problems in general, and often signals an opportunity for intervention before subsequent problems have a chance to become full-blown.* A lack of personal commitment to what is happening in the classroom is very often a youngster's initial cry for help, the first sign of a breakdown in his trust, optimism, and conscientiousness.

## SUPPORTING GOOD GRADES

Many of these difficulties would be identified sooner or perhaps even circumvented altogether if parents set higher standards for their children's grades and viewed anything below a *B* as a concern. Children who are truly responsible, hard-working, and invested in their futures get very good grades, even if their intellectual endowment is quite modest. They earn high marks because they try hard, they are anxious to do well, and they get down to work seriously on a daily basis. Teachers are usually delighted with such a child, even if the child is not especially bright—even if he is decidedly on the dull side. The child compensates for his lack of natural intellectual talent by over-achievement, over-learning, and endless drill on the basics.

Some children figure out on their own that they need to do this, but often it's the parents that need to support the child to make it happen. Some children will get straight As without their parents' help, but they are the minority. Most children get Bs and Cs without their parents' help, and the parents think this is fine because they recognize that the child is not a natural genius. The problem is, for a child to get Bs and Cs means he is not really mastering the material, although he's not failing miserably. On school tests that measure knowledge, the child actually gets a large number of wrong answers. There's a lot he doesn't know. The child is being carried along by the school system without drawing attention to himself as a failure, but he's failing to get the most out of the learning opportunity. As he gets older, there is a tendency for the gap between his achievement and his potential to widen.

It would be a great benefit for this youngster if his parents expected that he get As most of the time, and if his parents then gave him the personal support needed in order to do it. This approach has the effect of cementing a close bond between the child and the parent; it improves his school record, his level of skill and achievement, and his self-regard. He feels more secure, confident, and successful. It gives him a different identity. It prepares him for doing better on his own next year. It builds character. This is a different thing from having the parent *do* the homework for the child, and it is different from the parent farming this task out to a paid tutor. It is rather like the parent in the old days teaching his own child fine craftsmanship—how to make a quilt or shoe a horse.

This is how it's done: the child and the parent examine the school notebook every day and review each subject. If there is a spelling test, the parent tests the child on the word list, and helps in making flash cards to practice on the words that are missed. Reading assignments are read together—What's the story about? What's the main idea? The child is assisted in writing assignments, both in brainstorming out loud what he intends to express and in circling mistakes in red pen on the first draft. For math, the parent says, "Show me how you would go about doing this." They struggle together on the hard ones. For science, the parent can help the child write a fact sheet—with all the data summarized that are likely to be on the test—and review it daily.

The parent need not be a teacher, or even especially smart himself. He has only to be one step ahead of the child; this is easy since he is likely to have passed the fifth grade once himself, however long ago. It is a very enlightening process for many parents. If often lays bare, to the parent's horror, how frequently the child is lost or perplexed by his schoolwork, and how feeble is the child's confidence in his basic skills. It does not demand that the parent invent a curriculum, or dream up stimulating topics. It consists merely in doing the homework that's already there, including preparing for every test, with meticulous care and seriousness—problem by problem. The parent sits with the child quietly, every day, for as many hours as it takes to get that day's work done. If the child is doing a wonderful job tonight alphabetizing his spelling words, the parent might sneak a magazine onto his lap and relax for ten minutes. The process usually doesn't work if the parent is simultaneously trying to do the dishes or bathe the baby. The child needs the parent *right there* in a sustained way, providing encouragement and helping the child see that every detail matters because every detail matters to the parent.

The goal is that the child's abilities are supported and inspired by the parent in an intimate, personal, friendly, and helpful spirit. The child may not like the teacher and he may not like geography, but something valuable is passed on to the child when the parent and the child together have made flash cards with the state capitals on them, so that he does really well on the test. It tells the child that he can excel, and that his parent knows this and wants to help him do so. It tells the child that success that seems out of reach is actually accessible if the task is broken down into small pieces. It helps the child learn to be realistic about budgeting time. The immature youngster has a very inexperienced grasp of how long things take; his sense of the passage of time is strongly influenced by his own wishful thinking. His natural impulse to procrastinate and his naïve belief that his homework will only take a jiffy conspire to make him leave everything to the last moment.

This kind of parental homework support provides the reassuring presence of a love relationship just at the moment when the child's doubts about himself are most painful and disturbing. The homework problem that the child cannot solve points an accusatory finger at the insecure youngster, saying, "Ha! You're stupid!"—reinforcing his anxieties about his adequacy. This is a core experience for many youngsters who try to avoid their schoolwork. The parent's presence is an antidote to this; the parent helps the child contain his anxiety and lends the child courage to tolerate the self-doubts involved in each new challenge. In time, this courage becomes part of the child. Having experienced the encouraging parent, the child develops an inner voice that says, "You can do it!" He begins to face frustrations that require sustained effort with greater confidence and security. Homework support convinces the child that the parent cares enough about him to make a personal commitment of time and energy. It also communicates how important his education is to the parent. It tells the child that his education is more important to the parent than TV or sports or fast food or whatever it is that the parent usually takes the time to share with the child.

This support, to be sure, is a huge investment on the parent's part. There are going to be parents who cannot afford to do this because they are working two jobs or because they are busy single parents. Like anything else, it's a question of what is possible and also of priorities. A parent who feels victimized by life's responsibilities in general will not look with enthusiasm at the time-consuming prospect of making a mediocre student into a strong one. This kind of parent will say that it's up to the school or up to the child. Perhaps, above all, homework support may strike the parent as alien because many parents have become accustomed to the mentality of addressing their children's misbehavior, rather than their inner qualities, their competence, and their future. Parental "teaching" in our day often has been reduced to lecturing, preaching, and scolding. Many shy away from the teaching relationship between parent and child hallowed by the ages, in which the child was patiently tutored and initiated into the skills of his particular heritage. For many families, this function has become institutionalized and commercialized. Yet, if we are not pleased with the results thus achieved, if the skills become haphazard and the parent and child become relative strangers to one another, steps can be taken to repair these problems. The parent and child can spend time working together, constructively committed to a mutual goal: making the most of the child's opportunities.

# WHAT THE SCHOOL CAN'T DO

There are ways in which the school can enhance and broaden the role the parents have played for the child, but the school is not the parent. Social and family problems today have caused an epidemic of youngsters in every neighborhood who come to school in varying states of personal crisis—children who are beaten, suicidal, intoxicated, mentally ill, pregnant, sexually abused, violent, undernourished, and neglected. The school, to its credit, often recognizes that it is the only stable resource in the child's life, and feels obligated to do something constructive for the child. In any event, the child and his problems are right there, on the school's doorstep. But beyond taking emergency measures, there are considerable legal, logistical, financial, and ethical barriers standing in the path of the school in its wish to provide what the child fundamentally lacks—responsible adults taking care of him. In the absence of responsible adults caring for the child, the school is left in a quandary.

Because school performance is a sensitive barometer of a youngster's well-being, school personnel are often alert to a child's emotional difficulties and anxious for the child to get professional help. It is not too uncommon that the school is in fact more anxious than the parents for a child to receive treatment. The child's difficulties can be largely a reaction to family problems that the parents, at that moment, may be unwilling to examine or change. The questions raised by the evaluation are thus unwelcome, and the referral comes to naught. The following case illustrates some of the issues typically involved.

## *Clinical Considerations*

### Case

> *Crystal was referred by her junior high school counselor for evaluation at age 13 after a long series of unexcused absences. She was failing the eighth grade, although she had been a good student in grammar school.*

*When seen by the therapist, Crystal presented as an attractive girl wearing lots of makeup who readily described a chaotic home life. Her 19-year-old brother was a heavy drinker, and there was much yelling and conflict at home. The family never ate meals together; everyone was "sort of on their own." It appeared that father too frequently had quite a bit to drink. He was a real estate developer in a rural area and the family was ostensibly wealthy, but Crystal had the suspicion that bill collectors were harassing the family in mysterious ways.*

*To the therapist's amazement, Crystal hesitantly related how six months earlier, at the age of 12, she had had an abortion. She was still going steady with her 15-year-old boyfriend, but had sworn off alcohol and sex since that time. Crystal described feeling deserted by her mother throughout the experience; she explained how mother had accompanied her to the clinic on the day of the procedure, but had waited in the car because she could not bear the idea of running into someone she knew. As a result, Crystal went through the experience alone. "Boy, I'll tell you—that really took a lot of nerve," she said with a grin.*

*The therapist at this point told Crystal that he admired her "nerve," and stated that he could see that her life was not an easy one. He commented that he hoped she was prepared to protect herself since it didn't seem as though other people were protecting her very much at the moment. Crystal said, "Yeah, I'm getting better at that."*

*The therapist met with the parents, together and singly. Father was a huge, talkative, and very controlling man who denied that Crystal's troubles represented anything more than "a standard teenage attitude problem." Mother was a glamorous and anxious-appearing woman who indicated she was somewhat intimidated by her husband. Each minimized the father's drinking and dismissed the brother's problems as irrelevant. (The brother had been asked to come to the session, but had not shown up.) The therapist emphasized the need for the family to recognize serious problems with both offspring. The parents paid a general sort of lip service to the need for treatment, but then remarked that they were paying the fee out-of-pocket and could not anticipate a lengthy therapy.*

*Having suspicions that the evaluation would not progress beyond its initial phase, the therapist searched in vain for resources where Crystal might receive treatment on her own for a negligible fee, or some sort of local support group. Her small community offered nothing accessible by public transportation, and the nearest Al-Anon meetings were a lengthy car drive away from her home.*

*As the therapist feared, the family failed to keep all subsequent appointments, responding with excuses, rescheduling, and vague promises that extended over a period of weeks. The therapist next telephoned the local child protective services agency. Without naming the patient, the therapist described the situation and asked the agency whether it could proceed to investigate the home for neglect or abuse. The agency worker listened sympathetically but responded that unless the child was actually suicidal, homicidal, or in immediate danger, the state's law did not permit intervention. The agency worker suggested that the family press charges against the boyfriend (Crystal and her parents both had been opposed to doing this). She also recommended that the school pursue the issue of the truancy.*

*The therapist then called the school, fortunately having obtained signed consent for this communication from the parents at the initial visit. The therapist spoke frankly with the guidance counselor who had made the referral. The school did not have a program to support youngsters in such straits, she said, but she would try to keep an eye on Crystal's progress personally. At six months, the therapist phoned the counselor for a follow-up: Crystal's grades had improved to Cs and Ds and she was still absent, but less frequently.*

This case is typical of many referrals where the parents have not yet reached a frame of mind that makes treatment feasible. The parents' unavailability to the youngster often appears to be a significant part of the problem, so that their unavailability for treatment is not utterly unexpected.

The therapist is often faced with a dilemma between two styles of approach to treatment-resistant parents. The confrontational style attempts to emphasize the destructive parts of the reality, to grab the parents' attention, as when the therapist asks the father, "Are you really saying that a pregnant 12-year-old is 'business as usual'?" This sometimes provokes a breakthrough, but runs the risk of making it even easier for the parents to perceive the therapist as unsympathetic. The seductive approach, in contrast, downplays the immediate issue of the parents' poor judgment while attempting to establish rapport, for example if the therapist empathizes with the father in his exasperation at Crystal's attitude. Although these two approaches are in one sense antithetical, the most successful therapists manage to use both, often within the same moment, suspending their empathy midway between the parents' needs for a nonthreatening ally and the youngster's need for appropriate protection. The therapist's best hope in achieving this delicate balance rests in his awareness of his countertransference. Errors are often the result of the therapist's unexamined and condemnatory view of the parents' failures (which the parents are quick to pick up) or, sometimes, similarly negative views of the youngster.

It must be acknowledged, however, that even when approached with consummate therapeutic sensitivity, some families are not ready to begin or sustain a treatment. The therapist is then left with two avenues that may prove useful to the youngster. The first is to explore a potential network of helping adults with the goal that the youngster does not remain completely isolated. Clergy, hospital, emergency room staff, school personnel, remote family members, hot-lines, and community groups all can offer useful support to a young person in this situation, either in a crisis or sometimes in an ongoing way.

The final consideration is to recognize that struggling youngsters, like those small plants that cling tenaciously to the inhospitable face of a cliff, often make the most of the very smallest drops of nourishment that come their way. Even the evaluation, no matter how brief, presents the possibility that something genuinely inspirational can occur for the patient. Childhood memories of certain brief contacts may be treasured forever, exerting a powerful influence on the individual's self-image and outlook.

It is for this reason that at each initial visit, the therapist must endeavor to achieve not only a well-filled-out database, but a kind of personal magic. He must elicit clinical information, but also convey respect for the patient—and hope. It is his opportunity, and sometimes his sole opportunity, to actively reaffirm the patient's human goodness. This need not always be accomplished in words—sometimes it can be done with a look. For the professional to view the assessment chiefly as an impersonal affair focused on information can inflict a devastating hurt on the patient, whose deepest need (albeit not necessarily visible on the surface) is to be valued and validated as a human being.

Throughout life, but perhaps most notably from ages 10 to 20, the young person craves new influences, new people with whom to be in love, from whom enduring inner relationships can form. The poet's muse, the guardian angel, the inspiring teacher, the idealized older brother, the best friend, all represent these potent inspirational figures that have so much to give the developing personality. These influences are often especially poignant when the influence of the original parents leaves much to be desired and the new relationship takes on an element of rescue and healing beyond even its usual ardor. Lucky individuals may find this quality in their marriages.

The therapist at times has an opportunity to offer this kind of relationship, both to the child patient and to his parents. In this sense, all therapists are real people, engaged in real relationships with their patients. Both parties participate in a reciprocity of need—the therapist needs his work to be meaningful, and is often greatly moved and excited by what takes place in the office. In therapy, of course, the relationship is not in all aspects symmetrical: the patient comes seeking relief of suffering, and the therapist is a professional who is paid; he exercises abiding self-discipline with regard to a variety of ordinary impulses that are extraneous to the best interest of the patient's treatment—his own romantic impulses, or confessional impulses, or impulses to steal other people's children. But being there for the patient is very real, and the therapist provides not only commentary on the patient's introjects, he may become thereby an introject himself. The therapist may participate in the patient's inner world not only during the treatment, but after, and in some cases, ever after.

# 10

## The Adolescent's Needs

### THE GOOD BABY-SITTER

The long period that extends from the time of kindergarten to junior high—during which the child, year after year, has a certain sameness of body and mind—is a golden opportunity for a child to consolidate into his character the parent's love, values, and outlook. By junior high, the youngster has come a long way toward being able to truly manage and take care of himself. Of course, he still needs his parents to be there for him, but by now this has largely come to mean that he knows he has their trust and confidence, rather than that they are physically there.

The healthy child of 12 or 13, broadly speaking, doesn't need constant adult supervision—in fact, he can provide it to others. We acknowledge this by general consensus when we let a youngster of this age baby-sit for an infant or toddler. We are saying that the young teen is responsible enough to be the sole authority for a little person who cannot manage much of anything on his own, at least for several hours at a stretch.

The baby-sitter role is an excellent example of something that demands ordinary authentic maturity of character—the kind every young adolescent should have. It is a benchmark for what needs to be in place for a young person *well before* he undergoes the personal transformation of puberty and the physical, intellectual, and social changes that go with it. The child need not have an interest in baby-sitting or the technical expertise (it might be the furthest thing from the minds of many 12-year-olds), but he needs the head and heart to do it capably if he were called upon: a respect for the preciousness of that young life, a kind-heartedness, an ability to be duty-bound for a stretch of hours, and an iron-clad immunity to various temptations.

A child with this kind of normal personal maturity is well-prepared for the process of adolescence soon to come, and his parents should be proud. This young teen, no matter how level-headed and trustworthy, is still immature in a thousand ways and not beyond completely going to pieces in certain circumstances. Yet an early adolescent can have what it takes to be a responsible baby-sitter even if he is not particularly intelligent, or particularly independent in other areas, or particularly mature physically or socially. He may seem timid and child-like at times, yet have achieved a constancy of character and good sense that would make a splendid baby-sitter.

## THE TROUBLED TEEN

It is clear that a great many young people enter adolescence without the necessary backbone of a firm character, and that this is the common denominator that underlies a vast spectrum of adolescent problems that will become dramatic only later. Such a youngster is Jell-O inside. He has no resistance to the impulses coming from within, or to peer pressure coming from without. Disaster is always just around the corner because he lacks the judgment, self-protectiveness, and respect for others that would help him navigate around peril. Such a teenager is not bad—in the astute phrase of one father, "Oh, he's not looking for trouble. Trouble finds him."

There are many young teenagers one would not put in charge of an infant; one would not put them in charge of a potted plant. It is predictable that every aspect of the adult world that is suddenly spread out like a smorgasbord in front of this adolescent can be the focus of serious problems. This sad state of affairs is so commonplace that many people think it is normal. The parent is in a quandary, constantly waiting for the other shoe to drop, yet unable to provide supervision all day long. The piece of the picture that often does not come into focus is that the youngster has never been able to manage his own life from the inside; something that should have been consolidated by the time childhood was drawing to a close was never achieved. The youngster's body has become large and strong but his character hasn't.

The reason many teenage problems do not respond to a quick fix is that the development of the problem was not quick. The problem teen is often the end result of a long process in which the stability of the youngster's inner world failed to become anchored through strong positive relationships. These are teens who do not feel invested in their own futures, who feel empty and hopeless and angry. They are disinclined to master their impulses because they see no point in doing so; achieving relief in the moment seems to them a more reliable satisfaction than aiming toward some distant and abstract goal. They feel they have been betrayed by the world of adults and thus owe it no loyalty. The voice inside, which reassures each individual that he is good, and loved, and worthy of protecting, speaks rarely to these teens and only in a whisper; their memories of childhood are full of bitterness and hostility and a sense of loss. As school-age children, they kept in the background, only communicating their failure to invest in their futures by their mediocre schoolwork. This lengthy period of apparent calm was their parents' opportunity to furnish the bare rooms of the child's character through a rich, loving relationship. All the signs of the 8- or 11-year-old's inner impoverishment may have been there, but insofar as the youngster had not actually lit a fire in the principal's office, the observer may maintain that there was never any problem until puberty set in. Such an 8- or 11-year-old feels no real loyalty to doing things the way his parents would; he does them that way because he's made to. He'd be a motorcycle gang member if he could, but he can't. He doesn't have a motorcycle; he doesn't know how to pump gas, or to drive. He doesn't have the cash, the muscles, or the gumption. He bides his time.

Eventually he has the resources to do what he's wanted to do all along. Puberty, a widened sphere of opportunities, and the encouragement of other youngsters with similar difficulties provide the troubled adolescent with resources that make it possible for him to live out in reality the self-destructive, antisocial, and altogether foolhardy wishes that have been pent up as fantasy for years. The "problem" does not begin when he is picked up by the police.

The process of adolescence is like the removal of a scaffolding that has held up a building from the outside. Without the external support, it has to stand on its own or crumble. Fortunately, it is always possible that the troubled teen can find what he needs in a new positive relationship with relatives, friends, teachers, clergy, or in a treatment situation. At times, these lost souls have gained helpful information about how life's problems can be solved by reading books or even by watching television. It is not that each and every empty adolescent is surely doomed, but it is so much easier and less painful for the pieces to fall into place in a developmentally logical sequence, so that the youngster has adequate protection inside to meet the dangers of the outside world half-way during the period of time when he needs it most.

In most neighborhoods all across our great land, illicit drugs are being sold somewhere and any 15-year-old (and many a 9-year-old) who wants to can find them. This is itself disgraceful and scandalous, but it is not an excuse for concluding that it is the nature of all 15-year-olds to be drawn into drugs and that the problem rests exclusively on our neighborhoods and not at all on the 15-year-old. There is a trend at times in public discussion of troubled teens to lay all responsibility on the average environment and downplay the importance of the teenager's personal agenda in negotiating a safe passage through this environment. Naturally, in those neighborhoods where the drug lord truly reigns as king, many more teenagers will be drawn into crime, but even here many families succeed in preparing their offspring to resist it.

## LEAVING THE PARENT BEHIND

The adolescent, like the toddler, is learning how to manage *leaving the parent behind* for increasingly significant periods of time. Of course, he takes the parent with him inside, for guidance and support. This is why it is so important that the parent has paid heed to what kind of overall inner relationship his child is going to carry with him on these journeys: Is it packed with nourishment and energy, like a tasty lunchbox, or is it distasteful and sour? It is these inner relationships, based on the totality of the youngster's experiences and perceptions of his parents, that he will draw upon to sustain him in his journey.

To be sure, the push to venture forth into the world, for both the toddler and the adolescent, is driven by a certain grandiosity and heedlessness. Both the toddler and the teenager can be a little irksome to be around, since they suddenly have all the answers. But this heedlessness is necessary to propel the toddler or teenager over the hump, so to speak, of his enormous reliance upon his family. He needs, in fact, quite a fire under him at these times—like a rocket at take-off, gathering force to escape the huge gravitational pull of his dependency on his parents.

This fire, this heedlessness, is the very stuff of life. It is not rebellion. The parent who experiences his toddler's or teenager's thrust to push away from the parent as rebellion has missed the whole point. This parent has confused a personal power struggle between himself and his offspring with an awe-inspiring and beautiful explosion within the youngster that nature has put there for a purpose.

There are of course some toddlers and teenagers whose personalities have come to be dominated by actual oppositionalism and rebellion. The need to rebel is never healthy because its energy derives from disappointment in interpersonal relationships rather than a focus on the real world outside and the individual's healthy drive to conquer it. Rebellion in a teenager is a sign that something has deflected his energies away from his natural interest in mastering the world and taking his rightful place in it as a mature individual.

Thus it is the essence of adolescence to need to embrace some risks. This is necessary for the adolescent to take the biggest risk of all: to take his life in his own hands, no longer protected by the parent, and begin to make his way in the world. This leads every ordinary adolescent to do things from time to time that his particular parents would not choose to do because he is leading his own life and not theirs. The parents, on their side, need to withstand their feelings in response to this—including pride, worry, anger, and perhaps envy and a sense of being abandoned.

This is in contrast to those rebellious youngsters who enter adolescence without the stability of character necessary to navigate among risks, and are thus impelled to actions that not only their particular parents, but no sensible person would commit. This is the difference between normal adolescence and self-destructiveness. The normal adolescent can question authority because now he sees himself as an authority; he is ready to take his place among the elders in his community debating all the issues, large and small, upon which opinions may legitimately differ. He is ready for citizenship. The immature adolescent does not join the world of authorities as one voice among others—he is against authority in the abstract. He does not discriminate among issues; all he needs to hear is that some adult does it "this way" and he's prepared to resist it.

Many parents, especially those who have approached their children by trying to manage and control them, are bewildered by the needs of the adolescent, who is now too big to control. This parent has trouble distinguishing between the distress he feels at his teenager's ability to act on his own decisions and the distress he may feel at his teenager making what seem to him to be bad decisions.

The wise parent who has *controlled the situation* for his small child has been able to maintain a warm intimacy with the youngster; he has avoided, whenever possible, the need to control the child directly and thus minimized conflicts and power struggles within their relationship. The nature of the authority between the parent and child has been predominantly one of imparting wisdom and guidance, rather than constricting the child's activity. The child admires the parent and is inspired to model himself after the parent's leadership.

This approach pays off in adolescence, when of course the parent can no longer control the situation. The adolescent no longer inhabits special environments created by the parent; for the most part, he inhabits and participates in the ordinary outside world, with all of its problems and dangers. The parent, however, by virtue of his good rapport with the adolescent, maintains a considerable influence over him. But this is not control, because the adolescent has the power to make his own choices, based on his inner resources.

### Vignette

*Josh, age 14, belongs to a local roller hockey league. Official league policy demands protective helmets and padding for all practices and games. Josh and his chums, however, often gather at the hockey field at odd times for informal skirmishes. For these events, the boy explains, no one wears helmets or padding; the players are more mobile and see better without the protective gear. If one player wore a helmet, he would be at a disadvantage. But Josh's health-conscious parents want him to wear a helmet. What to do?*

Josh's parents need to make up their minds what *their* goal is. Josh is a rather cautious, studious boy, and secretly they are glad he enjoys this daring sport. They decide that the real goal is to produce a youngster with a realistic respect for potential injury. They recognize that their goal of forever protecting his head is no longer developmentally appropriate. Josh acknowledges that the situation is not ideal, but he is willing to take the risk.

The parents have the option of forbidding him to play, but in the end settle for a strong expression of concern about what they see as a pretty dangerous activity and send him off helmetless with their blessing. Josh is glad because he'd feel awful lying to his parents—telling them he'd wear the helmet when he planned to take it off anyway. Of course, if Josh is injured, his parents cannot turn around and say, "See, I told you so," since they had a legitimate opportunity to forbid it. They can't sanctimoniously disapprove of his decision, since they endorsed it themselves. If Josh is hurt, the parents would then wisely support him emotionally through the experience by reminding him that he was not misbehaving, that his parents and he had *agreed* that living vigorously means taking some risks. They could all concur that they were all unlucky, perhaps all mistaken, and will all know better next time.

Now if Josh were 11 years old, or if he were a notoriously reckless and immature 14-year-old, the parents might reasonably forbid him to play without a helmet. The goal of protecting the child who doesn't have the judgment to do it himself takes precedence. But Josh in general has good judgment; we notice that his act of risk-taking is innocent of any hidden agenda—lying to his parents or actually getting hurt is not part of the fun. He just wants to participate in an ordinary aspect of life that makes his parents cringe. He's not going without a helmet because he wants to rebel, he's going without a helmet because that's the nature of this particular hockey game. In a subtle way, it is important for him to make some choices that his parents wouldn't make and to survive these choices. It reassures him that there are other ways of living besides his parents' way, and that these ways are not singularly good or bad, or invariably delicious through being forbidden. It also reassures him that his parents can tolerate his living his own life, not living their life. And, importantly, he is able to be himself, without dishonesty, without feeling as though he can only grow up by keeping part of himself secret.

The adolescent whose character has developed in the normal way, who has the necessary Rock of Gibraltar sense of responsibility to be a good baby-sitter, has outgrown the parent who needs to "make" him do things. The parent is still an authority, but the authority consists of his greater wisdom about most matters. The parent is wiser because he's lived longer and seen more. He continues to be an expert on hundreds of intimate details of his teenager's existence. Yet the days when the parent physically lifts the child out of an imbroglio are over. A teenager who still needs to be lifted out of situations for his own good is stuck at a very immature level of development with regard to his ability to manage himself. Examples of this are school failure, drunkenness, unwanted pregnancy, reckless "accidents," acts of violence, and other crises that call for the authorities in one form or another. Yet just because the authorities are called doesn't mean there's a problem with the teenager. This can be part of normal living.

### Vignette

*Karen, age 17, was arrested at a community political demonstration for trespassing. The event was part of a protest movement led by responsible adults, including members of religious organizations. Karen was aware of the potential risk of arrest, as were the other participants, since the demonstration utilized the nonviolent principle of civil disobedience. She was a little frightened by the idea of having a record, but also thrilled to be taking, as she saw it, an active role in history. Her mother was anguished at what she viewed as a serious threat to her daughter's successful future. Because the deed was done and because she recognized Karen's need and right to make her own decisions, mother made a partially successful effort to keep*

*the extent of her anxieties from Karen. She shared her worries bit-*
*terly and at length with her husband, however. The father, who had*
*been a student activist himself a generation ago, was enormously*
*proud and felt that eventually Karen's personal resourcefulness would*
*turn this event into an asset.*

This vignette illustrates the need for adolescents to take risks, and
to foresee and accept the possible consequences of these risks. The
teen is in great need of moral support at these times to bolster the courage and independence of spirit that is needed take risks and accept
consequences. This support strengthens the teen's courage and independence, as well as the love relationship with the parents. This is in
contrast to the parent's praising or blaming the teen for doing what the
parent would or wouldn't have done, which undermines both the teen's
emerging character and the bond with the parent. *It is no contradiction*
*to say that while the adolescent is making his own serious decisions, he*
*still needs his hand held!* He needs it especially at these times. A parent who is so insecure that it becomes a personal insult when the teen
does not imitate the parent in every way is very likely to spitefully with-
draw support at this time, which is crushing to the teen's initiative and
confidence.

Karen's mother showed sensitivity to her daughter's need for moral
support by refraining from the temptation to scold, "Now, see what
you've done!" although she wanted to do exactly that. In healthy families, as here, the relationship between the parents acts as a shock ab-
sorber for parental emotions stirred up by the offspring. Mother knew
it was not constructive to criticize Karen, but let it out at her husband
who, as a mature adult, was able to take it in stride. An older and wiser
person, perhaps Karen herself at another phase of life, might have
passed up this opportunity to be a part of history, or assessed the long-
term risks differently.

This vignette also illustrates the strong interest many normal adolescents express in the sad state of the world and their sunny confidence that they would do a much better job if they themselves were
running it. This outlook itself can be infuriating to many grown-ups.

To many parents, the teenager's itch to take charge is a reminder
that the parent himself is not immortal. The adolescent's physical

strength, beauty, and energy are a premonition that the world cannot make room for both of them indefinitely. To the degree that the parent can come to terms with his own mortality, he welcomes the adolescent's vigor and ambition. To the degree that he fears or denies it, he may view the upstart with resentment.

## *Clinical Considerations*

### Clinical Case

*Kim was 17 when her parents brought her to treatment. Her mother stated Kim was "all over the place." Kim was a marginal high school student, impulsive and irritable at home. She had no direction, plans, or goals. She and her mother fought constantly over what seemed to both of them to be the silliest things. Kim had fits in which she became hysterical. Her long-term boyfriend, John, was given to jealous rages; their crowd was known for drunken partying, which often deteriorated further into fistfights and car chases because of John's suspicious possessiveness.*

*The parents owned a small grocery store where they seemed to toil around the clock. There were two older brothers. The children themselves had labored long hours in the store since they were small. Mother could not understand what was the matter with her daughter; she had been a studious and hardworking child. Kim had considerable talent as a singer, but had dropped out of voice lessons when she was 12. Mother said perceptively that she had often speculated whether Kim had been sexually molested, but Kim denied it.*

*Kim was an extremely beautiful young woman with a merry, action-oriented temperament. She was herself aware of the chaotic quality of her life, which she described as "a total mess." She could not identify what the trouble was; however, it had something to do with feeling overwhelmed and suffocated by her parents, especially her mother, whose very presence made Kim want to run away. Kim described her parents as grossly obese; their minds and lives were small. She felt as though she had to gasp for air when she was around them. All her parents did was play cards with the people upstairs and work themselves to death.*

*The therapist put some pressure on Kim to account for her own self-destructiveness, particularly her misadventures with John, who had serious problems with alcohol and the law and was often quite threatening to Kim. The therapist pressed Kim to consider why she was not more invested in her own best interest.*

*After several sessions meditating on these themes, Kim said haltingly that only one really bad thing ever happened to her, so absurd she had always tried to forget about it. She was 12. She had slept over at a friend's house across the street, but unexpectedly returned home late at night to get her wallet. When she entered her living room, she saw evidence of an abandoned card game. As she walked down the darkened hall, she was horrified to glimpse through her parents' open door her mother and father in bed with the neighbors, all apparently stark naked, laughing and obviously enjoying themselves. Kim fled from this appalling sight and was so overcome with nausea and dizziness that she had to sit down on the driveway. After a few moments, she caught her breath, crept away from the house, and vowed never to speak of this discovery to anyone.*

*Thereafter she felt excruciating discomfort in her parents' presence and indeed a kind of alienation settled over all her relationships. She felt she could trust no one. She became flighty and bold, provocative in the classroom, and a tease with boys. She attached herself to her classmate, John, an athletic star with a short fuse, who seemed to have the ambition to control her every move. From then on, nothing had been right.*

*Following this session, Kim spent a great deal of time in the sessions describing her difficulties with her boyfriend. In time she confronted him about his drinking (to no avail), displaying less and less tolerance for his controlling possessiveness, and soon announced to the therapist that they had broken up. She began taking voice lessons once more and was planning to graduate from high school.*

This case illustrates how a single traumatic event can shake a child's confidence in the parents—or, perhaps more accurately, how a traumatic memory can serve as the focal point and organizing principle for a variety of more subtle factors which are then, as a totality, experienced as disillusionment.

The shock of discovering that her seemingly strait-laced parents were lovers with the neighbors caused Kim to suffer a muddle of anger, shame and guilt, jealousy, and embarrassment—and most of all, a profound sense of isolation. She was breathless from panic and unwelcome excitement. Her parents could no longer offer comfort, guidance, and leadership; of course the actual parents did not know this, and continued to try to offer these things, all the while mystified that Kim did not profit from them. In particular, the person Kim's mother had become in her daughter's mind was unable to offer reliable guidance in matters of impulse. Kim could no longer make use of mother's "goodness"; it had been spoiled.

Thus some years passed in which Kim's judgment and her ability to assess what was in her own best interest languished. Indeed, if her parents could sink to this exploit, what could stop Kim from partying, drinking, and driving recklessly? The choice of John as a boyfriend clearly represented Kim's wish for containment (he made lots of rules); Kim knew she was afraid of her own impulsiveness and found someone who aimed to control her. At the same time, John himself embodied a kind of chaos and danger; moreover he accused Kim of romantic disloyalty. He was wrong on a literal level, but right about Kim's heart, where doubts about loyalty were an abiding concern.

Sharing this painful memory allowed Kim to reconsider her parents, especially her mother; more and more she recognized that, after all, her mother was "basically a nice lady." At the same time, Kim experienced a shift in her self-regard, saying that she had found "my own voice." Thinking and speaking, instead of self-destructive *doing*, then became available to her as a means of managing her own feelings, communicating her intentions to others, and investing in her own future.

# 11

❧

# Fostering Maturity

## THE NEW RELATIONSHIP

The teenage years can pose challenges for parents because the young-ster responds to them in new ways. The parents still treasure their adolescent offspring with the same depth of commitment and ideal-ism as they did when the child was born; the teenager, on the other hand, has recently made surprising discoveries about his parents' basic ordinariness. This does not mean the adolescent loves his parents any less, but it does mean that the parents are viewed all of a sudden as being rather like other people in the neighborhood, rather than the idealized demigods they seemed to be when the youngster was 8.

A parent who needs to remain admired eternally as all-knowing, all-powerful, or all-important will find the adolescent's broadening insight into the parent's mere humanity a painful come-down. The parent may feel the teenager has lost all respect for him because the teenager no longer respects his omniscience.

This is also a difficult time for a parent who sees himself as a vic-tim. The normal adolescent is for the most part leading his own life; the victimized parent can't help but be envious since he felt that his own youth was dominated by his deprivations, his own parents, or the unlucky stars that ruled and ruined everything for him. This in itself makes him resentful. On top of this, the independent teen wants his hand held? No, sir! The normal teen needs the parent to endorse his autonomy, to put a seal on it, so to speak. The envy that the victim parent feels makes him disinclined to do it—"If you're so independent, don't ask *me* to like it!"

This withholding is also set in motion by the fact that the parent who feels like a victim takes everything personally. If the child doesn't take his advice, his feelings are hurt. The existence of the child's independence is itself a kind of insult. The parent holds out to the child a choice, "My way, or you're on your own." The child needs to become a clone of the parent, or walk the plank in isolation. This can be extremely depressing for adolescents, and often provokes self-destructive impulses and acts.

Any young teen is still an exceedingly unfinished piece of work, however. This is why the parent needs to be very available for advice, guidance, discussion, and wise counsel. Teens usually love this; they like to be spoken with as equals and their newfound ability to think more abstractly is a toy they cannot resist playing with all day long—this makes them great conversationalists with each other (as is well-known) and with their families.

It is the teenager's new ability to think abstractly that leads to his capacity for both great joy and great woe. Fresh vistas of adventure open to him, with a sense of promise and excitement. At the same time, seeing the big picture brings a new realism that is often painful. The teenager's growing understanding of the complexity of adult life brings the sobering awareness that he may not always be fully equal to the challenge. It all suddenly looks harder than it used to. Moreover, the teenager's lack of true maturity tends to paint these issues in black and white. The parent's reassurances, which succeeded in comforting the 10-year-old and soothing all of his anxieties, don't go as far at 15 because the 15-year-old sees further than the 10-year-old. The parent can no longer fix everything with an embrace. The teenager recognizes that his parents are not so perfect and powerful as they once seemed. He recognizes that not only does he want to solve problems on his own, but that he *has* to. All of this leads to a sinking sensation.

The teen's natural inclination to talk things over with his parents, which he needs to do in order to complete his development, can be turned into its opposite by the parent who is determined to be coercive rather than wise. The teen's good judgment is like a little plant that needs careful tending and nurturing to make it grow, but also one that will wither with too much heavy tramping around in the vicinity. The child's character is in great need of parental guidance, but the spirit needs to be collaborative.

A parent who tries to "make" the normal teen do things will usually fail, certainly eventually if not right off the bat. It is usually physically impossible to achieve, and it is psychologically offensive to the youngster as well. The parental mentality of defining what one will "let" a teenager do is wrongheaded from the start; if he wants to, he'll do it anyway (sex, drugs, etc.), as is sadly all too well known.

The answer is not that one "lets" the teenager have sexual intercourse or use heroin; the answer is that one must abandon the ambition to be the gatekeeper of the youngster's experiences. The parent must work with all he has: the adolescent's current love relationship with the parent and the good sense the youngster already has inside. These things are the result of long years of childhood and the love relationship that was taken in during that time.

The parent's friendly availability to the teenager allows discussion that clarifies a thousand issues that the teenager may not have thought of, and these insights may have great impact on the youngster's decisions. Teenagers have trouble understanding, for example, how terrified parents are of drunk drivers and other nighttime dangers presented by the dating situation. Once they've been informed of this, the teenager's compassion for the worrying parent should inspire promptness or phone calls.

In contrast, the more aggressively the parent focuses on whether he will let the teenager stay out until 11:00 P.M. or 1:00 A.M. or whatever, the more he undermines his real relationship with the teen and the ultimate goal of furthering his well-being. He produces a youngster who can't wait to get out the door in order to be free of the parent; he produces a teen who is irritated at the parent and thus not especially inspired to feel empathy for the parent's worry. He may even enjoy worrying the parent out of spite. The interaction with the parent is angry and oppositional (the parent has made it that way), which undermines the parent's ability to offer needed support for the teenager's independence.

Because the parent does not provide this crucial kind of moral support, the youngster remains stranded at an unfinished and immature state. The parent and youth are at a stalemate. The youngster, lacking the moral support he needs, experiences the anxious emptiness so typical of these unfinished teens who seek the false support of other peers who are similarly afflicted. It also produces guilt over the unhappy relationship with the parent (whose love is still craved), so that the excitement of reckless actions that so often prove to be dangerous seems tempting as an antidote to his depressing mood. The teen feels bitterly as though he's been treated like a child, so he's provoked to drive dangerously and smoke and drink and make his girlfriend pregnant just to prove that he is not.

This does not mean that all the parents need to do is to let the youngster come in at 3:00 A.M. It means that parents who are concretely focused on the clock are barking up the wrong tree. What the parents should be after is a self-reliant young adult who still likes them, and who hopefully has learned from these wise parents a few things about both late-night dangers and compassion for worriers. Getting the youngster in at a particular hour was initially only a means to this end, but can itself become an obstruction to its achievement.

The problem is that the concrete *surface behavior* (coming home at a certain hour)—has become an end in itself to the parent. It has overshadowed the real goal, which is the youngster's eventual strong *character*; what is forgotten is that the surface behavior is only an approximate indicator of the character-to-be, and not always a very reliable one. In other words, the parent must be willing to abandon his loyalty to particular behaviors if this loyalty is going to conflict with his ultimate aim. In this way, struggles over what parents let teenagers do are like the falling apart episodes of a little child: parents who are stuck on evoking and maintaining good behavior all the time may end up with less satisfactory results than parents who are confident in the future product and thus more flexible about what constitutes acceptable behavior at specific times.

## Vignette

*Daphne and Kevin were 15 and 17 when the police took them in for parking past the legal curfew at a well-known lover's lane in Kevin's father's car. Kevin had entertained vague amorous designs on Daphne, who was, however, not at all romantically interested in Kevin. The two, good students in high school and great cynics, were passionately discussing a nineteenth-century novel when they were apprehended. These teenagers and their parents cooperated piously in the general police reprimand that followed, but secretly everyone thought the episode was hilarious.*

Here is an example of teenagers making a mistake in judgment that involved the police. The mistake was neglecting to think through the likelihood of the authorities policing a lover's lane and flaunting the curfew to boot. The whole episode reveals a typical normal adolescent silliness and, in their case, a sympathy with proud loners, artists, and other renegades from the conventional. Although what Daphne and Kevin did was wrong (or at any rate, was against the law), it was not really destructive. Their parents sensibly assumed that these conscientious teens had learned what they needed to know from the experience itself and said nothing further about it.

## TRUST

The wise parent makes the adolescent's long-term best interest his highest priority; *because the parent has integrity himself, his actions over the years have demonstrated to the adolescent that he is sincere in this focus and the adolescent believes him.* He has only used coercion and force when it was necessary to preserve safety, lifting the toddler physically off the brink of disaster, or making his 8-year-old have an emergency appendectomy when the child objected. The rest of the time, the parent was willing to lose battles in order to win wars. Thus it is that the parent and adolescent still trust each other, despite the fact that the offspring increasingly recognizes that the parent is not a godlike special being, but an ordinary person.

Any adolescent in a hot-headed moment may feel that his parents are his enemy. What is important is what he really believes underneath when he cools down. If the adolescent does not understand in his heart of hearts that his parents want the best for him, he is unlikely to be able to protect his own self-interest consistently on his own. Indeed, he is likely to behave self-destructively as a kind of public advertisement of his plight.

The teenager who lacks faith in his parents' good will develops a vacuum in his personality in precisely the area where the parents are perceived to be lacking—in the adolescent's management of his own long-term best interest. A teenager who truly feels he cannot trust his parents is a person without hope. He lives for *now*, vengefully or sadly— or both. This loads the dice for every kind of self-destructive choice, for which cigarette smoking is so often the classic and tell-tale indicator.

The parent may have hoped that his insistence on rules will prevent a youngster from behaving destructively, but this is an illusion. *Only a teenager's faith in himself, based upon his faith in his parents and their faith in him, can lead him to exercise good judgment.* Many parents consistently underestimate and remain curiously blind to the extraordinary capacity for angry and unhappy adolescents to engage in dangerous activities behind their backs despite "rules." The teenagers usually know that the reason they do these things is because they are disappointed in the parents whose love they crave, and the adolescents themselves are usually conspicuously aware that what they're doing is destructive. The lack of inner resources is in fact one of the things they often feel most angry about, blaming their parents (sometimes with some justice) for sending them off unprepared for living. This sad phenomenon is sometimes called typical adolescent rebellion, but it is not normal in the sense of *being healthy*; it is only considered normal because it is commonplace (i.e., it passes for the norm). Some people think these teenagers have no parents looking after them, but experience reveals that the parent is often tagging along right behind the teenager, complaining and arguing and demanding and getting absolutely nowhere.

Meanwhile, most parents faced with this are at wit's end, because they are basically good and love the adolescent. The parent is exposed to the self-destructive behavior, which is overt, and may miss the teenager's feelings, which are concealed. The behavior is taken at face value as pleasure-driven. The self-destructive choice, be it sexual involvement, drugs and alcohol, or truancy, becomes the focus of a pushing and pulling that goes: "I won't let you have this pleasure!" "I'm going to have it anyway." The parent, if he feels a strong sense of victimization, may express this with a certain envy of the pleasures of youth and contempt for the adolescent's lack of self-control.

This seals the adolescent's sense of isolation because, as he himself is only too aware (though he may not admit it), the self-destructiveness is mostly not pleasure-driven, it is driven by his hopelessness. This is the common thread in many stories of adolescent rebellion, each with its own particular twists.

The parent feels that he's trying his best, since he's hounding the adolescent to the point of mutual exhaustion. The hounding is completely ineffective, however, leading the parent to feel all the more angry and helpless. If the parent sees himself as a chronic victim, then he is already feeling angry and helpless, since that is the core of his experience on earth anyhow; the bitter disappointment in his teenager and his no-good ways is only consistent with many other similar disappointments, and is in this way inevitable. A commonplace situation is a parent with a helpless outlook on life doing battle with his unhappy teenager, many of whose problems with optimism originally arose from and are currently sustained by the parent's outlook.

The parent of a self-destructive adolescent also feels a very legitimate grief mixed in with his hostility, and the adolescent is often quite unaware of how much the parent craves to restore a feeling of cherished tenderness with him. In this way, both parent and child have certain ironic similarities, each being unaware of the other's closely guarded secret: they are brokenhearted because of the failed intimacy between them. They may indeed share certain problems with intimacy itself; one of the most basic of these is the recognition that other people are indelibly separate no matter how close they are, and will lead their own lives, no matter what.

The parent in this kind of struggle has no faith in his adolescent, an attitude that deprives the teenager of just what he especially needs. The adolescent's poor track record only serves to reinforce the parent's pessimism. In this way, *the more trouble the youngster is in, the less likely it is that he will obtain from his parents the kind of emotional support he needs to begin to repair his troubles.*

The more out-of-control the adolescent is, the more intent the parent usually is on taking control of the teenager's life. But often this is like putting the mercury back into the thermometer after it has shattered. Short of jail or involuntary psychiatric hospitalization (both of which usually involve a respect for due process legalities), there is little a parent can do to take control of the youngster, except in the short-term during an emergency, without the teen's collaboration. Even rigorous rehabilitation programs require the consent of the teenager. A parent with strong feelings of personal helplessness is going to find in the out-of-control teenager the consummate confirmation of his ineffectuality.

All solutions, short of permanent prison chains or a magic tranquilizing gun of some sort, must begin with the acknowledgment that the adolescent alone has the power to do what he wants with his own life, including doing his best to ruin it. All other human beings, including parents, can influence and persuade only to the degree that they establish a bond of trust and good faith with the adolescent—which exerts its extraordinary force only indirectly, through the adolescent's heart.

## Clinical Considerations

### Clinical Case

*Danny, at age 16, was seen by a therapist in a locked facility for juvenile offenders. He had been placed there following a series of drug-related offenses. This was a youth whose parents also had had significant drug problems. Danny's first out-of-home placement had occurred at the age of 10 months, when his father assaulted his mother. The father was jailed; the mother was hospitalized with a head injury from which she never fully recovered. Danny was placed in a temporary foster home for six months.*

*Danny then returned to his mother, where he remained until he was 3. At that time, mother entered a drug rehabilitation program and placed Danny with her sister, Carla, where he lived for the next two years. Carla was a woman with many problems; in this home also lived Carla's boyfriend Jerry, who had a record of convictions on vice charges. During this period, Danny's mother remained in touch with him but could not take him back because she lacked a stable place to live.*

*When Danny was 5, Jerry was arrested and Danny was placed in a foster home with several other children. It was here that Danny was sexually abused over a period of months by one of the older foster boys. Danny told no one about this and the foster home only came under investigation when another of the youngsters lit a serious fire. Thus Danny was removed from this setting and placed with the Eberlins in another foster home; he was now 7.*

*Mr. and Mrs. Eberlin were kindly older people and Danny was the only foster child currently placed with them. A period of relative stability ensued. Danny attended regular classes, where he received passing grades. During this time his mother was arrested for prostitution; there was some discussion of her voluntarily relinquishing parental rights and Danny's being adopted by the Eberlins.*

*When Danny was 10, Mr. Eberlin had a stroke. His wife was overwhelmed by the responsibilities of caring for him. At this point, Danny's mother, who had continued to see him at intervals, took him back. He had not lived with his mother for seven years.*

*Danny made a poor adjustment to this arrangement. A chaotic period followed, with many moves and many different men in mother's life. When he was 11, one of mother's boyfriends introduced Danny to the use of marijuana and began to utilize him as a go-between in the world of drug dealing. Danny, a bright boy, was skilled at this and readily rose in the ranks.*

*Danny was frequently apprehended by the police; at the age of 13 he was sent to a lockup. Danny quickly learned how to play the system and graduated from this setting to a less restrictive group home. The staff at the group home were delighted by his charm and he remained there for nearly two years. All the while, unbeknownst to them, Danny maintained his own clientele as a drug dealer.*

*At the age of 15, he was again apprehended and sent to a locked facility. He was identified by the staff as having leadership skills; a therapist on the premises took a special interest in Danny and offered to see him in individual psychotherapy. The therapy began enthusiastically with Danny relating vivid, colorful events from his past. The therapist was gratified to believe that they were forming a bond. After a while, however, Danny unaccountably began to miss sessions, arrive late, and fall asleep during the sessions. Danny could not explain what this meant. He apologized and tried once again to narrate entertaining stories.*

*When Danny had been in this facility for eight months, a tragedy occurred. He was notified that his mother had been found dead in her room. The cause of death was not known. The therapist was eager to be a support to Danny, who wept in his office, racked with sobs, for several hours. The following day, to the therapist's surprise, Danny seemed virtually his old self. It was eerie.*

*A few weeks later the institution underwent a change in administrative leadership. Certain corrupt goings-on involving the staff were exposed—among them, a collaborative enterprise between two staff persons and several of the youthful inmates in which cigarettes, drugs, and money were exchanged for various favors. There was a suspicion, never founded, that this included sexual favors. Danny had been one of the youngsters involved.*

*The therapist was appalled to have been part of an institution that abused its charges. At the same time, he was forced to reevaluate his understanding of his relationship with Danny. He had thought that Danny had trusted him. Now he recognized that Danny had not trusted him. Danny trusted no one. But before the therapist had an opportunity to discuss these matters with Danny, Danny approached him to state that he needed to end the treatment. He needed time to work with the reading tutor instead. The therapist, chagrined, realized that Danny had been a step ahead of him all along. He wished Danny well. He invited him to return to therapy, anytime.*

*The reading tutor was a cynical older woman whose approach to incarcerated youngsters was dry, droll, and detached. Danny did not open up to her, just as—as far as is known—he did not open up to anyone. All the same, he worked very hard at reading, moving from a fifth- to a twelfth-grade level of comprehension over the remainder of his two years at the facility. He left the facility at the age of 18 and attended a junior college. He continued to smoke marijuana and deal it as well, although on a relatively minor scale.*

This case illuminates some of the issues that arise in the treatment of youngsters who have suffered chronic neglect and abuse and whose early attachments have been characterized by massive disappointment and instability. Like Danny, many of these children display great resilience and appear relatively free of overt symptoms. Their major areas of difficulty lie in establishing three-dimensional relationships with other people and submitting to the rules of society.

The therapist did not make headway with Danny for several reasons. He presumed that his institution offered Danny safety, but in fact Danny was being victimized by the staff. This arrangement, while an ethical wrong perpetrated by adults, also served Danny as an outlet for his own acting-out; it provided him with a justification for keeping the therapist at arm's length. Danny had "nothing to say," like many patients whose thoughts and feelings find avenues of discharge through various destructive activities.

To treat the acting-out individual, one must, so to speak, stuff the acting out back into the head. If the routes to acting out are blocked, the patient is forced to *experience something*, something that can then be talked about. Thus, firm external structure, with few avenues for mischief, is often a necessary precursor to treatment.

In addition, as an ethical wrong, Danny's abuse by the staff prevented him from having faith in the therapist; the therapist, as part of a untrustworthy institution, was naturally viewed by Danny as untrustworthy himself. Until the staff participation in wrongful activities was exposed and justice was done (i.e., through a process of restitution), there would not be much reason for Danny to believe that any of the authorities had integrity. And of course, everything he had experienced in life disposed him to the opposite conclusion, including the manifest failure of the multiple agencies that had had the responsibility for his protection (child welfare, public assistance, hospital and rehabilitation staff, courts, foster arrangements, and so on). Like the therapist, most of the workers in this vast administrative apparatus had been honorable and well-intentioned people. But their good intentions did nothing for Danny because children do not experience their good intentions but only concrete outcomes. The outcomes for Danny were a pattern of violation and abandonment.

The child who has experienced this kind of intense and sustained failure on the part of society is very likely to make identifications that are saturated with aggression. His inner world is often made up fairly exclusively of victims and perpetrators, since this is what he has known; to the degree that he has his wits about him as he matures, he is bent on being one of the perpetrators and not one of the victims.

The naïve therapist thinks he can offer such a youngster a relationship. But often the youngster does not know what to do with a relationship. He sees it in terms of what he can get out of it: a pass to the cafeteria, a better pair of sneakers. For many of these youngsters, it goes further to define the relationship (as the youth himself does) in instrumental terms, by setting an explicit goal that the youngster wants for himself. For Danny, learning to read was one such goal.

A further consideration is a developmental one: the yearning for deep and genuine attachments cannot continue to be frustrated indefinitely. Small children, when abused, typically show considerable hunger for nurturing figures, even if these love relationships are rendered stormy by their primitive aggression. But for older children and adolescents, some portion of this yearning becomes progressively sealed off. The door closes. The abused individual loses the childish qualities of turmoil and warmth, and narcissistic solutions come to the fore. It is for this reason that with each passing year the abused youngster becomes less accessible to real intimacy and the work of treatment becomes much harder.

# 12

## Male and Female

### SEXUALITY AND CHARACTER

Sexuality is one of the most comprehensive elements in the personality, going through and through—from the basics of animal drives to the most culturally determined attitudes. It is a modality of expression in which human beings exhibit their great diversity as individuals; it is closely linked to the conviction of being alive. Sexuality is interwoven in myriad ways with a person's identity, his goals and values, his joys and despair; it is one of the most revealing mirrors of our character.

A person's sexuality is like a piece of music—like a jazz quartet or orchestral symphony it unfolds throughout the life cycle with different instruments taking prominent parts at different times, yet *meaning something* because of the various voices working together. True mature sexuality, which involves responsibility for sexual pleasure in relationships and for reproductive decisions in all of their implications, is a sphere of adulthood. The component parts, however, have been developing since infancy; each, like the orchestra's violins, horns, and wind instruments, has a different history, a different melody. It is because of this complexity that there are many opportunities for inner confusion and conflict along the way.

Of course, many parents will focus attention on the narrow question of their teenager's potential for sexual intercourse because it presents acute risks. But to have any real understanding of this potential it is necessary to place it in a broader context: the meaning that each growing individual gives to sexual pleasure, its aims and characteristics; his concepts of romantic love and commitment; and the individual's gender, sexual identity, and sexual role identification. Equally important is the manner in which these questions fit harmoniously into the totality of the person's character: his self-image, aspirations, loyalties, plans, and goals.

The physical process of puberty intensifies the capacity of the sexual organs and the body generally, as well as the emotional sphere, to experience excitement and desire and to experience orgasm. What the mind makes of this desire, however, is subject to external elaboration and remains to a considerable degree as much of a mystery to scientists as to poets. Of course, desire itself is nothing new to the pubescent child because the wish to hold and be held, to possess, to control, to caress, and to kiss, have been present (and gratified to a partial degree) since infancy. *One might say that loving a child and providing it ordinary physical care are inseparable from one another and provide a necessary basis for mature sexuality.*

Such early love experiences are especially important because they tie the phenomenon of the child's physical sensations of pleasure to an enduring human love relationship. We see the breakdown of this process in unfortunate persons who have had relationships of poor quality with their parents and who, as adults, may pursue a sequence of unrelated sexual encounters without the experience of loving any one partner, so to speak, *between* sexual encounters. Such an individual's sexual performance may appear normal from a biological perspective. What it lacks is a mature involvement with the other participant on an emotional and psychological level.

*Sexuality and character have an intimate, two-way relationship.* Without sexual energy, a personality is constricted and perhaps somewhat joyless, unspontaneous, or even lifeless. Of course, circumstance or choice may lead some adults to a lifetime of celibacy, but it is often easy to see how their innate sexuality is diverted to other pursuits and lends them passion and ardor despite the absence in their daily life of the sexual act as such. On rare occasions, one also meets dry individuals, often capable and talented in other areas, who seem never to have heard of sex. This personality type was perhaps more common in the past, when child-rearing practices and society generally were considerably more repressed than they are today and it was possible to come of age with few points of reference in sexual matters.

The totality of a human being's personality has an enormous impact on his or her sexuality. This is true both in regard to broad questions, such as a person's role as a wife, husband, and parent, and to the specifics of lovemaking. The prominence of character traits such as integrity, loyalty, courage, kindness, and idealism go a great distance to attract romantic partners and to sustain relationships. Keeping these priorities in mind helps buffer youngsters (and adults) against the crosscurrents in our culture that foster undue anxiety about and emphasis upon superficial physical features.

Parents can encourage their offspring to be alert to the inner beauty of their childhood friends and members of their family circle by making note of good-heartedness and valor when they make their appearance. A mother who sincerely appreciates her daughter's best friend for her warmth and pluck will reap many rewards: it conveys her empathy for the daughter's feelings, at the same time reinforcing the importance of such personal qualities in all relationships. It gives the mother credibility in the daughter's eyes, especially if, further down the road, the mother may feel concerned that the daughter is attached to someone less worthy. A mother who ridicules her daughter's best friend behind the friend's back for her unwashed hair or her big nose is teaching her child that the personal qualities that make the friendship valuable to the child are trivial in mother's view.

Stability of character, closely tied to the capacity for shouldering responsibility, is crucial to love relationships. Children who have experienced a home life where people are reliable and constant, both in their behavior and their moods and attitudes, are likely to offer and expect reliable behavior later on in their relationships.

Parents teach their children what is worthy of love, in every area. Parents can inform their children that they deserve someone responsible and considerate. The message is best delivered *in the abstract* and in an appreciative context: "Such a lovely person you are! Make sure your sweetie gives you the kindness and tenderness that you deserve!" The best way to convey this message is by the parents being considerate to each other and to the teenager. That way, a relationship between the teen and an inconsiderate or irresponsible person is unlikely to get a foothold from the beginning.


## ENVY


A person's capacity for love is always intimately connected to his capacity for hostility. Anger, envy, and jealousy inescapably enter the picture. Little children express these fundamental human emotions very directly—first in infancy by grabbing what appeals to them, and then by grumbling about what they cannot have once the idea of ownership is comprehended. This sometimes expresses itself by exaggerated contempt for the owner or for the very thing owned. If these attitudes dominate the personality, they can distort all love relationships. A person who cannot acknowledge to himself the existence of powerful feelings of envy may become poisoned by them; he may lose the ability to enjoy what he does possess and become chronically bitter and resentful. This is often transparent in the hatred that a person who is self-conscious about his appearance feels for individuals he believes to be especially good-looking, or in the criticism many people express towards others who have a great deal of success, skill, money, luck, influence, intellect, or whatever quality has stirred up their jealousy.

Feelings of envy normally become especially strong in a small child just at the age when the recognition of differences between male and female is taking place, when the child recognizes himself or herself as one or the other. This collides with the child's natural ambition to be everything all at once: "When I grow up I'm going to be a policeman, a princess, a movie star, and the President." For every small girl or small boy, there is a period of life when the recognition sinks in that it's not possible to be everything. The child is disappointed in having to relinquish the ambition to be *just like* the parent of the opposite sex. Fortunately, the parent of the same sex inspires the child with joy and excitement to be *just like* him or her.

*In a home where there is a general atmosphere of love, respect, and security, the feeling of pride in being who one is wins out over envy of what one is not.* The child accepts the fundamental biological limitations inherent in being either male or female. Men cannot bear children and nurse them at their breast; women cannot impregnate other women with a penis, or become a parent at the age of 90 as men can do. Beyond these biological limitations, the child gradually incorporates into his or her character many of the various features of feeling and action that are part of being a man or being a woman in his or her particular family and culture. It is obvious that in addition to this, most people have a number of characteristics from the parent of the opposite gender; after a while the small boy, secure that he is going to be a man like Daddy, wants to play the violin or raise tropical fish like Mommy. Only the nursery-age child is troubled by a woman senator or astronaut, because the role stereotypes that were (and are) so deeply ingrained in our beliefs still seem to him a law of nature. His thinking is concrete. A mature person feels at home in his or her body and its many potentials and feels free to take up needlepoint or fencing, neurosurgery or nursery school teaching.

Health in sexual as well as in other dimensions of life consists of harmony between the various elements in the personality, and harmony can be achieved, even enhanced, where there is variety. What is unhealthy is a state of envious discord between elements in the self: desire which is at odds with shame in such a fashion that gratification and self-punishment alternate.

## HOMOSEXUALITY

Early in life sexuality is enriched by all manner of influences, not the least of which is identification with the parent or a loved person of the opposite sex. As every human being has the potential for a multiplicity of such identifications, in every personality there are features which, if taken in isolation, would seem to belong to the parent of the opposite gender. In this sense, all people are fundamentally bisexual.

In some persons, the capacity for sexual excitement and romantic love seems focused on others of the same sex; sometimes this trend is partial and transient, and sometimes total and permanent. New situations, new priorities, and new stimulations may have an uncovering effect on latent sexual wishes even in middle life, although often by adulthood a person's pattern of romantic response is pretty well established. Our society has found it convenient when a person's sexual desire, the impulse to fall in love, and his or her sexual identity as a man or a woman all line up in the conventional direction. However, this does not always happen. In most societies throughout the ages there have been a substantial number of men and women whose sexual love is focused mostly or entirely on members of the same sex. Sometimes other features of their personality seem patterned on the stereotypes from the other gender, sometimes not.

Our culture has looked upon homosexuals and lesbians with extraordinary bigotry and hatred—with so much venom that one might wonder if there wasn't an element of envy mixed in. In the past, many individuals whose lives were otherwise paragons of virtue, or at least paragons of ordinariness, were hounded into secrecy and misery by public consensus that homosexuality was evil and sick. The causes of homosexuality are unknown, and there is no scientific evidence today that it is either a sickness or an evil. Many people at this time are rather confused in their attitudes toward gay and lesbian individuals, and there is still great prejudice in many areas of public and private life.

Sometimes a youngster is clearly very aware of being homosexual or lesbian early in childhood. This may not seem normal to the parents but it is normal to the child. Forcing a youngster into behavior that is unnatural for the child is not good. Parents may rightly feel that life is easier for people who are conventional than it is for people who are not—but the important thing is not that the child's life always be easy so much as that it should be authentic.


## SEXISM

Most children struggle with sexism and parents are often befuddled about how to respond to it. When a small child echoes a stereotype, "I don't want to be in the school play—that's for girls," one could answer lightly that the school play is for anybody, but maybe not for him. Because the idea of a level playing field in occupations and society is a recent development, many parents today are especially concerned about bolstering their children's confidence in endeavors beyond traditional roles. It is good to encourage all children to be whatever they aspire to be and for parents to actively assist them to accomplish their goals.

Most children want to be parents. It is especially helpful to have raised the issue of integrating parenthood and work into the future lives of both girls and boys, since society's expectations set these categories up in rather mutually exclusive ways. Sons, especially, need to see their fathers involved in the care of small children in order to assume this role as natural later on. Boys and girls should be invited to get to know infants (if the family does not have one handy) and the joys of caring for them.

There is a big difference between helping a child to take joy in being *who he is*, and pushing a child into a stereotyped mold. In the past the qualities of the ideal man and the ideal woman were almost mutually exclusive traits; today, we tend to think of an ideal *person*. The ideal man of the past was dominant, ambitious, and fearless; the ideal woman tender, submissive, and nurturing. Today we see these as potential aspects of *every* personality, with some features more vivid in certain individuals than in others.

Parenting attitudes have not always kept pace with this development, however—some parents are made nervous by a boy who snuggles lovingly with a baby doll, or a girl who plays cowboy. Many parents without realizing it set entirely different expectations for their sons and daughters with regard to emotion. Boys are sometimes sternly pressured not to cry or to express anxiety, lest they seem like sissies. But of course the forbidden emotion goes somewhere, and is liable to express itself eventually in drunk driving, violence, and other "masculine" avenues— ways of losing control that are socially sanctioned and stereotypically patterned even though acknowledged as lamentable at the same time.

Similarly, girls are sometimes pressured not to compete or to express aggression, lest they seem unladylike. But again, the stifled emotion is likely to emerge through an indirect route: masochistic or passive-aggressive ways of handling these impulses.

If children make sexist remarks, one can say, "Oh, that's a silly idea people used to have." There is no disputing the fact that in the past women were prohibited access to most areas of power, including decision-making within their own marriages. We believe today that this

inequality is wrong, yet the reality under our noses is still far from equi-
tably balanced. Shrewd youngsters may observe this contradiction and
we cannot blame them for seeing what is there to be seen. We can
reassure children that it is our present intent as a nation to make
opportunity as fair as possible and to work towards that goal. The
family also demonstrates this by operating from the principle of equal
partnership between parents, within which any particular roles of
wage earning and child care may then be delegated as seems best to
all concerned.

## SEX AND VICTIMHOOD

The actual historical problem of women's professional, financial, and
political inequality can be grievously confused with the psychological
war between the sexes, which is somewhat different. The war between
men and women is part of a mentality of victimhood—the victim
expresses his envy, resentment, and helplessness in terms of the battle
of the sexes.

We recognize this sense of victimization in the man who is con-
temptuous and bitter about every feature of women, including the fact
that he is drawn to them by erotic desire. He thinks of them as animals; he likes to humiliate and hurt them. His view of women reduces
them to sex objects. His perception may be that men slave away heroically to earn money that which women then squander in their laziness
and greed. The underlying sense of helplessness is obvious. He really
believes underneath that women have all the power and that men are
their toys on a string. These impressions tend to go back to early childhood. A father whose attitude toward women is disrespectful in this
way is likely to convey these ideas to his children. His sons may copy
these attitudes of superiority and hostility. His daughters may feel
ashamed and inadequate, taking on the role of victim or perhaps avoiding all men as hurtful.

The counterpart is the "castrating" woman who sees all men as the
enemy, as juvenile and irresponsible subhumans who demand to be
catered to and who then betray, abuse, humiliate, and martyr the women
who attempt to do so. For them, it's a man's world from top to bottom.

Here again, the children's sexuality will develop in an atmosphere warped by envy and anger. This woman's daughter is raised to mistrust men; her son quite naturally concludes that all women aim to dominate and punish him, just as his mother did.

A man or woman who feels victimized by the opposite sex is very often married to—or perhaps, these days, divorced from—someone with a similar sense of victimization. Their mutual attraction is only natural since they share a fundamental perspective on life. Sometimes the warfare is overt and physical, sometimes subtle and psychological. Such individuals may find endless apparent justification for their respective worldviews, but at bottom, in both cases, is a sense of personal inadequacy, resentment, and jealousy of others. It is typical indeed that any person who has strong victimized trends in his or her personality, whatever the cause, will experience the victimization in sexual terms. This has devastating effects on children of either sex because the child is often cast in the gender role appropriate to the parent's preconceived expectations. Sometimes the story line develops first with a theme of idealizations: "Mama's little boy is the one man who will never desert me." Then pow! the dreaded consequence emerges; it just goes to show you that no man can be trusted. Another mother fills her daughter's head with distrust of boys: "They're all the same. All they want is one thing."

These problems often become visible as a crisis at the point when the child begins to develop a love interest outside the home—a father explodes when his daughter is found with her boyfriend, calling her a slut and a tramp. One can be misled by a focus on the virtues or shortcomings of the particular boy when the issue is more fundamentally that this father believes all women are sluts the minute he perceives that he cannot control them.

Such parents often were raised in families that encouraged these destructive attitudes. Many women feel that their parents were more generous and supportive of their brothers' education and careers, because in fact they were. Many men feel that their parents were ashamed when they cried, but eager to comfort their sisters, because in fact the parents did so. It is one of the tragedies of such sexual stereotyping that it perpetuates resentments and the stereotypes themselves by producing irresolvable envy. A teenager or adult with a troubled sexual life often emerges from a background in which envy and a sense of victimhood interfered with his developing sense of confidence, security, and trust. As he goes through life, romantic idealization gives way to disappointment, promise to betrayal.

## *Clinical Considerations*

### Clinical Case

*Lauren, age 9, was brought was brought to therapy by her mother after she revealed that her father had attempted to have intercourse with her. Father was unemployed and had had a history of mental illness; when mother confronted him with Lauren's accusation, he abruptly left the house. He was found later that week in a hotel room, having stabbed himself in the neck; despite significant blood loss, he survived this wound. However he never returned to the home.*

*The case was investigated by the police and children's protective services. Lauren had two younger brothers; mother worked in a fast-food restaurant. Lauren, a conscientious girl, had hitherto been an excellent student. Now her grades were barely passing; she had nightmares, flashbacks, and fears of being separated from mother.*

*Lauren and her mother were seen in therapy; Lauren was a pretty and neatly dressed youngster who looked extremely sad, constricted, and subdued. At the initial session, she expressed reluctance to enter the therapist's office, pointing out that she did not like the sign on the door. When the therapist inquired why this might be, she stated, "See, it says 'The Rapist'" (i.e., THERAPIST).*

*Her subsequent sessions were characterized by much similar evidence of quick intellect in the service of pessimistic vigilance. At times, like a different person, she behaved seductively—lying on the floor and opening her legs, or asking the therapist if he liked to "talk dirty."*

*Meanwhile, a court date was set in which Lauren was expected to give testimony in the presence of her father. The therapist met with Lauren and her mother, both together and individually, to discuss the implications of this plan.*

*The therapist was at first appalled that Lauren was, as he conceptualized it, "forced to go through all this again." But as he spoke with his young patient and her mother, he began to understand that they saw positive meaning in her day in court. Lauren rather liked the idea of taking the stand. She played out this role in therapy repeatedly, each time articulating more details of the traumatic events.*

*When the court date arrived, the therapist accompanied her to the courthouse and sat with her mother while Lauren entered the witness box. The father's lawyer objected to his presence, claiming that the therapist had coached her responses. But the judge overruled this, stating that the therapist's presence was "humane and proper." The father was found guilty but mentally ill. His illness was taken into account in sentencing.*

*In treatment one year later, Lauren spoke of her experience in court with pride. She said she felt sorry for her father but glad he was getting both treatment and punishment. She wanted to be a doctor or a lawyer herself one day, to "help anybody who is under a lot of unhappiness."*

This case illustrates the significance for the child victim of actual restitution, as well as therapeutic working-through. Clinicians often regard with horror the entry of the child victim into the law court, where the child may be victimized yet again by an inefficient bureaucracy, a dehumanizing public display, aggressive tactics on the part of the defense lawyers, or an eventual adverse judgment. These considerations, while very real, must be balanced by a strong argument on the other side, one readily overlooked. While a victim may need therapy, he often needs more than therapy. He needs justice. He deserves justice. The abuse of children is not only dysfunctional, it is illegal. Its larger meaning, not only to society but above all to the young victim, is that it is a crime.

It is for this reason that going through the legal motions (even when it may be in vain) is often of immense benefit to the child. It puts the perpetrator into the larger context of other perpetrators, other acts, and a larger society that has already thought of the problem and dealt with it before. This often astonishes the child, whose inclination is to see himself as isolated, the only person on earth who ever experienced abuse.

Various personalities along the way—attorneys, case workers—reinforce the child's position as having rights, as deserving respect. This conveys that not only the therapist and friends and family are concerned about the child, but that society as a whole is concerned about him and concerned about other children with similar problems.

The goal of legal action is not to make the perpetrator suffer (although this wish is worthwhile exploring in treatment); its goal is to give truth its day in court. This process reintegrates the youngster into the fabric of society because the good faith of the public institution is there to be tested and examined. If, unfortunately, truth should not always carry the day, the child will find that he has company here as well.

The danger for the child is that his trauma remains lodged in the personality like a foreign body, preventing him from developing a complete and coherent sense of himself. His boundaries, once transgressed, remain incomplete. Having been violated, the child becomes both privately and socially something of a non-person. He ceases to take up psychological space, and easily falls through the cracks of the social contract. The poorly socialized or antisocial outcomes seen so commonly in sexually victimized children can be understood as a pathological solution to this problem. The child comes to terms with the assault on his identity through repetition compulsion and intrapsychic fusion with the aggressor. In addition to these mechanisms, however, the inability of the adult world to respond with due deliberation to the wrong done to the child is a powerful factor in the child's destructive choices: he gives up not only on himself but on the society that had failed to protect him. For this reason, therapists must be alert to the patient's potential to do something active as well as contemplative to redress his injury. The child lives not just in his head, but in the world, and deserves efforts at restitution that are both private and public.

# 13

## ॐ

# Romance and Marriage

## TEENAGE SEX

A child's love affairs are unrealistic and they dismiss the laws of reality—one loves a movie star, or another youngster glimpsed on the school bus to whom one has never spoken a word. The mature adult loves realistically, with lifetime commitment. The love affairs of adolescents lie often somewhere in between; indeed much of the confusion surrounding adolescent sexuality today seems to reflect the unclear dividing line between the immature and the mature form of the human personality. Most traditional societies, including America's until the mid-twentieth century, had a fairly clear definition of these boundaries. A youth was financially and psychologically dependent upon his parents; an adult wasn't. From this perspective, although young people engaged in sex play of all sorts, they usually refrained from intercourse because the psychological, biological, and social weight it conveyed was too much for them. In 1945, intercourse was for grown-ups.

We must note, however, that in the past an individual of 16 or 18 was often quite grown-up. Because life was less complex and opportunities more limited, many teenagers had gone as far as they would go by the age of 16 in terms of intellectual, social, professional, and personal development. They were ready for marriage because they had already attained their personal goals, and the rites of passage to adult-hood were timely. They were ready to relinquish the dependent position with regard to their parents, and ready to be self-sufficient in relation to their own commitments. We find this today in many parts of the world, including parts of our own country where options for ex-tended growth beyond puberty are restricted.

In this sense, a large number of the mothers who have lived on this earth throughout the ages were teenage mothers, and this was not necessarily bad. The sexual act and the typical consequences—a baby and responsibility for the baby's future—occurred in a con-text of a man and woman committed to each other and to the baby, even if the man and woman were still in their teens. They were chro-nological teenagers, but not psychological adolescents.

Especially in their teens, many girls actively yearn for a husband and a baby. This is not a disorder in itself. It is a problem only when it is carried into action while the rest of the girl's personality is not mature enough to be fully devoted to these goals. Then we have a person at odds with herself. The conflicted wish for a baby—or an accidental pregnancy—is most liable to crop up at the wrong time for young girls who are having trouble becoming psychologically inde-pendent from their parents and who feel resentful that they did not finish the process of getting what they needed from their parents, especially their mothers.

The daughter may hold her mother accountable for deprivations and injuries that she suffered that were actually altogether beyond her mother's control; we observe that this is a normal although immature phase of a child's response to any deprivation or injury. On the other hand, the girl may be quite accurate in her assessment of her mother's failures as a mother. In either case, the attachment to her mother in-volves a relationship that often seethes with disappointment, frustra-tion, and anger. The girl is stuck in her development, unable to move forward until she gets what's coming: justice, retribution, and fulfill-ment of all her unmet needs.

This inner state of affairs is very frightening to teenagers because it threatens to push the personality back toward the dependency of babyhood. Here it is very typical for the girl's mind to make a kind of flip-flop: instead of experiencing directly a burning involvement with her mother, she lets herself believe that she is unconcerned with her mother—in fact she is not troubled at all if her mother is made to feel unimportant, unloved, and ignored. This allows the girl to go through the motions of separating herself from her mother in a show of independence. The pigeons come home to roost, however, in that the move towards independence tends to be more sham than genuine. The girl reveals her continuing dependence on her mother—indeed, her focus on her—through activities that somehow always call for her mother to become reinvolved.

A teenage girl who is prematurely sexually active is often transparently enacting this conflict. Her relationship with her young man is marked by the intensity, neediness, and rage that she carries over from the unfinished business with her parents. As a result, the romance is a rocky one, contributed to by the fact that the young man often has corresponding problems of his own. The angry young man who has deep doubts about his ability to establish himself as an adequate adult is especially liable to compensate for this by engaging in, advertising, and bragging about sexual activity.

This is the perfect recipe for the production of an unplanned pregnancy, since the baby serves so many purposes at once. The young father shows everyone that he's truly a man. By having a baby, the girl demonstrates conclusively that she cannot possibly be the incomplete, unsatisfied child she fears herself to be, since she is now a mother. There is an element of triumphant competitiveness with her own mother in the act too, both in announcing that the girl is a sexually functioning adult (whereas her own mother may be on the waning side of her own youthful attractiveness), and in demonstrating that the girl will be indeed a superior mother. At the same time, the girl humiliates her mother, by showing her to have failed to produce the idealized daughter, a virginal bride. This causes the mother social shame and casts public doubt on her goodness as a parent, since her daughter is "wayward." Not incidentally, for many girls the pregnancy, delivery, and care of the new baby may bring about an outpouring of attention, nurturing, admiration, sympathy, and cash gifts—often more of these things than she may have experienced at any other time. She has something to love that will love her back, magically free from the hurts and losses she has experienced with other people.

Often there are surprise twists in the plot. Sometimes the girl has perceived her mother as overly engulfing, intrusive, and insistent that the teen remain firmly under her thumb. By handing over the grand-child as a kind of hostage, the girl frees herself to lead her own life while providing her mother with something new to control and pos-sess. Sometimes the grandmother's pleasure with this arrangement is obvious to the onlooker. Alternatively too, one may see a grandmother and mother settling down together quite collaboratively to raise the little one, sometimes accompanied by the shared belief system, "Men are no good!" Here the twosome seem to have buried their differences by finding a common enemy.

The outcome for the baby depends a great deal on what the baby means to the mother. The adolescent mother who is personally unready for the role is likely to be less patient, joyful, talkative, physically lov-ing, and flexible with her baby than a more emotionally mature mother. Her basic commitment to the baby is compromised, as are her level of skill and satisfaction with mothering itself. The overall negative emo-tional flavor is often evident in a demanding, punitive, physically re-strictive approach to interacting with her baby. This is a carryover of her relationship with her own mother because she is treating the baby the way she experienced being mothered—with underlying hostility. Sometimes this resembles the aggressive doll-play one sees in little girls who have been abused.

In the case of the young unmarried mother, it makes a great deal of difference whether we are dealing with a fundamentally mature person-ality or an angry adolescent embroiled in her own problems. The needs of the teenage mother and the child presented by each situation are very different. All the same, many situations have some features of both.

### Vignette

*Josie at 18 was a good student in high school when she became preg-nant by her employer at her after-school job. Clearly he had taken advantage of her through seduction, although he had not actually forced her. She was a quiet, subdued girl living with her parents. The atmosphere in the home had been painfully constricted ever since a tragic car accident when Josie was 10, in which her older sister had been killed and Josie herself had been seriously injured; as a result she walked even now with a slight limp.*

*With the news of her pregancy, Josie's family banded together, blaming her employer. The atmosphere in the home came alive once more. Her mother sewed maternity clothes and prepared an elaborate layette. Father, a carpenter, redesigned and repainted the deceased daughter's bedroom in preparation for the new baby. The infant was born amid great joy (and with some comparison to the baby pictures of Josie's dead sister). Josie supported her baby by working part-time. A few years later, Josie married a young man her own age and the young couple went off to live independently with their little daughter.*

This vignette illustrates the way in which an unplanned and unwanted pregnancy may have multiple levels of meaning. Although completely unintended, and experienced on the surface as a disaster, the pregnancy allowed Josie to relive a portion of her childhood with her parents, permitting her to finish her girlhood by reestablishing an intimacy between them that had been damaged by the losses this family had experienced. Josie, the injured girl, was able to be loved and recognized after all. The production of the new baby filled a void in this home, allowing everyone to let go of the past and invest in the future. The entire family experienced a fresh start.

The fact that the family had both psychological and economic resources to support this unmarried teen mother and her baby during a period of vulnerability contributed to the good outcome. In particular, Josie's mother and father were *actually* able to provide for her the emotional involvement that Josie had missed in the past due to preoccupation with their grief.

## HONORING MARRIAGE

A teenager who is pursuing a sexual aim needs to do so on his own, for himself, as an adult would do. If he needs his parent to make it work, to make it safe, or to "undo" the consequences of it, he is simply showing us that he is not adult enough to be engaging in the activity to begin

with. If a teen is not prepared to shoulder the consequences of accidental pregnancy on his own, he has no business having intercourse.
This is something that teens even today seem to understand.

Naturally, the young teenager is often caught in the dilemma of
physical maturity and social timidity. The desire for some sort of sexual
activity is strong while the nature of the youngster's real relationships
does not give an opportunity for its expression. This inspires the young
teenager to find makeshift satisfactions in masturbatory fantasy, pinups, and explorations of the media for forbidden materials. This sometimes takes place in small groups of youngsters who lend each other
courage. Parents may catch wind of this because the child feels guilty
about this activity and wants to get caught.

This is one of the few areas in life where a parent's wisest position is
one of a certain degree of hypocrisy. The parent says of the pinups, "I
don't want to catch you doing that!" This means the parent fully expects the youngster to keep doing it, but wants it done behind his back.
The parent understands the child has lurid and graphic tastes in pinups. The parent is suitably shocked and horrified, or at least seems so.
The child gets the important message that his sexual fantasy is something he cannot share with his parents. If he's big enough to engage in
it, he needs to shoulder its risks on his own. This establishes the bound-
ary where it ought to be: that the parents cannot be partners in any
sense in their teenager's sexual lives. It is up to the teenager to handle
sex with self-reliance. His parents have made it clear to him that it is
his private and personal responsibility.

There is in this area (as in many others) an apparent contradiction
between what is ideal for the individual child and what is helpful to the
community from a public health perspective. The message from the
parent and from the public agency is not quite the same. Of course, this
is inevitable, insofar as public agencies are not parents. Because condoms
clearly save lives through prevention of HIV infection, and rescue lives
from serious trouble through other sexually transmitted diseases and
unwanted pregnancy, it is crucial that all Americans—including teenagers—have ready access to them as well as to empathic and accurate
contraceptive information. Reproductive health resources, including
abortion, need to be user-friendly for all teenagers to prevent needless
deaths and needless suffering. This is the public health message.

It would not be wrong for a parent to address these public health concerns with his teenage children in some detail as a general issue, a piece of wisdom about the world. His son (or daughter) might save someone he knows from an early death from AIDS by being able to advise others where and how a condom might be purchased in his community. This is a very different thing from a father giving his son a wink and a condom to keep in his wallet, which practically pushes the youngster to have sex. Many parents, fearful of pregnancy, themselves bring their teenage daughters to the doctor's office to be equipped with contraceptive materials. Although, in this situation, use of contraception is surely better than a lack of use which leads to an unwanted pregnancy, thoughtful postponement of intercourse until the girl is old enough to manage her own life independently is better still.

Reproductive health care services need to be readily available to teenagers, but the parent should not be the middleman for this exchange, unless the parent wants to encourage his teenager to have sex. The fact that minors have considerable trouble getting their own medical care (legally, logistically, and financially) is only another manifestation of the fact that grown-up sex is for grown-ups.

It is true that a large number of teenagers still living at home are having sexual intercourse. What parents do not always recognize is that the youngsters often do not feel very good about it. The parents' envy makes them imagine the youngsters are drawn by the irresistible ecstasy of the experience, but when you get right down to it, these early participants usually feel quite neglected, as if no one cared enough about them to see to it that their lives were properly sheltered and protected. Under the surface bravado there is often great anxiety and confusion. No wonder! The sexual act, undertaken to prove that the youngster is independent, capable, and securely loved, in fact delivers no such magic at all. Quite the contrary; because it is developmentally out-of-step with the rest of the teenager's capabilities and resources, it is likely to generate more serious worries and insecurities in place of those it was intended to solve.

Teenagers engage in sexual activity of all sorts with one another, but it stops short of intercourse, since that could lead to pregnancy. Their sexual activity is private and is not brought to the attention of the parents. In this way it resembles the parents' sex life with each other, which is not discussed with the teenager for reasons of tact, modesty, and common sense.

A teenage couple may engage in intercourse when they are fully committed to one another and when they are able and willing to shoulder all the potential consequences. This applies mainly to couples who plan to marry eventually, and who would not be greatly disturbed by the early arrival of a baby. It is obvious that many young people today in various stages of commitment (or lack thereof) often have sexual intercourse when they are fully emancipated, living independently, managing their own money, and keeping their internal affairs to themselves. Whether it is wise for young people to be doing this is a matter of both individual choice and public debate, but it is not, strictly speaking, a parenting issue. Such persons are functioning like adults, and many are parents themselves.

It is teenagers living at home, whose moods and finances and comings and goings from the house are still inescapably the parents' intimate business, who are liable to involve their parents in their confusion about sex, and parents are frequently confused right along with them. From the parents' awareness that many adults today have sexual relations outside of marriage comes insecurity about whether it is "natural" for their adolescents to do so. Parents recognize that their children may not find committed life partners until they are 25 or even 35, and parents accept that some intimate experience may take place before the adult offspring is led to the marriage-bed.

Parents need to understand, however, that children have very conservative moralistic ideas; this is part of their rigid thinking. *Children need to be reassured about the sanctity of marriage.* It is an excellent thing for children to be taught that sex belongs in marriage and that marriage is final. It is part of their sense of the world as a safe place, regulated by rules. When adolescents are old enough to begin to understand the true complexities of adult life, they will be prepared to see that, like many rules, this one involves a large number of exceptions. The parent need not express condemnation of adults who don't follow the rules; the goal is not to encourage the child to criticize others, but to encourage him to want fidelity for himself.

Parents should indicate to children of 5 and 10 and 15 that sexual intercourse is for married adults. They can do this cheerfully, kindly, firmly, and frequently. The fact is that the youngster will see a great deal of evidence to the contrary on TV and in real life, and will want to discuss this with the parents. The parents can explain that many unmarried young people do engage in intercourse, but it probably isn't so good for them. The public school system will back up this message.

A healthy adolescent, the kind who would be a trustworthy babysitter at 12, has the judgment at 14 and 16 to postpone intercourse if not until marriage, at least until financial and physical emancipation, and does not involve the parents in the act. His sexuality is his private business and he takes full responsibility for it. The fact that the parents become aware that a teenager living at home is having sex is itself clear evidence that the teenager is not managing his sexuality as an adult would. If the parents blandly endorse this by providing the teenager with contraception or other mechanical assistance, then they only confuse him further. It's that simple, because sex is for adults, not for teenagers living at home.

Adolescent sexuality is properly expressed through a range of foreplay activities that may include petting to orgasm, but that do not involve intercourse as such. A teen who does not participate to some degree in kissing and fondling until he leaves home is unusual these days, although probably normal for a few timid souls. Naturally, teenagers are entitled to their privacy to engage in sexuality, so that parents snooping suspiciously or imposing prissy artificial hoopla, such as rules about not closing doors, just convince the teens that their parents have a prurient interest in their relations, and force them into inconvenient venues.

Because teenagers are not ready for intercourse, they have an opportunity to explore their growing passion in developmentally appropriate ways. This puts the focus on communication, on extended excitement, and on mutuality of pleasure. It also tends to keep in center stage the issue of whether the boy and girl really like each other, which with teenagers is liable to change. By benefiting from a period in life that is full of sexual feeling but without the risk of total lifetime commitment or pregnancy, the adolescent becomes more at home with verbal and physical expression of romantic passion and more knowledgeable about his responsiveness as well as that of the opposite sex. Teenagers who are technically and psychologically virgins make better lovers because of this practice period.

In contrast, the very young teenagers who are fully sexually active are usually in a race for the boy to ejaculate. There is a kind of short circuit to this "goal" that greatly reduces the incentive or opportunity to explore the truly creative and expressive aspects of lovemaking. The emotional and psychological depth of the sexual experience is impoverished because the interpersonal context is usually rather shallow. It is often true that younger girls who engage in intercourse do not particularly enjoy the act itself so much as they are desperate to prove to the world and themselves that they no longer crave their parents' warmth and tenderness, since they are all grown-up now. The relationship with the boy in these cases is often mutually exploitative, with some trade in security, money, power, status, or protection for the rights of sexual entry.

It is for all these reasons that parents can tell their teenagers clearly that the completed sexual act belongs in marriage, and that the reason for this is that it is better for everyone that way. There is virtually nothing a parent can do to enforce this, and efforts to enforce it regularly seem to impel the teenagers to have sex, even if there is little pleasure in it.

### Clinical Considerations

#### Case

*Greg, 19, came to treatment after dropping out of a small private college during his freshman year. This occurred shortly after being dumped by his on-and-off girlfriend of six months. The conclusion of their stormy affair had been especially bitter: Greg had made several angry telephone calls to this young woman, and had been mortified the following day when the campus security officers called him in to admonish him for harassment; if he did not desist she would press charges.*

*Greg was outraged and humiliated; he felt publicly defamed. Wild fantasies of vengeance kept him agitated during the day and awake at night. He was unable to eat or concentrate on his studies. He could not tolerate that his ex-girlfriend remained at the school. One of them would have to leave the scene in defeat. After a week of this turmoil, he impulsively notified the school of his immediate withdrawal.*

*Greg returned home to his parents and took a job in a restaurant. His home life was not an easy one. His parents were factory workers and Russian immigrants. As a youth, his father had been a soldier in World War II; he had been captured by the Germans, and subsequently starved and tortured in prison camp. These were experiences about which the father apparently spoke very little.*

*In addition to Greg, there were two older sisters. The oldest had moved away. The other, Irene, remained bedridden at home with multiple disabilities; she was unable to speak comprehensibly, sit up, or feed herself. The parents managed to care for her by working in the factory on alternating shifts. Greg was often called upon to assist his beleaguered parents with Irene's care, an obligation that he loathed.*

*Greg had been an honors student in high school and was also a competitive chess player. He had been attending college on a full scholarship.*

*Greg presented to treatment as a pale, thin, unsmiling, and intense young man who appeared younger than his 19 years. At first he used the therapy to vent his enormous rage at his ex-girlfriend; he never really liked her, he maintained, and had found his experience of their sexual encounters "overrated." She was vain, cold, shallow, touchy, and less intelligent than she thought.*

*The focus of Greg's seemingly inexhaustible scorn rapidly enlarged to include almost everyone in his field of vision. He had endless contempt for what he viewed as the ordinary, well-intentioned bumbling he saw all around him. His parents were utterly inadequate fools: after a quarter of a century in the United States, they still spoke broken English. He harbored many doubts that the psychiatrist had the abilities to help him.*

*Persons who were not viewed as complete idiots were experienced as dangerous enemies. This fantasy lay behind much of his preoccupation with chess. He soon acted out similar themes of attack by provoking a feud with a chess official over a technicality; the dispute escalated until Greg was threatened with serious official reprisals. During this period of treatment, Greg described his image of the psychiatrist as a leather-clad dominatrix in stiletto high heels, menacing him with various medical instruments and condemning him with a cruel pleasure.*

*Over time, intensely shameful, negative feelings about himself
began to emerge. Greg spoke of himself as a "monster," like his sister
Irene, the hopeless and inarticulate cripple. Neither of them should
have been born. His disappointments in love had been only natural—after all "beggars can't be choosers." He confessed to perverse
and disturbing sexual dreams. It was difficult to respond to Greg's
assessment of himself at this time because he literally could not bear
to hear anyone else's voice address these subjects. He was desperate
to talk but intolerant of any and all replies.*

*Very slowly, Greg began to see that much of his consuming anger,
his fears of retaliation, and his self-hatred were connected to his
overpowering disappointment in his parents. He viewed them bitterly as inaccessible, impoverished, "defeated" personalities—ground
into dust by history, their own limitations, and biology itself. Gradually he recognized how frustrated he felt by their failure to understand what he needed: their ineptitude and ignorance (as he perceived
it) seemed to him like personal insults. At the same time, he experienced much guilt in despising these people who, he knew, only
wanted what was best for him.*

*In a moment of great tension, he recalled how one day years ago
his mother had complained to his father about a long-forgotten scuffle
between Greg and his oldest sister. His father had stepped in, pulled
Greg away, and shoved him in a closet that the father then barred
shut with his own body. Greg shook with emotion remembering his
terror at that time.*

*Later in the same session, Greg spoke of his sister Irene; he now
saw that she was truly a person despite everything, and recognized
that he loved her. He was beginning to find that he actually enjoyed
her company. He was making an effort to teach her things and she
was learning them. With tears running down his face he said in a
ringing defense of her, "She knows her colors."*

*Following this session, Greg seemed to loosen up as a person and
the therapy lost its quality of urgency. For the first time, Greg began
to express a genuine curiosity in areas beyond chess. He was able to
respond to his parents' limitations with more detachment and dis-
missed his unhappy love affair with a certain humor as "one of those
disasters of youth."*

*Some months later, having won a local chess tournament, he decided to return to college and terminate treatment. In his final session, he recalled with bemusement his previous fantasy of the psychiatrist as a sadistic temptress. He had trouble imagining why he had thought of her in those terms. It seemed to him ironic that now he felt grateful to her.*

This case illustrates how an apparent crisis in young adult sexuality rests upon long-standing developmental vulnerabilities that may remain relatively silent until revealed by the widened opportunities of physical and social maturity (Waelder 1936). Until "grown-up" romance presented itself as an actual possibility, the patient was not forced to acquaint himself with the degree to which his love relationships were infiltrated with fears of being attacked, and his own hostility.

Greg came to treatment in response to an immediate crisis and a generalized regression in functioning: like the poet, he could neither study, eat, nor sleep. Unlike the poet, however, this was not because he was overwhelmed by love, but by the opposite emotion.

This was a young man who had probably needed more from his parents all along than they were able to provide. There were multiple reasons for this, including the father's history of profound brutalization, the parents' relative isolation as immigrants, and their preoccupation with his disabled sister's needs. The patient had an aggressive temperament, and was also exceptionally intelligent; these factors placed special demands for empathy upon his parents, who were indeed somewhat overwhelmed and unimaginative personalities.

As a result, the patient spent his childhood frequently seething with frustration. His wounded narcissism, envy, and rage led to intense sadistic wishes. His father's episodic loss of control and the frightening echoes of his unspeakable war experiences reinforced Greg's fears of annihilation. The example of his sister's impairments further threatened Greg's confidence in his own integrity. Fear, guilt, and rage towards himself and these primary objects were then projected and displaced all over the environment—his vituperative skills earning him some actual enemies as well. His vengeful impulses towards others generated a deep conviction that he could not love anyone and that no one could love him.

Against this backdrop, evolving sexual impulses could not be integrated, and, in particular, served as a symbol to the patient of everything "monstrous" about him. But what emerged as monstrous in the end was his sense of himself as heartless, exiled from the circle of human attachments, a "beggar" at the threshold of love.

Treatment allowed Greg to come to terms with the gap between his own needs and his parents' capacity to fill them, and to accept this reality with more empathy for himself as well as for them. As a result, he was able to see people not as sadomasochistic puppets, but as they really were. Life became an opportunity for more than attack and counterattack. Through his narcissistic identification with his sister, who at first appeared to him damaged, isolated, helpless, and devalued, he eventually experienced a capacity for true contact, nuturance, and tenderness towards something outside himself.

# 14

## Towards the Eternal

### SPIRITUAL VALUES

What we give each child that becomes his character is based on intimate love of the most precious and personal kind. All values begin here, in the capacity for emotion that binds individuals to one another—not in spite of their uniqueness, but because of it. The depth and permanence of this devotion between parent and child are what allow the development later on of the child's capacity to be devoted to other things—to art, religion, science, and to other people, and to put his heart in it.

The parent who is secure in his ideals conveys his own honesty, integrity, and loyalty to his children. The parent demonstrates that he values these things by living with them as reference points, by acting with good faith and expecting this from others. A parent who lives by these values has confidence in his self-reliance, without needing to be all-good or all-knowing. His example, as well as friendly instruction, conveys to children that it is good to be alive and to live among people you love and who love you in return. This is an outlook that many religions seek to engender in people; a scientist might call it mental health. It is historically derived from religion, but no longer today necessarily bound to any particular religion. A child can grow up without specific religious loyalties yet full of the spirit of these values.

The confident parent is not overly troubled by the commonplace bad influences that exist everywhere in the outside world. He knows his child is protected from harm by the child's own good judgment, not by the parent's effort to stand between the child and the world. The parent knows that these negative forces—whether modern commercialism, materialism, or sensationalism in the media—can only act destructively on the troubled youngster who needs something to fill an emptiness inside, who seeks a substitute for a human relationship that is missing. The parent who has faith in his relationship with his youngster knows his child takes these bad influences with a grain of salt.

The confident parent invests himself above all in the intangible aspect of life: the relationship between our spirits and things and people that really matter. Make no mistake: there is nothing wrong with enjoying the things that money can buy, or wanting to have them. Parents want their children to be safe, to be educated, to be fed and housed and dressed. All this takes money. Not only that—our ideas of beauty and value are excited by finery of all sorts: children and adults get deep pleasure from lovely belongings, art on the walls, as well as stimulation from travel, music, art, dance, and broad cultural exposure. These things are not free either.

Yet the most spiritual thing on earth is a baby, because its interests are strictly personal. The infant is born valuing the human face and human love and needs these things to grow as much as it needs food and warmth. The wise parent knows the greatest gift and reward he can give his children is his simple joy at their existence and growth.

In the past, families seemed to have fewer things underfoot. A little child might have one or two dolls, a ball, a bicycle, checkers, and a box of watercolors, and be set for life. Not long ago, children spent hundreds of happy hours in the backyard with pie pans and mud, putting stones and bugs into jars. The simple exposure of the child's fantasy to the richness of the natural world is important to the child's feeling part of nature and at home in it as an imaginative, creative force. Many parents eager to give the best to their children are quick to purchase the expensive toy "designed by experts to stimulate the child's imagination"; such a parent lacks faith in himself and in the conviction that it is the *parent's attitude* towards life that stimulates the child's imagination. The purchased paraphernalia may actually impede rather than further the creative process, especially when the purchase or the newness of the thing becomes an end in itself. Then the child is easily bored and needs a new thing to feel stimulated and alive.

What keeps a child (or an adult for that matter) from being bored is being in psychological contact with the infinite depth and variety of inner creative experiences as they occur with people or in solitude with memories and thought. Some of these experiences are necessarily wistful. There are important growing experiences for children in which they are aware of unfulfilled yearning, and in which they are not directly smiling or having fun.

A parent who is made anxious by a child's experience of wistfulness will fill up his child's schedule with sports and structured activities, and fill his child's room with things. This teaches the child that he must have an activity or a new thing at all times in order not to feel, even for a moment, empty. What it really teaches the child is that he *is* fundamentally empty when he holds still and that this is a condition to be feared. This robs the child of his capacity to tolerate the momentary formlessness of his own inner experience, like the artist's anxiety at the blank canvas before he is inspired by the next creative idea. What any artist will tell you is that it is necessary to come to grips with the terrible blankness on the canvas in order to reach down into the personal richness inside and give it shape.

Not all children are going to grow up to be professional artists because few of them have the specific gifts that can develop into a mature talent. But all children have creative originality because they have personal uniqueness and an urge to express it; we foster this by an attitude towards the child's time and activities that meets the originality half-way, giving it materials to work with that allow the originality to take the lead over the materials. Adults present in the background allow this process to develop because they have confidence in it. The child's imagination then makes a horse out of a broom, a witch's cape out of an old scarf. The free play of children who are not overly pushed around by the specific qualities of their playthings is enriching to their characters in ways that play with highly directive playthings is not. Relatively formless playthings can be used to express, chew over, and resolve problems of concern to the child—which strengthens and consolidates the youngster's emotional life as *real, personal, and inside*. This in turn links the child's experience of reality to the eternal values because it allows the child to deal symbolically with the issues of deepest relevance to him: the great polarities of life and death, man and woman, love and hate.

## MEMORY AND MEANING

A man who is a classical musician once observed that part of the impulse he felt for learning and performing cherished masterpieces came from his sense that without people playing them, the pieces might die and be forgotten. Through his devotion to music, he sensed that he helped keep alive the greatness and beauty of the past. This is a man whose mother was quite ill both physically and mentally when he was growing up and whose childhood was dominated by the anxiety that he would lose her.

The feelings that we recognize when we are deeply moved—by the sublime in art, by acts of courage, by religion, by the extraordinary beauty of the natural world—hearken back to an early period in our lives when we experienced deep feelings without words to express them. Very often these deep emotions are an inexpressible mixture of pleasure and pain, desire and regret. We notice that some individuals— not necessarily particularly talented themselves—have a great capacity to respond to the emotional meaning of nature, of works of art or music, and of human events generally. This capacity to be moved, to find the experience of living deeply meaningful, is an important element of character. It has great impact on one's interpersonal relationships, but is also an important feature of solitude and that portion of the personality that cannot to be shared with anyone else.

The development of this dimension, whatever we choose to call it— depth, sensitivity, reverence, imagination, empathy—depends upon the richness of the first intimate bonds between parent and child. With joy and love there is anguish and loss under the best of circumstances, since life is not an easy thing. No parent can protect his child against all pain and hurt, however hard he tries. We cannot know whether this musician, had his mother not been ill, would have been sensitive to the sublimity of art as well as to its fragility, or whether he would see himself as rescuing it from death. We can easily see, however, that the poignance he experienced in his relationship with his mother heightened his sensitivity to everything that is precious, and gave an urgency to yearning and nostalgia.

*What matters for our children is not that we be perfect but that we be intensely real.* The authentic parent who fails the child or who is lost altogether leaves the child devastated. This nonetheless does less insidious damage than the parent whose failure or loss is well-tolerated because the attachment itself was shallow or impersonal.

There comes a time for all parents when active involvement in their children's lives comes to a close. Active parenting comes to an end when the child takes charge of his own life and responsibly launches forth into the world. Yet there is in all bonds between parents and children an ebb and flow, and a depth of attachment such that even into adulthood, middle age, and in some cases old age, the tie between them continues to be deepened by new shared experiences.

The gift of every child enriches the life of the parent, and the emotional growth that this stimulates is also precious. We learn from our children, and our characters are made broader by their love and, very often, by their astute reactions, observations, and advice. In our tendency to find children cute, we may fail to adequately respect a child's penetrating observations; even a small child may contribute wise counsel. Values are reinterpreted by every individual and the unique outlook each child brings to a family enlarges the experience of all its members.

It is the eternal function of families to care for children and the infirm, with the adults in mid-life bearing the most active responsibility for those too little, too sick, or too old to do so. Parents may live long enough to have their grown children care for them in some stage of their lives where much of the parent's authority, even his authority over his own affairs (reflected in a power of attorney), is delegated to the child. The so-called sandwich generation is as old as time, since it has always been the duty of the strong to care for the weak. This task perhaps came as less of a surprise in ages past to families that were not accustomed to delegating so many roles out of the home.

It is our greatest joy and legacy to see our children grow up fit to *take care*—of themselves, of their own families, of us as aged parents, and of their society and their world. When we see this happen, we know that we have done our job well. Our children's greatest inheritance from us is not what we leave them in the bank, and not even what they may remember of us, but who they are.

In the great river of life, our love—for our children and the people that our love has allowed to grow and mature—is our real immortality. No person who has touched the inner life of a child, even if childless himself, is excluded from this. In this way, our love for our children becomes the child himself and his children and his children's children. This can be part of our answer to the child who asks, "What happens to us when we die?" We can reassure this child, and reassure ourselves if we ever doubted it, that each human being has the opportunity to participate in the deepest and most eternal mystery there is—the human heart. Our spirits on this earth have been merely loaned to all of us, for us to pass on to others in an embrace that is beyond memory and beyond death.

# References

Bender, L. (1947). Childhood schizophrenia. *The American Journal of Ortho-psychiatry* 17:40–56.

Bleuler, E. (1911). *Dementia Praecox or the Group of Schizophrenias*. New York: International Universities Press, 1968.

Fenichel, O. (1945). *The Psychoanalytic Theory of Neurosis*. New York: Norton.

Freud, A. (1936). *The Ego and the Mechanisms of Defense*. New York: International Universities Press.

Freud, S. (1917). Introductory lectures on psychoanalysis. *Standard Edition* 16:243–462, 1963.

Jacobson, E. (1964). *The Self and the Object World*. New York: International Universities Press.

Kernberg, O. (1975). *Borderline Conditions and Pathological Narcissism*. New York: Jason Aronson.

Klein, M. (1932). *The Psycho-Analysis of Children*. New York: Norton.

Kraepelin, E. (1919). *Dementia Praecox and Paraphrenia*. New York: Robert E. Krieger, 1971.

Mahler, M. S., Pine, F., and Bergman, A. (1975). *The Psychological Birth of the Human Infant: Symbiosis and Individuation*. New York: Basic Books.

Waelder, R. (1936). The principle of multiple function. *Psychoanalytic Quarterly* 5:45–62.

Winnicott, D. W. (1965). *The Maturational Processes and the Facilitating Environment*. New York: International Universities Press.

# Index